# CLOSE UP IN CLASS: CURRENT ISSUES

*Close Up in Class: Current Issues* is a library of print and interactive resources for exploring national and international debates. Close Up's curriculum is designed to expose students to the historical foundations, institutional structures, and government processes necessary to engage in informed discussion about public policy.

Close Up's curriculum is closely aligned with Common Core Standards and the C3 framework—our resources help students to draw connections between historical tensions and current controversial issues; evaluate, synthesize, and debate policy from multiple perspectives; and apply new knowledge through actual civic engagement.

Our nonpartisan interactive resource center examines critical policy questions on a variety of levels:

- **Foundational Units** review the structure of U.S. government and explore long-standing tensions within American democracy.

- **Current Issues Units** give students a broad understanding of key policy issues and relevant modern-day debates.

- **Monthly Discussions** examine today's pressing controversies and discuss how current events impact individual communities and inform federal, state, and local policy.

- **Teacher Resources** include a variety of reading guides, essay questions, surveys, and community engagement activities that challenge students to develop a point of view and practice active citizenship.

Our *Current Issues* textbook includes central Foundational and Current Issues Units to help frame classroom discussions and research.

**To access your online resources please enter your Close Up ID and password at www.closeup.org.**

P9-CEP-424

# TABLE OF CONTENTS

# U.S. GOVERNMENT:
## STRUCTURE, PRINCIPLES, AND TENSIONS

# INTRODUCTION

> "I know no safe depositary of the ultimate powers of the society but the people themselves."
> —Thomas Jefferson

> "And it is long since I have learned to hold popular opinion of no value."
> —Alexander Hamilton

The United States is not a finished project. The Constitution established a blueprint for building a government, but the document is not as clear or easy to make sense of as a blueprint for a building. For one thing, it was not created by one architect but by 47. And the 47 architects all had very different ideas about the type of government that should be created. For that reason, what emerged is a compromise document—the Constitution incorporates different ideas about power, democracy, and the role of government that do not naturally fit together. If the nation had been a building, there is no guarantee that it would have lasted. However, the founders included a process for amending the Constitution and, over time, through amendment, court decision, executive action, and legislation, a stable—but still contested—form of democracy has emerged.

This chapter provides an overview of the structure of the federal government in order to inform your understanding of the political and policy debates that make up the remainder of the book. More importantly, this chapter attempts to illuminate some of the long-standing tensions that are hardwired into our system. Although a few modern examples are sprinkled throughout the chapter, the major intent is to show the continuing debates that have shaped American politics and democracy for centuries, and still do today.

## THE CONSTITUTION

A "Living" Document. The drafters of the Constitution knew what they wanted to accomplish. In a single document, they wanted to create a democracy in which the people elect their leaders and government is managed by the people for the people. They also wanted to establish certain individual rights that government could not take away and certain areas in which states could make their own decisions.

Yet, when the drafters gathered in Philadelphia for the Constitutional Convention in 1787, they disagreed about how to accomplish these goals. For months, they argued over states' rights and issues relating to which branch of government, if any, should be most powerful. They also disagreed over whether to list citizens' rights in the initial document, who should be allowed to vote, what the role of the courts should be, and how leaders in the executive, judicial, and legislative branches should be chosen.

After months of negotiations, however, the drafters reached an agreement: a Constitution replaced the Articles of Confederation in 1788 as the nation's framework for government. Remarkably, they did it in less than 4,500 words. The document has many features and ideas that were ahead of their time, including a process for making amendments so the document could be altered over time. That process paved the way for key additions such as the Bill of Rights. The Constitution created the important guiding principles that deeply shape life in the United States as we know it today. These principles include the separation of powers and federalism.

**Separation of Powers.** The drafters were nervous about vesting too much government power in any one person or institution, such as a king or a parliament. Because of this fear, they created three branches of government: executive, legislative, and judicial. To ensure the proper balance of power between the branches, they also created a system of checks and balances. James Madison explained it well when he wrote, "Ambition must be made to counteract ambition.... If men were angels, no government would be necessary. If angels were to govern men, neither external nor internal controls on government would be necessary. In framing a government which is to be administered by men over men, the great difficulty lies in this: you must first enable the government to control the governed; and in the next place oblige it to control itself."[4] For more than 200 years, the separation of powers and system of checks and balances has achieved the drafters' goal of dispersing power among the government's various branches.

## CHECKS, BALANCES, AND TENSIONS
## IN THE 21ST CENTURY

Politics, it is often said, ends at the water's edge. Since the presidency of William McKinley during the Spanish American War, Congress has frequently shown deference to the executive branch when it comes to developing alliances, engaging in military action, or forging trade agreements. In recent years, however, Congress has been more vocal.

For example, in early 2015, the State Department engaged in negotiations with Iran and six other nations to curb Iran's nuclear program in exchange for relief from political and economic sanctions. Israel, a close ally of the United States, opposed the deal, as did many Republicans in Congress. In January, Speaker of the House John Boehner, R-Ohio, invited Israeli Prime Minister Benjamin Netanyahu to address Congress without informing the executive branch about the invitation.[1] In the prime minister's address, he urged the U.S. electorate not to accept a deal with Iran.[2] In March, 47 U.S. senators, all Republicans, signed a letter to Iran's leaders written by Senator Tom Cotton, R-Ark., explaining the limits of executive authority in the United States and claiming that Congress or a future president could ignore any agreement that Iran reached with President Barack Obama's administration.[3]

Both the invitation to Netanyahu and the letter from Senator Cotton raised questions about the appropriate balance of authority between the executive branch and the legislative branch in regard to foreign policy. Both instances also highlighted a gray area in the structure and procedures of the U.S. system of government: the Constitution contains no explicit provisions regarding the nuances of diplomacy, except insofar as it mentions treaties, war, and the role of the president as head of state.

**Federalism.** In keeping with the founders' desire to make sure that no branch of government could ever achieve full control of the U.S. citizenry, the Constitution divides powers between the federal government and the states. For example, states were given the power to establish their own forms of government, consistent with the Constitution; to pass and enforce laws; to educate their citizens; and to build roads. After the Constitutional Convention, Madison wrote, "The powers delegated by the proposed Constitution to the Federal Government, are few and defined. Those which are to remain in the State Governments are numerous and indefinite. The former will be exercised principally on external objects, as war, peace, negotiation, and foreign commerce; with which last the power of taxation will for the most part be connected. The powers reserved to the several States will extend to all the objects, which, in the ordinary course of affairs, concern the lives, liberties and properties of the people; and the internal order, improvement, and prosperity of the State."[5] Today, virtually every state has a three-branch system that mirrors that of the federal government. The Tenth Amendment to the Constitution clarified that powers that were not specifically given to the federal government, or specifically prohibited to the states, are reserved for the states. The intent behind this amendment was to continue to ensure that the United States would remain a federation of individual states operating together under certain guiding principles of democracy and individual rights. Accordingly, for example, states make their own laws regarding the minimum age requirements for driving.

Although federalism has preserved the autonomy of states to govern in a number of areas, it has caused much debate. For example, states have the power to educate their citizens. Some critics of this power say that the federal government should establish a uniform set of learning standards that would apply to all states. This, they say, would help the United States compete in an increasingly globalized world. Others say that the federal government already has overstepped its bounds in many areas, including tax policy. Both the federal and state governments have the power to tax citizens in order to raise funds to run their respective governments. Some state advocates say federal tax policy discourages growth in their states and that the combined federal tax rates—for income, Social Security, and other taxes—are too high. In effect, they argue that their citizens should not have to fund a disproportionate share of the costs to run the federal government. Other people say the federal government is simply too big and tries to regulate too much. They cite the fact that the federal government employs almost two million civilian Americans and is the largest employer in the country.[6]

Key principles such as the separation of powers and federalism remain among the fundamental beacons guiding the relationship between the government and the people. They also guide the relationships between the various branches of government. Given the complexity of governing in today's changing world, it is likely that debate over these principles will continue well into the future.

# THE LEGISLATIVE BRANCH

**Congress.** The legislative branch is defined in Article I of the Constitution. This was the article that the framers of the Constitution debated the most. During the Constitutional Convention, delegates debated how states should be represented, how legislative members would be elected, and how slaves would be counted, if at all. Ultimately, the Constitution established a two-house Congress, one based on state population size (the House of Representatives) and one based on equal representation for each state (the Senate). The intent was to ensure sufficient representation for each state. Today there are 435 members of the House and 100 members of the Senate. The number of senators remains the same for each state; however, the number of representatives per state can change over time based on periodic results of the U.S. Census.

It is important to note that members of the House come up for reelection every two years; senators come up for reelection every six years on a rotating basis. Thus, every two years, the entire House and one-third of the Senate is up for reelection. Often, it is difficult to pass legislation in an election year, when many members focus on getting reelected. Yet, members can face pressure from their constituents if they perceive that members have been part of a "do nothing" Congress.

So just what is Congress supposed to do to meet its duties as the legislative branch? The Constitution gives Congress a wide range of powers, including the power to declare war, regulate interstate and foreign commerce, ratify treaties, and confirm presidential nominations such as Supreme Court justices. Perhaps the most significant, though, are the powers to approve the president's annual budget and to propose legislation that becomes law. The latter most often happens when a bill is passed by both houses of Congress and then is signed by the president. The president may veto a bill, but Congress can override that veto with a sufficient number of votes.

**Making Laws.** The Constitution's drafters were concerned about giving the legislature too much power to make laws. As a result, they set up a series of processes—involving both houses of Congress—that a bill must survive in order to be sent to the president for signature. In practice, far more bills are proposed than are enacted into law.

Typically, the process begins when a member proposes a bill. If the chairperson of the appropriate congressional committee thinks the bill is worthy of consideration, a subcommittee may hold public hearings in which witnesses testify. If the subcommittee approves the bill, it gives the bill to the full committee. The full committee may or may not approve the bill. If approved, the bill may be sent to the House or Senate for debate. In reality, bills are often amended during committee hearings and floor debates, and at some point, a final vote is called. If the bill does not pass, it is sent back to its original committee. No action is taken on the vast majority of bills. If the House and Senate pass different versions of the same bill, a conference committee of representatives and senators works out the differences. The new bill is then returned to each chamber for final debate and a vote. If both the House and Senate pass the same version of the bill, it goes to the president. The president can sign the bill into law or veto it. Congress may override a veto by securing a two-thirds majority vote in both houses.

# THE LEGISLATIVE PROCESS

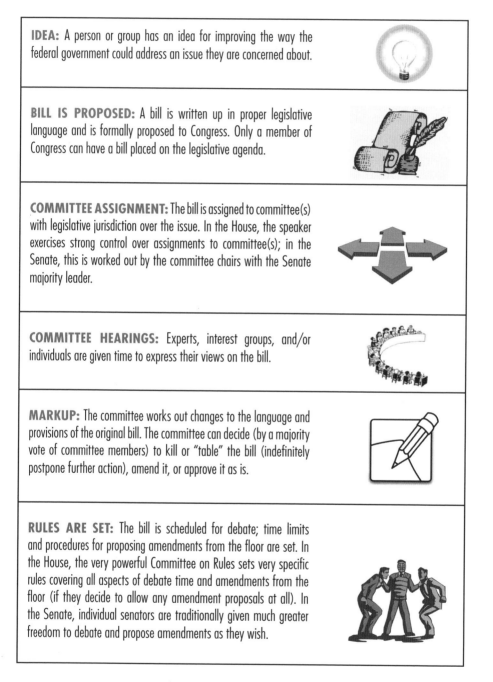

**IDEA:** A person or group has an idea for improving the way the federal government could address an issue they are concerned about.

**BILL IS PROPOSED:** A bill is written up in proper legislative language and is formally proposed to Congress. Only a member of Congress can have a bill placed on the legislative agenda.

**COMMITTEE ASSIGNMENT:** The bill is assigned to committee(s) with legislative jurisdiction over the issue. In the House, the speaker exercises strong control over assignments to committee(s); in the Senate, this is worked out by the committee chairs with the Senate majority leader.

**COMMITTEE HEARINGS:** Experts, interest groups, and/or individuals are given time to express their views on the bill.

**MARKUP:** The committee works out changes to the language and provisions of the original bill. The committee can decide (by a majority vote of committee members) to kill or "table" the bill (indefinitely postpone further action), amend it, or approve it as is.

**RULES ARE SET:** The bill is scheduled for debate; time limits and procedures for proposing amendments from the floor are set. In the House, the very powerful Committee on Rules sets very specific rules covering all aspects of debate time and amendments from the floor (if they decide to allow any amendment proposals at all). In the Senate, individual senators are traditionally given much greater freedom to debate and propose amendments as they wish.

**FLOOR DEBATE:** The whole body debates the merits and drawbacks of the bill and votes on passage. At this stage, the whole body can vote to kill or "table" it, pass it as is, or (if the rules allow amendments from the floor) pass an amended version of the bill.

**THE OTHER CHAMBER ACTS:** The other chamber of Congress must take the bill through the same process. Both chambers of Congress must take the bill through the steps of the legislative process. The Constitution requires all "money bills" to originate in the House; other types of bills can originate in either chamber.

**CONFERENCE COMMITTEE:** A conference committee composed of members from both chambers comes together to work out differences between the two versions of the bill. This is typically a time of intense negotiations (and lobbying).

**CONGRESS CONSIDERS THE CONFERENCE BILL:** Both chambers of Congress must vote on the final version of the bill. Members may debate the final version, but no amendments are allowed; each chamber must cast a straight up or down vote.

**TO THE PRESIDENT!** The president may either sign the bill into law or veto it. The president may also use a procedure known as the "pocket veto."

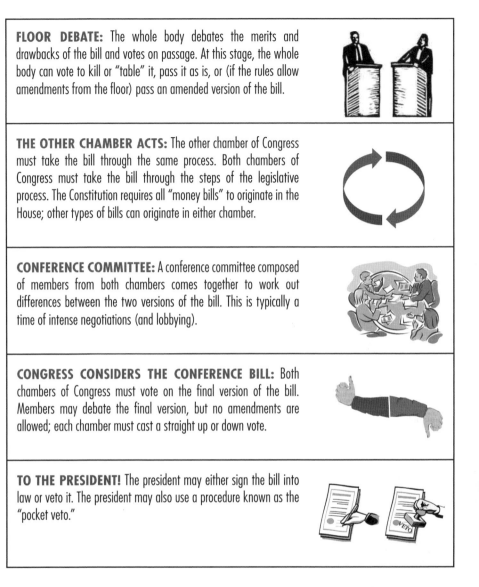

Many people believe it is easier to kill bills in Congress than to pass them. Powerful committee chairs can decline to consider bills, and committees can change a bill's intent by adding amendments. Furthermore, senators with different viewpoints or party alliances can hold up votes with filibusters or other delaying tactics. There is often pressure on members to vote along party lines and to deal with industry lobbyists and the media as well.

A good example of how difficult it is to make laws is the recurring discussion of immigration reform. Since the 1990s, lawmakers have consistently tried to pass laws to reform the immigration system. These proposed laws have focused on two main priorities: establishing a pathway to citizenship for undocumented immigrants and increasing border security. Republican lawmakers have consistently introduced bills that would increase border security, while Democrats have consistently attempted to pass bills that would offer citizenship to different groups of people.[7] In 2013, in an effort to compromise, a bipartisan group of eight senators gathered to create a bill that would address both of these concerns. The group's bill received support from both parties and passed in the Senate. However, the Republican-controlled House never took up the bill, and thus almost all momentum to reform immigration was lost.[8] Although the 114th Congress may debate immigration reform, any reform bill would need to be reintroduced in both the House and the Senate.

## ATTEMPTED SENATE CLOTURE* VOTES, 96TH-112TH CONGRESS (1979-2012) *Bars are colored according to the minority party*

Average cloture votes when REPUBLICANS are in minority:   57.25

Average cloture votes when DEMOCRATS are in minority:   41.63

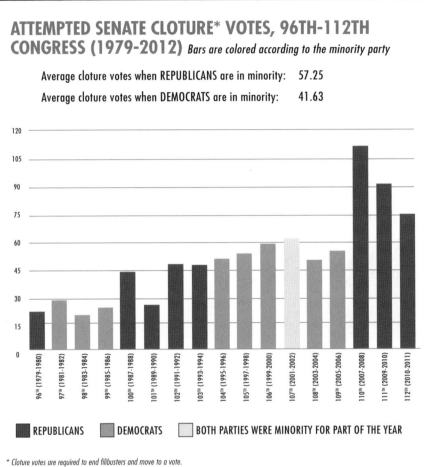

REPUBLICANS      DEMOCRATS      BOTH PARTIES WERE MINORITY FOR PART OF THE YEAR

*\* Cloture votes are required to end filibusters and move to a vote.*
*Source: The Brookings Institution*

# SENATE LEADERSHIP

President of the Senate
Joseph Biden
Vice President of the
United States

Senate President Pro
Tempore
Orrin Hatch,
Republican, Utah

Senate Majority
Leader
Mitch McConnell
Republican, Kentucky

Senate Minority Leader
Harry Reid
Democrat, Nevada

Senate Majority Whip
John Cornyn
Republican, Texas

Senate Minority Whip
Richard Durbin
Democrat, Illinois

# HOUSE LEADERSHIP

Speaker of the House
John Boehner
Republican, Ohio

House Majority Leader
Kevin McCarthy
Republican, California

House Minority Leader
Nancy Pelosi
Democrat, California

House Majority Whip
Steve Scalise
Republican, Louisiana

House Minority Whip
Steny Hoyer
Democrat, Maryland

# THE EXECUTIVE BRANCH

The executive branch is defined in Article II of the Constitution. It consists of the president, the cabinet, and all of the federal agencies. It is by far the largest branch and includes an estimated 2,000 agencies and subagencies.

Officials in the White House and the rest of the executive branch both advise the president and help to implement laws. Although the president appoints many of the leaders of the executive branch (such as cabinet members, secretaries, and agency directors), most of its employees are career civil servants whose tenures are not affected by who controls the White House. This enables the work of the federal government to continue even when the presidency changes hands.

According to the Constitution, the role of the executive branch is to carry out the laws passed by Congress by issuing regulations and administering programs. This is a large and complex task implemented by a variety of agencies. It involves complicated allocations of federal funds to states for specific types of programs and constant coordination with states and with other countries in the implementation process.

The president also relies on the executive branch to advance policies that may be at odds with those put forth by Congress. This push-and-pull between Congress and the executive branch illustrates the system of "checks and balances" laid out in the Constitution. At times, checks and balances can cause gridlock, a situation that arises when Congress and the president cannot agree and policy does not move forward. In response to the gridlock on immigration reform, President Obama issued two executive orders to temporarily halt deportations of young people who entered the country illegally without their knowledge, as well as the families of those young people.[9] Despite protests from many lawmakers, executive agencies moved forward with the programs—until they were temporarily blocked by a federal judge in February 2015.

Ultimately, a major question is how far the executive branch can go in doing its job. For example, how much domestic surveillance should federal agencies be able to do? In recent years, the public has become more aware of the extent of government surveillance, largely owing to whistleblowers such as Edward Snowden and Chelsea (formerly Bradley) Manning. Because of information provided by these whistleblowers, organizations such as the Central Intelligence Agency (CIA) and the National Security Agency (NSA) have been criticized for violating the rights of American citizens.[10] The Obama administration has either defended the actions of these organizations or claimed that the United States is not spying on ordinary people who do not threaten national security, but some members of Congress are concerned. Congressional members have held multiple hearings to investigate both the extent of government surveillance and the legality of the government spying on American citizens. Many people argue that there should be more congressional oversight of domestic surveillance. They believe that this is an important check that the legislative branch provides on executive authority. Others argue that in matters of national security, the executive branch should be able to act quickly and decisively, and that oversight could either slow or complicate the process of keeping the United States safe.[11]

President of the
United States
Barack Obama

Vice President of the
United States
Joseph Biden

# THE CABINET MEMBERS

**Secretary of State**
John Kerry

**Secretary of the Treasury**
Jacob Lew

**Secretary of Agriculture**
Tom Vilsack

**Secretary of Homeland Security**
Jeh Johnson

**Secretary of Housing and Urban Development**
Julián Castro

**Attorney General**
Loretta Lynch

**Secretary of Labor**
Thomas E. Perez

**Secretary of Health and Human Services**
Sylvia Mathews Burwell

**Secretary of Transportation**
Anthony Foxx

**Secretary of Education**
Arne Duncan

**Secretary of Defense**
Ashton Carter

**Secretary of Energy**
Ernest Moniz

**Secretary of Commerce**
Penny Pritzker

**Secretary of the Interior**
Sally Jewell

**Secretary of Veterans Affairs**
Robert A. McDonald

# THE JUDICIAL BRANCH

Article III of the Constitution establishes the Supreme Court and the lower federal courts. It is the shortest of the articles describing the branches of government. However, its brevity contrasts greatly with the powerful federal judiciary that exists today. Its power is largely due to the work of the early 19th century Court, led by Chief Justice John Marshall. Through decisions in cases such as *Marbury v. Madison,* Justice Marshall established the Supreme Court's right to decide the legality and constitutionality of the actions of the other two branches of the government.

**The Supreme Court.** Cases that come before the Supreme Court are mostly on appeal from lower federal or state courts and chosen by the justices. Each year, the Court receives roughly 8,000 petitions, from which the justices select fewer than 100 cases to hear. The cases usually involve matters of great public importance or issues on which lower courts have offered conflicting decisions. The Supreme Court session typically runs from October through May, with many decisions announced during the summer recess.

An excellent example of how the Constitution's system of checks and balances works is the appointment of federal Supreme Court justices. The president nominates justices, but the Senate must approve the appointees. These justices serve for life, unless they resign or are impeached. This allows a justice to make a decision without having to worry about how others perceive his or her rulings. In this respect, the appointment system is supposed to operate much like the tenure system in place in many educational institutions in the United States and abroad.

# THE SUPREME COURT

Chief Justice
John Roberts
Appointed by President
George W. Bush, 2005

Associate Justice
Stephen Breyer
Appointed by President
Bill Clinton, 1994

Associate Justice
Antonin Scalia
Appointed by President
Ronald Reagan, 1986

Associate Justice
Samuel Alito
Appointed by President
George W. Bush, 2006

Associate Justice
Anthony Kennedy
Appointed by President
Ronald Reagan, 1988

Associate Justice
Sonia Sotomayor
Appointed by President
Barack Obama, 2009

Associate Justice
Clarence Thomas
Appointed by President
George H. W. Bush, 1991

Associate Justice
Elena Kagan
Appointed by President
Barack Obama, 2010

Associate Justice
Ruth Bader Ginsburg
Appointed by President
Bill Clinton, 1993

# SIZE AND SCOPE OF FEDERAL GOVERNMENT

A major argument in American democracy centers on the proper size and scope of government. The size of government is measured by its revenues and expenditures and by the sheer number of its employees and programs. The scope of government is harder to measure, but it relates to the number of things that the government attempts to regulate, promote, or address. For instance, how active a role should the government play in regulating or trying to expand Internet access?

In many ways, arguments over the size and scope of government form the very basis of American politics. Conservatives tend to believe that government should play a smaller role in people's lives and particularly in the marketplace. In contrast, many social conservatives argue that the government should play a role in moral or social issues, by banning gay marriage, regulating alcohol purchases and consumption, or limiting access to abortion. Liberals or progressives are more likely to argue that the government has a larger role to play in people's lives. They advocate for strong consumer protection laws and push for programs that are intended to promote equality or economic growth. Yet, many liberals feel that the government should stay out of what they view as private moral decisions such as gay marriage, marijuana usage, and abortion access.

The federal government's power to take action on as many issues as it does largely rests on a few parts of the Constitution and one amendment added after the Civil War.

**Necessary and Proper Clause.** Under Article I, Section 8 of the Constitution, Congress has the power "to make all Laws which shall be necessary and proper for carrying into Execution the foregoing Powers, and all other Powers vested by this Constitution in the Government of the United States, or any Department or Officer thereof."[12] In many Supreme Court cases, this clause has been used to uphold challenges to federal authority, but in recent years, the Supreme Court has begun to reinterpret and narrow the meaning of the clause, limiting congressional authority.[13]

**Interstate Commerce Clause.** Article I, Section 8, Clause 3 of the Constitution gives Congress the power "to regulate commerce with foreign nations, and among the several states, and with the Indian tribes."[14] The commerce clause has been used to regulate market activity, but it has also been used in more controversial ways. For example, civil rights legislation passed in the 1960s used the commerce clause as justification. In one case (*Katzenbach v. McClung*, 1964), the Supreme Court ruled that the federal government could force a family-owned restaurant in Alabama to desegregate. In recent years, the more conservative Court has narrowed the scope of this clause.[15]

**Taxing and Spending.** Article I, Section 8, Clause 1 states: "The Congress shall have Power to lay and collect Taxes, Duties, Imposts and Excises, to pay the Debts and provide for the common Defence and general Welfare of the United States; but all Duties, Imposts and Excises shall be uniform throughout the United States."[16] The Supreme Court declared in two separate cases that the spending authorized by the Constitution must be for the general welfare.[17] Unlike the two clauses described above, this clause has received little scrutiny in recent years. In fact, this clause was central to the Court's decision to uphold the Patient Protection and Affordable Care Act, the law more commonly known as Obamacare.[18]

**Equal Protection Clause.** Section 1 of the 14th Amendment states: "All persons born or naturalized in the United States, and subject to the jurisdiction thereof, are citizens of the United States and of the state wherein they reside. No state shall make or enforce any law which shall abridge the privileges or immunities of citizens of the United States; nor shall any state deprive any person of life, liberty, or property, without due process of law; nor deny to any person within its jurisdiction the equal protection of the laws."[19] The equal protection clause plays a large role in federal civil rights protection programs, arguments about affirmative action, and even debates over abortion.

# CONCLUSION

The understanding of these parts of the Constitution has changed over time. The founders knew that this would be the case; Alexander Hamilton said, when arguing for ratification, "Constitutions should consist only of general provisions; the reason is that they must necessarily be permanent, and that they cannot calculate for the possible changes of things."[20] On this point, his most bitter political rival, Thomas Jefferson, agreed; he wrote, "Laws and institutions must go hand in hand with the progress of the human mind. As that becomes more developed, more enlightened, as new discoveries are made, new truths disclosed, and manners and opinions change with the change of circumstances, institutions must advance also, and keep pace with the times. We might as well require a man to wear still the coat which fitted him when a boy, as civilized society to remain ever under the regimen of their barbarous ancestors."[21]

It is up to all Americans to discuss, deliberate, argue, and take action to shape government today. In so doing, we play the fundamental role required in any democracy—that of the citizen. In the remainder of this book, you will have an opportunity to explore current political tensions and issues facing the nation. As you engage with the book and with others, remember that many of these debates are as old as the nation itself.

---

[1] Nakamura, David, Sean Sullivan, and David Fahrenthold. "Republicans Invite Netanyahu to Address Congress as Part of Spurning of Obama's State of the Union Plans." *Washington Post.* 21 Jan. 2015. Web. 5 May 2015. http://www.washingtonpost.com/politics/in-state-of-the-union-obama-takes-credit-as-republicans-push-back/2015/01/21/dec51b64-a168-11e4-b146-577832eafcb4_story.html.

[2] Rosenberg, Matthew. "Netanyahu Addresses Congress on Iran." *New York Times.* 3 Mar. 2015. Web. 5 May 2015. http://www.nytimes.com/live/netanyahu-address/.

[3] Editorial Board. "'Dear Iran' Letter Subverts Nuclear Talks: Our View." *USA Today.* 10 Mar. 2015. Web. 5 May 2015. http://www.usatoday.com/story/opinion/2015/03/10/iran-47-republican-senators-president-obama-editorials-debates/24733603/.

[4] Madison, James. "The Federalist No. 51." 6 Feb. 1788. Constitution Society. Web. 29 Apr. 2015. http://www.constitution.org/fed/federa51.htm.

[5] Madison, James. "The Federalist No. 46." 29 Jan. 1788. Constitution Society. Web. 29 Apr. 2015. http://www.constitution.org/fed/federa46.htm.

6   "Data, Analysis & Documentation Federal Employment Reports." U.S. Office of Personnel Management. Federal Government. Web. 8 May 2015. http://www.opm.gov/policy-data-oversight/data-analysis-documentation/federal-employment-reports/historical-tables/total-government-employment-since-1962/.

7   Weiner, Rachel. "How Immigration Reform Failed Over and Over." *Washington Post*. 30 January 2013. Web. 1 May 2015. http://www.washingtonpost.com/blogs/the-fix/wp/2013/01/30/how-immigration-reform-failed-over-and-over/.

8   Everett, Burgess, and Seung Min Kim. "Immigration Reform Looks Dead in this Congress." *Politico*. 3 March 2015. Web 1 May 2015. http://www.politico.com/story/2015/03/immigration-reform-congress-115880.html.

9   U.S. Citizenship and Immigration Services. "Executive Actions on Immigration." Web. 1 May 2015. http://www.uscis.gov/immigrationaction.

10  Bowden, Mark. "What Snowden and Manning Don't Understand About Secrecy." *The Atlantic*. 23 August 2013. Web. 1 May 2015. http://www.theatlantic.com/politics/archive/2013/08/what-snowden-and-manning-dont-understand-about-secrecy/278973/.

11  Council on Foreign Relations. "U.S. Domestic Surveillance." 18 December 2013. Web 1 May 2015. http://www.cfr.org/intelligence/us-domestic-surveillance/p9763.

12  "Necessary and Proper Clause." Legal Information Institute. Web. 29 Apr. 2015. https://www.law.cornell.edu/wex/necessary_and_proper_clause.

13  Baude, William. "Sharing the Necessary and Proper Clause." *Harvard Law Review*. 10 Nov. 2014. Web. 29 Apr. 2015. http://harvardlawreview.org/2014/11/sharing-the-necessary-and-proper-clause/.

14  "Commerce Clause. Legal Information Institute. Web. 29 Apr. 2015. https://www.law.cornell.edu/wex/commerce_clause.

15  Ibid.

16  "CRS Annotated Constitution." Legal Information Institute. Web. 29 Apr. 2015. https://www.law.cornell.edu/anncon/html/art1frag26_user.html.

17  Ibid.

18  Goodwin, Liz. "Supreme Court Upholds Obamacare Individual Mandate as a Tax." ABC News. 28 June 2012. Web. 29 Apr. 2015. http://abcnews.go.com/Politics/OTUS/supreme-court-upholds-obamacare-individual-mandate-tax/story?id=16669186.

19  "14th Amendment." Legal Information Institute. Web. 29 Apr. 2015. https://www.law.cornell.edu/constitution/amendmentxiv.

20  Annenberg Classroom. "Our Constitution." The Leonore Annenberg Institute for Civics. Web. 29 Apr. 2015. http://www.annenbergclassroom.org/ibooks?bookId=1.

21  "Quotations on the Jefferson Memorial." Monticello.org. Web. 29 Apr. 2015. http://www.monticello.org/site/jefferson/quotations-jefferson-memorial.

# DEFENSE AND SECURITY

## CURRENT CONTROVERSIES

- Should the United States reduce its defense spending?

- Should the United States use enhanced interrogation techniques to protect the country?

# INTRODUCTION

"If we desire to avoid insult, we must be able to repel it; if we desire to secure peace, one of the most powerful instruments of our rising prosperity, it must be known that we are at all times ready for war."
—George Washington

"A nation that continues year after year to spend more money on military defense than on programs of social uplift is approaching spiritual death."
—Martin Luther King, Jr.

The Constitution's preamble tells readers that a major goal of the document is to "provide for the common defence."[1] However, even during the presidency of George Washington, there was significant debate over alliances and military matters. As the United States' role in the world has grown, so too has the intensity of debate about military and security matters. In this chapter, we will consider some enduring tensions that shape our approach to defense policy and examine two current controversial issues:

- Should the United States reduce its defense spending?

- Should the United States use enhanced interrogation techniques to protect the country?

**Why Is Defense Policy Controversial?** Defense spending is a huge part of the federal budget. In fact, it makes up more than half of the nation's discretionary spending.[2] So it is natural that Americans would seriously disagree about how to allocate those funds, and whether so much money should go toward defense at all. Additionally, many different beliefs, values, and goals influence the debate over defense and national security.

- *Competing Goals.* What should be the goal of U.S. defense spending and policies? To play an active role in the international community? To protect American business and economic interests? To advance democracy and human rights?

- *Competing Priorities.* What should be the highest priorities of U.S. defense policy? Stability in regions such as the Middle East and sub-Saharan Africa? Protection of shipping lanes near the Horn of Africa? Coming to the aid of allies?

- *Competing Means.* Should the United States use military force to achieve its goals, or is it more effective to use covert actions and intelligence gathering? Should the United States work closely with other nations or independently? Should Americans use conventional forms of military engagement or focus on weapons such as unmanned aerial vehicles?

**Why Is Defense Policy So Complicated?** The community of nations is becoming more diverse and more interconnected. Actions taken by nations such as Iran and North Korea have ripple effects around the world; domestic disputes in Syria, Nigeria, and the Democratic Republic of Congo create regional and even global instability.

Meanwhile, in the United States, the pressure to cut the budget deficit and to pay off more than $18 trillion in national debt is bringing the military budget under greater scrutiny. The Department of Defense is being asked to make cuts and to set new priorities for future investments while maintaining a global presence and responding to emerging threats. In short, the U.S. military is being asked to "do more with less."[3]

# THE ONGOING DEBATE

## How much should the United States invest in defense?

In many ways, defense spending has been shielded from the kind of intense scrutiny that other federal programs and expenditures have faced since the height of the Cold War.[4] Threats and perceived threats posed by the Soviet Union during the 1960s, 1970s, and 1980s compelled lawmakers to maintain funding for military programs. During the 1990s, the United States continued to invest in defense at higher rates than other nations, but overall defense spending dipped significantly. However, the terrorist attacks of September 11, 2001, and the subsequent U.S. invasions of Afghanistan and Iraq made national defense a top priority again.

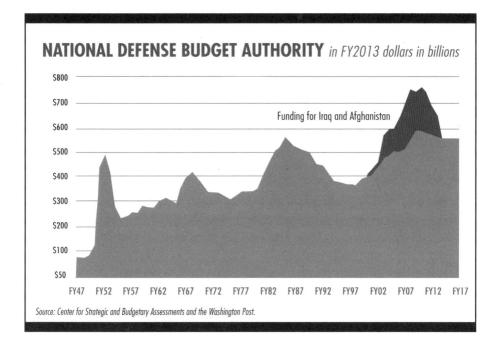

**NATIONAL DEFENSE BUDGET AUTHORITY** *in FY2013 dollars in billions*

Funding for Iraq and Afghanistan

FY47  FY52  FY57  FY62  FY67  FY72  FY77  FY82  FY87  FY92  FY97  FY02  FY07  FY12  FY17

Source: Center for Strategic and Budgetary Assessments and the Washington Post.

Compared with most other nations, the United States spends significantly more money on military and defense—more than the next seven biggest defense spenders combined.[5] However, the United States plays a different role in the world than other nations; for example, the U.S. Navy plays an outsized role in keeping the world's waterways safe for trade. The United States also deploys troops to stabilize regions in crisis and uses its military to assist other countries in the wake of natural disasters. Finally, the United States maintains a global military presence, with active-duty troops in almost 150 countries and ships deployed across the world's oceans.[6]

Though the United States allocates a significant portion of its budget to defense, defense issues can be difficult to debate. Few argue that national security should not be a top priority of the United States, or of any nation. According to a 2015 Pew Research Center poll, Americans ranked national defense and terrorism as the nation's top policy priority.[7] However, Americans remain sharply divided over how much should be spent for national defense. A February 2014 Gallup poll revealed that 39 percent of Americans favored cutting the Department of Defense budget. Meanwhile, 32 percent of respondents said current spending levels were appropriate while 28 percent thought spending should be increased.[8]

And debates about military spending are not only about money; they are about desired outcomes and priorities. Americans have largely failed to agree over what role the United States should play in the world—a role largely represented by its military might and presence.

# THE CURRENT CONTROVERSY
## Should the United States reduce its defense spending?

For the past several years, each round of budget debates in Congress has raised new questions about the appropriate level of funding for the Department of Defense.[9] But changing such an enormous bureaucracy does not occur overnight, and several proposals are being studied and debated. The most prominent—and the one against which other proposals are compared—is the plan put forward by former Defense Secretary Chuck Hagel and President Barack Obama in 2014. That proposal would:[10]

- Reduce the troop force from 520,000 to 440,000.
- Increase Special Forces troops from 65,000 to almost 70,000.
- Reduce the size of the Army Reserves and National Guard by five percent.
- Eliminate the A-10 warplane and U-2 spy plane fleets, and replace the U-2 with unmanned aerial vehicles.
- Close certain military bases.

Advocates of reductions in military spending point to the conclusion of the wars in Afghanistan and Iraq; the development of new technologies in surveillance and drone warfare; the diminished need for a large, constant military presence in Europe; and rising U.S. deficits and debt. They argue that the defense budget should be subject to the same high level of scrutiny as other budget items and that the United States can no longer afford to maintain such a large military force.

Those opposed to reducing the defense budget argue that national security is the most important priority of any nation. They point to security threats such as Russia's belligerence in Europe, the Syrian civil war, and the presence of major terrorist organizations such as the Islamic State of Iraq and the Levant (ISIL) and al-Qaeda as evidence that the United States cannot afford to relax its defense capabilities.

## Should the United States reduce its defense spending?

### YES: The United States cannot afford to be the world's police.

Senator Richard Durbin, D-Ill., made it clear during an appearance on CNN: "We have to acknowledge the obvious.... If we are going to reduce our debt for future generations, we have to cut spending on...defense."[11]

We vastly increased our defense spending in the wake of the 9/11 terrorist attacks in order to fund military incursions in Afghanistan and Iraq, and to beef up our national defense systems. Now, we are withdrawing our troops from Afghanistan and Iraq; war is no longer the major feature of our political landscape.

Mitch Daniels, a former Republican governor of Indiana and former director of the Office of Management and Budget, told a gathering of conservative activists, "I served in two administrations that practiced and validated the policy of peace through strength. It has served America and the world with irrefutable success. But if our nation goes over a financial Niagara, we won't have much strength and, eventually, we won't have peace. We are currently borrowing the entire defense budget from foreign investors. Within a few years, we will be spending more on interest payments than on national security. That is not, as our military friends say, a 'robust strategy.'"[12]

Others have put it more succinctly: Rising debt is the single greatest national security threat the United States faces.

As we examine our budget, we can afford no sacred cows. Military spending represents a significant portion of total government spending, and for too long, conservatives and Republicans—typically keen to cut government spending—have shielded defense spending from scrutiny.

Meanwhile, the United States' genuine need for a global footprint is in decline. We have established better intelligence and alliances in regions such as the Middle East since 9/11. We have also rapidly increased our inventory of lower-cost technologies such as unmanned aerial vehicles.

With two wars drawing to a close, now is the perfect time to begin reducing military spending to pre–9/11 levels while also making the kind of smart investments that will protect the country in the future.

## NO: The United States plays a vital role in global stability.

"Political leaders in Washington need to be reminded that our defense is the single most important responsibility of the federal government." Senators Tom Cotton, R-Ark., and Marco Rubio, R-Fla., penned these words in a joint op-ed during recent budget debates to remind the United States— and Congress—of our priorities.

The most important thing that a government can do is defend its citizens; other concerns are secondary. What's more, write Michele Flournoy and Eric Edelman, both former undersecretaries of defense, recent events "have reminded us all that the United States faces perhaps the most complex and volatile security environment since World War II."[14]

This is not a good time to reduce troop levels to pre-World War II levels, as many Democrats, including the Obama administration, would prefer. This is not a time to signal weakness or reticence on the part of the United States.

Some have argued that debt is a more pressing priority than defense, even contending, as Senator Rand Paul, R-Ky., did, that "part of our national security is trying not to overburden the country with debt."[15]

However, as Senator Lindsay Graham, R-S.C., appropriately responded, "I agree with Senator Paul that one of the threats to our nation is the debt. But I reject the idea that defense spending has anything at all to do with that."[16]

In an unstable world, the United States has a responsibility to protect both its citizens and the international order. The United States does not spend its entire defense budget to make war, as some liberals would have you believe. It spends a significant amount of its budget enforcing international agreements and laws, ensuring safe passage of goods and people through international waters, and assisting in the wake of natural and human-created disasters. No nation or international organization stands ready to fill the vacuum that would be created by a significant reduction in the global presence of the U.S. military. But terrorist organizations, rogue states, and militia groups most assuredly stand ready to exploit such a vacuum to advance their agendas and spread chaos. We cannot let that happen.

# THE ONGOING DEBATE
## When it comes to national security, do ends justify means?

While many public policy debates consider the appropriate roles and responsibilities of government, important debates also rage over *how* the government should pursue its objectives. Many of these debates relate to how the United States ought to behave as part of the international community. Often, the United States faces questions of whether to use force or coercion to achieve its aims when developing and implementing foreign policy.[17] In recent years, the United States has grappled with how to combat terrorism and defend the homeland without resorting to means that betray American values.

However, these issues are not new. Political scientists, philosophers, politicians, generals, and theologians have argued over the definition of a just war for at least two millennia. Augustine of Hippo, also known as St. Augustine, laid out the first formal theory on just war in the fourth century when he argued that adherence to Christianity is not incompatible with being a soldier so long as the wars, and the actions taken in the wars, are just.[18] Just war theory has evolved over time through the works of philosophers and politicians.

Afghan President Ashraf Ghani reacts to the Senate Select Committee on Intelligence report on CIA torture practices: "The Afghan government condemns in the strongest language the inhuman and unjustifiable practices detailed in the report."

# MODERN JUST WAR THEORY[19]

Just war theory has two sets of criteria, the first establishing *jus ad bellum* (the right to go to war), and the second establishing *jus in bello* (the right conduct within war).

***Jus ad Bellum:*** Criteria that must be met in order for a war to be considered just:

**Just cause:** War is permissible only to confront "a real and certain danger," such as protecting innocent life; for example, to preserve conditions necessary for decent human existence or to protect basic human rights.

**Competent authority:** The right to use force must be joined with the common good; war must be declared by those with responsibility for public order, not by private groups or individuals.

**Comparative justice:** No state should act on the basis that it has "absolute justice" on its side. Every party to a conflict must acknowledge the limits of its "just cause" and the consequent requirement to use only limited means in pursuit of its objectives.

**Right intention:** War can be legitimately intended for only the reasons set forth as a just cause.

**Last resort:** For war to be justified, all peaceful alternatives must have been exhausted.

**Probability of success:** This is a difficult criterion to apply, but its purpose is to prevent irrational resort to force or hopeless resistance when the outcome of either will clearly be disproportionate or futile.

**Proportionality:** The destruction to be inflicted and the costs incurred by war must be proportionate to the good expected to be achieved by taking up arms. Destruction applies in both the temporal and the spiritual senses.

***Jus in Bello:*** Criteria that must be met in order for actions within war to be considered just:

**Discrimination:** This criterion requires that actions within a war must never be "total war"— nuclear war—and must never target civilian populations or non-military targets.

**Proportionality:** Destruction caused by actions in war must be proportionate to the good expected to be achieved by the actions. Destruction applies in both the temporal and the spiritual senses.

**Fair treatment of prisoners of war:** Enemy combatants who surrender or who are captured no longer pose a threat. It is therefore wrong to torture them or otherwise mistreat them.

**No means *malum in se* (evil in itself):** Combatants may not use weapons or other methods of warfare that are considered evil, such as mass rape, forcing enemy combatants to fight against their own side, or using weapons with effects that cannot be controlled.

Advances in technology in the 20th and 21st centuries forced ethicists, statesmen, military leaders, and others to debate the best interpretation of the *jus in bello* criteria for actions during war. During World War I, for example, combatant nations experimented with chemical weapons. Germany was first to use them, causing the commander of the British Expeditionary Force, Sir John French, to call the use of gas "a cynical and barbarous disregard of the well-known usages of civilized war."[19] Months later, after the British deployed similar weaponry, Sir John explained, "Owing to the repeated use by the enemy of asphyxiating gases in their attacks on our positions, I have been compelled to resort to similar methods."[20]

During World War II, countries raced to develop technologies that would give them an edge over one another. Germany, seeking to cut off supply lines to Great Britain, caused great concern by torpedoing civilian ships with its advanced U-boat fleet of submarines.[21] Both Allied and Axis powers bombed civilian targets, such as the German raids over London and the Allied firebombing of Dresden and Tokyo.[22] Most notably, the United States' decision to use two atomic bombs in Japan shocked the world.[23]

The destruction caused by World War II led world leaders to create new rules to regulate international conflict. For example, the fourth Geneva Convention sought to protect civilians from harm and provide guidelines for the proper treatment of prisoners of war.[24] In the years since World War II, international leaders have expanded, altered, and updated international agreements and frameworks to keep pace with changes in technology and warfare. However, new technologies such as drones, borderless wars against extremism, and the rise of non-state actors such as al-Qaeda challenge our understanding and application of these principles.

# THE CURRENT CONTROVERSY

## Should the United States use enhanced interrogation techniques to protect the country?

One practice specifically banned by the fourth Geneva Convention is the torture of prisoners of war.[25] During the hunt for Osama bin Laden and the ongoing fight against terrorism, the United States has grappled with the definition of both prisoners of war and torture. During much of President George W. Bush's administration, the government argued that detainees held as part of the War on Terror were not prisoners of war because they did not belong to any state's military; in essence, they were not soldiers. Instead, the administration labeled them "unlawful enemy combatants" and argued that neither U.S. constitutional and legal protections nor international protocols such as the Geneva Conventions applied to them.[26] In an effort to distinguish between torture and techniques that the administration asserted were necessary intelligence gathering tools, the administration labeled some aggressive questioning practices "enhanced interrogation techniques."[27]

In December 2014, the U.S. Senate Select Committee on Intelligence issued a report condemning as torture the actions of the Central Intelligence Agency (CIA) under the Bush administration.[28] The debate caused an uproar on Capitol Hill, within the intelligence committee, and among former members of the Bush administration. It also caused Americans to reexamine the issue of torture and the extent to which the government should go to protect American citizens.

### Should the United States use enhanced interrogation techniques to protect the country?

## YES: There is too much at stake not to use all tools available.

The recent Senate report has raised a lot of hoopla in Washington, D.C. But amid all the debating about the morality of enhanced interrogation, which the Senate has mistakenly labeled torture, is the most important, indisputable point: it worked.

Former Vice President Dick Cheney summed it up well when he said on NBC's *Meet the Press*, "I have no problem as long as we achieve our objective....I was prepared and we did. We got authorizing from the president and authorization from the Justice Department to go forward with the program. It worked. It worked now for 13 years."[29]

Echoing this sentiment, three former CIA directors and three other high-ranking officials wrote in the *Wall Street Journal*, "Between 1998 and 2001, the al Qaeda leadership in South Asia attacked two U.S. embassies in East Africa, a U.S. warship in the port of Aden, Yemen, and the American homeland—the most deadly single foreign attack on the U.S. in the country's history. The al Qaeda leadership has not managed another attack on the homeland in the 13 years since, despite a strong desire to do so. The CIA's aggressive counterterrorism policies and programs are responsible for that success."[30]

In addition to the success of the program, it is important to note that the methods used by U.S. intelligence agencies are not torture. No fingernails were pulled, no one was electrocuted, and no one was intentionally harmed in a permanent way.

And, finally, terrorists present a special case. They cannot be considered protected by international rules because they exist outside the structure of those laws. They exist entirely to cause harm to civilians. As Charles Krauthammer wrote in the *Weekly Standard*, "Breaking the laws of war and abusing civilians are what, to understate the matter vastly, terrorists do for a living. They are entitled, therefore, to nothing. Anyone who blows up a car bomb in a market deserves to spend the rest of his life roasting on a spit over an open fire. But we don't do that because we do not descend to the level of our enemy."[31]

## NO: Enhanced interrogation is torture, and we are above that.

Even the CIA was not ready to come to terms with the evil it was perpetrating under the banner of "enhanced interrogation techniques." Instead, the CIA misled Congress about the extent of its torture program[32] and leaked and exaggerated stories to convince the public and politicians that the program was effective.[33]

In fact, the CIA has destroyed evidence of its misdeeds, including at least 92 tapes of waterboarding incidents that would enable the public to judge whether that technique counts as a form of torture.[34] The CIA's efforts to hide its most egregious abuses confirm what we already know: enhanced interrogation *is* torture and it is wrong.

An example of the techniques that we are supposed to believe are not torture? Sleep deprivation, which included keeping 9/11 conspirator Khalid Sheikh Mohammed awake for more than seven straight days.[35] The fact that Mohammed is a monster does not mean Americans must become monsters as well. Other examples include rectal feeding, which it is now clear the CIA used as an interrogation tool, not just to nourish prisoners who refused to eat.[36]

That the torture program was poorly managed seems obvious. At least 26 people were wrongfully held, and one mentally challenged man was held as leverage to get his brother to cooperate with the CIA.[37] Finally, the report concludes that the torture provided very little in the way of actionable intelligence that was usable or accurate.[38]

However, the effectiveness of these programs is not the most important thing. The most important thing is that we are a nation of laws, a nation that respects human rights, and a nation of values.

Senator John McCain, R-Ariz., said it best in a speech to the Senate. "In the end, torture's failure to serve its intended purpose isn't the main reason to oppose its use. I have often said and will always maintain that this question isn't about our enemies, it's about us. It's about who we were, who we are and who we aspire to be...Our enemies act without conscience," he said. "We must not."[39]

# CONCLUSION

These complicated issues highlight only a few of the tensions and challenges that the United States faces in determining how to defend the nation and interact with the global community. So long as there are threats to national security, American policymakers will continue to grapple with the best means of combating those threats and preserving stability.

[1] *U.S. Constitution.* Preamble.

[2] Griffith, Courtney. "A Closer Look at Discretionary Spending: Spending that Lawmakers Control through Annual Appropriation Acts." Ed. Jonathan Schwabish. Congressional Budget Office. 1 Apr. 2012. Web. 16 Mar. 2015. http://www.cbo.gov/sites/default/files/BS_Discretionary_print.pdf.

[3] "U.S. Military Must Do More with Less Money." The Brookings Institution. 11 Nov. 2013. Web. 16 Mar. 2015. http://www.brookings.edu/research/opinions/2013/11/11-us-military-budget-ohanlon.

[4] "Defense Spending No Longer Exempt from Scrutiny." Committee for a Responsible Federal Budget. 19 May 2010. Web. 2 Mar. 2015. http://crfb.org/blogs/defense-spending-no-longer-exempt-scrutiny.

[5] Peter G. Peterson Foundation. "The U.S. Spends More on Defense than the Next Seven Countries Combined." 13 April 2015. Web. 14 Apr. 2015. http://pgpf.org/Chart-Archive/0053_defense-comparison.

[6] "U.S. Military Personnel by Country." 1 Jan. 2012. Web. 14 Apr. 2015. http://www.cnn.com/interactive/2012/04/us/table.military.troops/.

[7] McCarthy, N. "These Are Americans' Top 10 Policy Priorities for 2015." Infographic. 6 Jan. 2015. Web. 14 Apr. 2015. http://www.forbes.com/sites/niallmccarthy/2015/01/16/these-are-americans-top-10-policy-priorities-for-2015-info-graphic/.

[8] Newport, F. "Americans Remain Divided on Military Spending." 27 Feb. 2014. Web. 14 April 2015. http://www.gallup.com/poll/167648/americans-remain-divided-military-spending.aspx.

[9] Pappas, Sandy. "Congress Needs to Scrutinize Pentagon Spending." *Minnesota Post.* 17 Apr. 2015. Web. 22 Apr. 2015. https://www.minnpost.com/community-voices/2015/04/congress-needs-scrutinize-pentagon-spending. Tilghman, Andrew. "Lawmakers Talk Big Cuts for Pentagon Budget." *Military Times.* 11 Feb. 2015. Web. 22 Apr. 2015. http://www.militarytimes.com/story/military/capitol-hill/2015/02/11/budget-cuts-hearing/23231453/. Pincus, Walter. "Pentagon Cancer Research Budget Comes under Scrutiny." *Washington Post.* 13 Mar. 2011. Web. 22 Apr. 2015. http://www.washingtonpost.com/world/pentagon-cancer-research-budget-comes-under-scrutiny/2011/03/10/ABq7S5R_story.html. "The Pentagon Budget and the Deficit." *New York Times.* 26 Sep. 2011. Web. 22 Apr. 2015. http://www.nytimes.com/2011/09/27/opinion/the-pentagon-budget-and-the-deficit.html.

[10] Simeone, Nick. "Hagel Outlines Budget Reducing Troop Strength, Force Structure." DoD News, United States Department of Defense. 24 Feb. 2014. Web. 22 Apr. 2015. http://www.defense.gov/news/newsarticle.aspx?id=121703.

[11] Sevcik, J.C. "Obama Scales Back Military Spending, Requests Defense Budget Cuts." United Press International. 4 Mar. 2014. Web. 20 Apr. 2015. http://www.upi.com/Top_News/US/2014/03/04/Obama-scales-back-military-spending-requests-defense-budget-cuts/9611393958680/.

12  Daniels, Mitch. "Keynote Speech to the Conservative Political Action Committee." Transcript-video. American Rhetoric. 1 Feb. 2011. Web. 20 Apr. 2015. http://www.americanrhetoric.com/speeches/mitchdanielscpac2011.htm

13  Rubio, Marco, and Tom Cotton. "Why Defense Budget Must Grow." CNN.com. 26 Mar. 2015. Web. 20 Apr. 2015. http://www.cnn.com/2015/03/26/opinions/rubio-cotton-defense-cuts/.

14  Flournoy, Michele, and Eric Edelman. "Cuts to Defense Spending Are Hurting Our National Security." *Washington Post.* 19 Sept. 2014. Web. 20 Apr. 2015. http://www.washingtonpost.com/opinions/cuts-to-us-military-spending-are-hurting-our-national-security/2014/09/18/6db9600c-3abf-11e4-9c9f-ebb47272e40e_story.html.

15  Raju, Manu. "Budget Debate Could Prove Awkward for 2016 Hopefuls." *Politico.* 18 Mar. 2015. Web. 20 Apr. 2015. http://www.politico.com/story/2015/03/fiscal-hard-liners-vs-defense-hawks-budget-splits-16-hopefuls-116211.html.

16  Ibid.

17  Byman, Daniel, and Matthew C. Waxman. *The Dynamics of Coercion: American Foreign Policy and the Limits of Military Might.* New York: Cambridge University Press, 2002.

18  "Just War Theory." Oregon State University. Web. 4 May 2015. http://oregonstate.edu/instruct/phl201/modules/just_war_theory/criteria_intro.html.

19  "Catholic Just War Theory." Catholic Peace Fellowship. Web. 4 May 2015. http://www.catholicpeacefellowship. org/nextpage.asp?m=2198.  "Just War Theory." Wikipedia. Wikimedia Foundation. Web. 4 May 2015. https:// en.wikipedia.org/wiki/Just_war_theory#Criteria_of_Just_War_theory.

20  Ibid.

21  Sarty, Roger. "The Royal Canadian Navy and the Battle of the Atlantic, 1939–1945." Dispatches: Backgrounders in Canadian Military History. Canadian War Museum. Web. 5 May 2015. http://www.warmuseum.ca/education/online-educational-resources/dispatches/the-royal-canadian-navy-and-the-battle-of-the-atlantic-1939-1945/.

22  "Germany Bombs London." BBC News. Web. 5 May 2015. http://www.bbc.co.uk/history/events/germany_bombs_london. Taylor, Alan. "Remembering Dresden: 70 Years After the Firebombing." The Atlantic. 12 Feb. 2015. Web. 5 May 2015. http://www.theatlantic.com/photo/2015/02/remembering-dresden-70-years-after-the-firebombing/385445/.

23  "The Atomic Bombings of Hiroshima and Nagasaki." Avalon Project. Yale Law School. Web. 5 May 2015. http://avalon. law.yale.edu/20th_century/mp25.asp.

24  "Geneva Conventions." Legal Information Institute. Web. 5 May 2015. https://www.law.cornell.edu/wex/geneva_conventions.

25  "Geneva Conventions." Council on Foreign Relations. Primary Sources. Web. 5 May 2015.  http://www.cfr.org/human-rights/geneva-conventions/p8778.

26  Haynes, William. "Enemy Combatants." Council on Foreign Relations. 12 Dec. 2002. Web. 5 May 2015. http://www.cfr.org/international-law/enemy-combatants/p5312.

27  Siems, Larry. "Why We Know the Decision to Torture Prisoners Started at the Top." Slate.com. 20 Apr. 2012. Web. 5 May 2015. http://www.slate.com/articles/news_and_politics/politics/2012/04/george_w_bush_and_torture_america_s_highest_officials_are_responsible_for_the_enhanced_interrogation_of_prisoners_.2.html.

28  "The Senate Committee's Report on the C.I.A.'s Use of Torture." *New York Times.* 8 Dec. 2014. Web. 5 May 2015. http://www.nytimes.com/interactive/2014/12/09/world/cia-torture-report-document.html?_r=0.

29  Bouie, Jamelle. "If Republicans Think Obama Is a Monarch, Why Are They OK With Cheney Being a Despot?" Slate. com. 15 Dec. 2014. Web. 5 May 2015. http://www.slate.com/articles/news_and_politics/politics/2014/12/dick_cheney_defends_cia_s_torture_republicans_angry_at_obama_s_executive.html.

30  Tenet, George, Michael Hayden, Porter Goss, John McLaughlin, Albert Calland, and Stephen Kappes. "Ex-CIA Directors: Interrogations Saved Lives." *Wall Street Journal.* 13 Dec. 2014. Web. 5 May 2015. http://www.wsj.com/articles/cia-interrogations-saved-lives-1418142644.

31  Krauthammer, Charles. "The Truth about Torture." *Weekly Standard.* Web. 5 May 2015. http://www.weeklystandard.com/Content/Public/Articles/000/000/006/400rhqav.asp.

32  Mazzetti, Mark. "Panel Faults C.I.A. over Brutality and Deceit in Terrorism Interrogations." *New York Times.* 9 Dec. 2014. Web. 5 May 2015. http://www.nytimes.com/2014/12/10/world/senate-intelligence-committee-cia-torture report.html?action=click&contentCollection= World&region=Footer &configSection=article&isLoggedIn=false&moduleDet ail=undefined&pgtype=Multimedia&_r=0.

33  Ashkenas, Jeremy, Hannah Fairfield, Josh Keller, and Paul Volpe. "7 Key Points from the C.I.A. Torture Report." *New York Times.* 8 Dec. 2014. Web. 5 May 2015. http://www.nytimes.com/interactive/2014/12/09/world/cia-torture-report-key-points.html.

34  Davidson, Amy. "The Torture Report: Inhumane Scenes from the C.I.A.'s Prisons." *The New Yorker.* 9 Dec. 2014. Web. 5 May 2015. http://www.newyorker.com/news/amy-davidson/inhumane-scenes-cia-prisons.

35  Taibbi, Matt. "10 Craziest Things in the Senate Report on Torture." *Rolling Stone.* 10 Dec. 2014. Web. 5 May 2015. http://www.rollingstone.com/politics/news/10-craziest-things-in-the-senate-report-on-torture-20141210?page=2.

36  Ibid.

37  Mazzetti, Mark. "Panel Faults C.I.A. over Brutality and Deceit in Terrorism Interrogations." *New York Times.* 9 Dec. 2014. Web. 5 May 2015. http://www.nytimes.com/2014/12/10/world/senate-intelligence-committee-cia-torture report.html?action=click&contentCollection= World&region=Footer &configSection=article&isLoggedIn=false&moduleDet ail=undefined&pgtype=Multimedia&_r=0.

38  "20 Key Findings about CIA Interrogations." *Washington Post.* Web. 5 May 2015. http://www.washingtonpost.com/wp-srv/special/national/cia-interrogation-report/key-findings/.

39  Engel, Pamela. "John McCain: The Brutal CIA Interrogations 'Stained Our National Honor.'" *Business Insider.* 9 Dec. 2014. Web. 5 May 2015. http://www.businessinsider.com/john-mccain-statement-on-cia-torture-report-2014-12. "John McCain Calls Out the Torture Apologists." Daily Kos. Web. 5 May 2015. http://www.dailykos.com/story/2014/12/09/1350555/-John-McCain-Calls-Out-the-Torture-Apologists.

# THE ECONOMY

## CURRENT CONTROVERSIES

- Should Congress raise the federal minimum wage?

- Should Congress increase taxes on top earners?

# INTRODUCTION

> *"The political problem of mankind is to combine three things: economic efficiency, social justice and individual liberty."*
> —John Maynard Keynes

> *"It is because every individual knows so little and, in particular, because we rarely know which of us knows best that we trust the independent and competitive efforts of many to induce the emergence of what we shall want when we see it."*
> —Friedrich von Hayek

Ever since the founding of the United States, Americans have been at odds over what role the federal government should play in directing economic policy, and which goals and priorities those policies should reflect. In this chapter, we will consider several enduring tensions in American economic policy and examine two current controversial issues:

- Should Congress raise the federal minimum wage?

- Should Congress increase taxes on top earners?

**Why Is Economic Policy Controversial?** The state of the American economy affects everyone. It governs how much money we earn, how much money we save, and what we can afford to purchase. Consequently, the economy is a vital issue to most Americans—and one of the most likely to influence the way they vote. When President Barack Obama won a second term in 2012, CNN exit polls suggested that 60 percent of voters believed the economy to be the most important issue facing the United States.[1]

Government involvement in the economy also has profound impacts on the lives of all Americans. Tax policies directly affect how much money the government collects, while tax revenue funds programs that individual Americans may or may not support. Interest rates—controlled by the Federal Reserve, the central bank of the United

States—determine how much Americans pay for homes, cars, and other goods purchased with the assistance of loans. And government regulations have far-reaching effects on wages, the ease of starting or operating a business, and the prices of goods and services.

As a result, economic policy is not crafted without controversy, as American policymakers, business owners, workers, and consumers have struggled for years to reconcile competing goals, priorities, and means of economic development.

- *Competing Goals.* What should be the most important goals of American economic policy? To create a system that allows the free market to flourish? To ensure that American workers, business owners, and investors are protected?

- *Competing Priorities.* What should be the priorities of American economic policy? To guarantee Americans access to gainful employment? To make it easier for businesses to grow and prosper?

- *Competing Means.* What means and methods should we employ to spur economic development? Should the government reduce taxes on workers and business owners? Should policymakers boost federal spending to try to stimulate economic activity? Should the United States forge new trade agreements? Should Congress raise the federal minimum wage?

**Why Is Economic Policy So Complicated?** The American economy—which encompasses the production, distribution, and consumption of goods and services—is the single largest national economy in the world. The total value of all goods and services produced in the United States—the nation's gross domestic product (GDP)—reached $17.7 trillion in the fourth quarter of 2014.[2]

Because the economy is such a large and significant force, lawmakers and economists often struggle to determine how to regulate it. The available tools include:

- *Fiscal Policy.* The federal government aims to promote growth through fiscal policy—the use of government spending and taxation to influence the economy. In addition to raising or lowering taxes, Congress and the president may attempt to stimulate the economy by spending taxpayer dollars on programs that provide jobs or grant subsidies to certain industries.

- *Monetary Policy.* The federal government also manipulates interest rates—the cost of borrowing money—and controls the amount of money in circulation. These functions, known as monetary policy, are entrusted to the Federal Reserve.

- *Trade Policy.* Congress and the president set rules regarding trade—the exchange of goods and services between nations. Trade policy may include import or export taxes, quotas, product safety regulations, or agreements between nations to reduce such restrictions. The government may place higher burdens on importers in order to protect domestic industries, or it may remove trade barriers to encourage the importation of foreign goods.

Regulation of the economy is further complicated by the fact that it is not an exact science. Throughout the course of American history, the federal government has used a variety of economic approaches that have achieved success. At times, the government has allowed the free market to operate largely without intervention, spurring innovation and creating competition. At other times, government economic programs have provided work and financial security for Americans in need. Furthermore, many unpredictable factors—such as consumer confidence or anxiety—contribute to economic booms and crises. As a result, policymakers face a complex and volatile landscape when they implement policies to regulate the economy.

# THE ONGOING DEBATE

## What is the appropriate role of government in regulating the labor market?

Although the framers of the Constitution protected Americans' rights to own property and to conduct private commercial affairs, they devoted few words to the exact role of government in the national economy. In its early years, the federal government largely refrained from regulating private business, developing a culture that celebrated free-market capitalism. But as the United States grew, some policymakers believed it necessary to expand the government's role, often in response to economic downturns or national concerns about labor standards, unemployment, or poverty.

The role of government grew dramatically in the 1930s, as the Great Depression brought widespread need to the forefront of American society. Faced with an unemployment rate of 25 percent when he took office in 1933, President Franklin Delano Roosevelt promised a "New Deal"—a series of government-led initiatives aimed at providing immediate relief, temporary work, and long-term economic reforms—for the American people.[3] Under various New Deal programs, Congress and President Roosevelt put millions of Americans to work on public

President Franklin Delano Roosevelt explains key components of the New Deal to the nation.

AP PHOTO

# NEW DEAL ERA LABOR REGULATIONS

**The Federal Minimum Wage.** The Fair Labor Standards Act of 1938 (FLSA) guaranteed a federal minimum wage of 25 cents per hour to workers in certain industries.[4] Since 2009, the federal minimum wage has stood at $7.25 per hour for:

- Employees of businesses with an annual gross volume of sales of at least $500,000.

- Employees of small firms who are engaged in, or produce goods for, interstate commerce.

- Guards, janitors, and maintenance employees who perform duties closely related to interstate activities.

- Employees of federal, state, or local government agencies, hospitals, and schools.

Under specific circumstances, several types of employees earn hourly wages below the federal minimum, including workers who earn tips, full-time students, student learners enrolled in vocational programs, youth under the age of 20, and workers with disabilities.[5] Many states also have their own minimum wage laws; when the state wage differs from the federal wage, employees are entitled to the higher of the two.

It is the responsibility of Congress to pass—and the president to sign—bills that raise the minimum wage, which they did 22 times between 1938 and 2014.[6] According to the Bureau of Labor Statistics (BLS), 1.6 million hourly workers earned exactly the federal minimum wage in 2012, while another two million earned lower wages due to their exempted types of employment. Together, these workers earning the federal minimum wage or less represented two percent of all American workers.[7]

**Overtime Pay.** The FLSA also guaranteed overtime pay for certain American workers. As of 2015, non-exempted employees were entitled to receive overtime wages—a rate of at least 1.5 times their regular rate—for all hours worked over 40 in a single work week.[8]

**Child Labor Rules.** The FLSA contained provisions to ban abusive child labor and to ensure that when youth work, their jobs are safe and do not interfere with their education. As of 2015, the federal government had set 14 as the minimum age for most non-agricultural work, although youth were permitted to work certain jobs—such as delivering newspapers or babysitting—at any age.[9]

**The National Labor Relations Board (NLRB).** The NLRB, established by the National Labor Relations Act of 1935, works to guarantee fair labor practices and to protect employees' rights to organize.

projects, established national rules for wages and working hours, and guaranteed workers' rights to organize.

Supporters of robust labor regulations argue that private industries cannot always be trusted to act on behalf of the public interest and, therefore, the government has a responsibility to protect its workers. But critics of strict labor regulations argue that they are an unnecessary interference in the efficiency of the free market and, therefore only increase costs for consumers and business owners. These critics believe that if the free market is allowed to operate naturally, the forces of choice and competition will compel private industries to treat their employees fairly and operate their businesses with integrity.

And the debate is far from finished, as Congress and the president have disagreed in recent years about whether to increase the federal minimum wage.

## THE CURRENT CONTROVERSY

### Should Congress raise the federal minimum wage?

In February 2014, President Obama signed an executive order increasing the minimum wage to $10.10 per hour for federal government contract employees—a policy that would affect several hundred thousand workers, according to White House estimates.[10] The president also endorsed the Fair Minimum Wage Act of 2013, which, if passed by Congress, would raise the federal minimum wage from $7.25 per hour to $10.10 per hour incrementally over two years; allow automatic annual increases to the wage, linked to changes in the cost of living; and gradually raise the wage for tipped workers to 70 percent of the federal minimum.[11]

But Congress and economists were deeply divided over the potential impacts of raising the federal minimum wage. Proponents of the wage increase argue that it would not only help the nation's poorest and most vulnerable citizens, it would provide millions of Americans with extra income to spend and invest, thus increasing economic activity and stimulating growth. Supporters also note that the current wage is woefully insufficient for full-time workers, trapping many people in poverty and contributing to record levels of income inequality.

But critics of increasing the minimum wage insist the policy would damage the economy and make it more difficult for businesses to hire and retain employees. Opponents note that the measure would only increase costs for employers and small businesses, forcing many of them to cut jobs, while reducing the jobs available to the least-skilled workers who need assistance the most. Furthermore, critics argue that few Americans are supporting their families with full-time minimum wage jobs—the minimum wage is primarily an entry-level, part-time wage for young people.

## Should Congress raise the federal minimum wage?

### YES: Lift Americans out of poverty and guarantee a decent living wage.

In the United States, the largest economic power in the world, a person who works full-time in a minimum wage job makes an annual income of $15,080.[12] To place that number in perspective, the 2014 measure of poverty in the United States was an income of $15,730 for a family of two, or $19,790 for a family of three.[13]

Therefore, the federal minimum wage, which has stood at a mere $7.25 per hour since 2009, is not even sufficient to keep American workers out of poverty. "This shouldn't happen in the richest nation on Earth," said former Senator Tom Harkin, D-Iowa, who introduced the Fair Minimum Wage Act of 2013. "No one who works hard for a living should have to live in poverty."[14]

At $7.25 an hour, the minimum wage traps many Americans in poverty and dampens social mobility, contributing to record levels of income inequality. In 2014, the National Low Income Housing Coalition reported that in order to pay fair market rent on a two-bedroom apartment, minimum wage workers in Alaska, California, Connecticut, Delaware, Florida, Hawaii, Maryland, Massachusetts, New Hampshire, New Jersey, New York, Virginia, and the District of Columbia would need to work at least 98 hours each week.[15]

But if Congress raises the minimum wage to $10.10 per hour, the Congressional Budget Office (CBO) has estimated that 900,000 people would be lifted out of poverty and 16.5 million low-wage workers would see increases in their average weekly incomes.[16] This policy would not only help the nation's most vulnerable citizens—it would provide millions of Americans with income to spend and invest, thus increasing economic activity and stimulating growth. "Raising the minimum wage to $10.10 an hour will put more money in workers' pockets, and more green in the tills of businesses across the country," said former Representative George Miller, D-Calif., who co-sponsored the Fair Minimum Wage Act. "It's time for $10.10 because a bigger paycheck will go right back into the economy, back into local small businesses that are always looking for new customers."[17]

President Obama also made his own appeal in his 2015 State of the Union address. "To everyone in this Congress who still refuses to raise the minimum wage, I say this: If you truly believe you could work full-time and support a family on less than $15,000 a year, try it," he said. "If not, vote to give millions of the hardest-working people in America a raise."[18]

## NO: Slashing job creation will harm the economy, small businesses, and the poorest Americans.

"When you raise the price of employment, guess what happens? You get less of it," Speaker of the House John Boehner, R-Ohio, said in 2013. "Why do we want to make it harder for small employers to hire people?"[19]

Ever since the Great Recession, which lingered for 18 months between 2007 and 2009, the United States has been making a slow economic recovery. In February 2015, 8.7 million Americans remained unemployed, while an additional 2.2 million people wanted work but had not searched for a job in the past month. Another 6.6 million were involuntarily employed part-time because their hours had been cut back or they were unable to find a full-time job.[20] Therefore, it is hardly the time to enact a policy that would slash total employment by 500,000 workers by 2016, according to the CBO.[21]

"It's a classic election-year ploy to make the Democrats look like they're protecting low-income workers," said Randel Johnson, senior vice president at the U.S. Chamber of Commerce. "I think it's well understood that raising the minimum wage hurts workers on the lower end of the pay scale in that it does kill jobs."[22]

Small businesses created 64 percent of the net new jobs in the United States between 1993 and 2011, while accounting for half of private-sector employment in 2012.[23] But in October 2013, 45 percent of surveyed small business owners told Gallup that a minimum wage increase would lead them to reduce their workforce, shrink employee benefits, decrease capital spending, or some combination thereof.[24]

It is also important to remember that the minimum wage is primarily an entry-level, part-time wage for young people—not a means of providing for an entire family. In fact, more than half of the workers who earned hourly wages at or below the federal minimum in 2012 were under the age of 25.[25]

"The majority of these workers are younger people just getting into the workforce," said Representative Paul Ryan, R-Wis., chairman of the House Committee on Ways and Means. "We want to get people into the workforce. A job is the bridge to a better life. And what we don't want to do is support ideas, especially in this kind of an economy, which will reduce the availability of jobs, number one, but more importantly, reduce the availability of jobs for the very people we want to get into jobs so they can start climbing that ladder of life."[26]

# THE ONGOING DEBATE
## How high should taxes be in the United States?

Perhaps no issue in American history has been more frequently and passionately debated than taxation. Article I of the Constitution states, "The Congress shall have Power to lay and collect Taxes, Duties, Imposts and Excises, to pay the Debts and provide for the common Defence and general Welfare of the United States; but all Duties, Imposts and Excises shall be uniform throughout the United States."[27] But like many powers outlined in the Constitution, the taxation authority of Congress is broad and unspecific, and Americans do not always agree on what level of taxation is appropriate, which goods and services should be taxed, and which government programs tax revenue should fund.

Under the current system, the federal government collects a variety of different taxes from American citizens—nearly $2.9 trillion in fiscal year 2013—in order to pay for its spending commitments.[28]

**Individual Income Tax.** Individuals pay taxes on the income they earn, which may include wages; salaries; tips; profits on the sale of assets or investments, also known as capital gains; income from royalties, trusts, and estates; interest payments on investments; and alimony. In 2013, the individual income tax accounted for 47 percent of federal revenue.[29]

**Social Security and Other Payroll Taxes.** Workers and employers are required to contribute to certain federal programs, most notably Social Security and Medicare—the benefits of which Americans are eligible to receive at a qualifying age. In 2015, workers and employers will each pay 6.2 percent of workers' first $118,500 in wages to Social Security, while each paying 1.45 percent of all wages to Medicare as well. In 2013, payroll taxes accounted for 34 percent of federal revenue.[30]

**Corporate Income Tax.** Businesses must pay taxes to the federal government—the level of which is determined by their profits. Corporations do not pay taxes on the costs of doing business, such as materials, wages, and the depreciation of their assets. In 2013, the corporate income tax accounted for ten percent of federal revenue.[31]

**Estate and Gift Taxes.** When individuals die, the federal estate tax is levied on the sum of their assets. The gift tax, meanwhile, is a tax on the transfer of property for less than full value—thus preventing Americans from avoiding the estate tax. In 2013, estate and gift taxes accounted for nearly six percent of federal revenue.[32]

**Excise Taxes.** Excise taxes are levied on the consumption of certain goods and services, such as gasoline, air travel, alcohol, and cigarettes. In 2013, excise taxes accounted for three percent of federal revenue.[33]

The American tax system, however, is vast and complex, and contains many caveats that specify which types of income are taxed at which rates. The income tax system is progressive, meaning that higher earners are subject to higher marginal rates of taxation. In 2014, for example, single Americans faced a ten percent marginal tax rate for the first $9,075 they earned, but a 39.6 percent marginal tax rate for certain portions of their income over $406,750.32. The tax structure is further complicated by tax credits that many workers claim, such as the earned income tax credit for low-income Americans, credits for first-time homebuyers, and credits for those with child or dependent care expenses.

Congress, for its part, has had several debates over the appropriate level of taxation in recent years. In 2001 and 2003, Congress sought to jumpstart the contracting economy by passing $1.7 trillion in across-the-board tax cuts at the urging of President George W. Bush.[35] Supporters hailed the policy for increasing Americans' take-home pay and stimulating the economy, while critics expressed concern that the tax cuts—along with surges in entitlement and military spending— were leading the government to spend more than it took in. But with the policy set to expire in January 2013, most Republicans pushed for the extension of all of the Bush tax cuts, while President Obama and most Democrats insisted on abolishing the cuts for top earners. In early 2013, the two sides reached a compromise agreement— increasing tax rates on top earners while making permanent the tax cuts for most families earning less than $450,000 annually—but the taxation debate raged on.[36]

# THE CURRENT CONTROVERSY

## Should Congress increase taxes on top earners?

In February 2015, President Obama sent Congress a $4 trillion budget blueprint for fiscal year 2016, which called for roughly $1.5 trillion in tax increases on top earners.[37] Among its provisions, the president's plan would:

- Increase the top taxation rate of capital gains from 23.8 percent to 28 percent.

- Implement the so-called "Buffet Rule," which would require Americans who earn at least $1 million per year to pay at least 30 percent of their income, after charitable contributions, in federal taxes.

- Require Americans to pay capital gains taxes on their appreciated assets at death, before those assets are passed to their heirs.

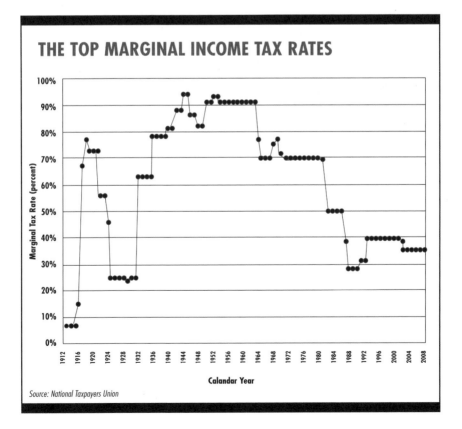

**THE TOP MARGINAL INCOME TAX RATES**

Marginal Tax Rate (percent)

Calandar Year

Source: National Taxpayers Union

Of the new revenue in President Obama's plan, roughly $640 billion would go toward reducing annual deficits, while the rest would fund new government initiatives.[38] And although it was unlikely that the Republican-controlled Congress would pass President Obama's proposal, the budget plan reopened the debate about whether the government should increase taxes on top earners.

Supporters of the tax increase believe it is only fair for the wealthiest Americans to pay more in taxes, especially as the United States grapples with a national debt that stood at more than $18 trillion in early 2015.[39] Proponents argue that higher taxes on the rich would allow the government to reduce taxes on low-income and middle-class Americans, providing them with purchasing power to stimulate the economy. Supporters also insist that prosperity does not trickle down from the highest earners—it begins with working Americans who are given a fair shot at success.

But critics of higher taxes on the wealthy disagree and argue that such policies only discourage investment, harm fragile economic growth, and punish success. These critics say that by increasing taxes on the nation's biggest business owners and investors, the government would only persuade job creators to either take their investments abroad or to reduce their total investments. Furthermore, critics believe that higher taxes would only feed the federal government's spending problem, while stoking dangerous class warfare.

## Should Congress increase taxes on top earners?

### YES: Encourage tax fairness and ease the debt crisis.

"Being asked to pay your fair share isn't class warfare," then-Newark Mayor Cory Booker said in 2012. "It's patriotism."[40]

"While the poor and middle class fight for us in Afghanistan, and while most Americans struggle to make ends meet, we mega-rich continue to get our extraordinary tax breaks," wrote Warren Buffett, the billionaire chairman of Berkshire Hathaway. "Last year my federal tax bill—the income tax I paid, as well as payroll taxes paid by me and on my behalf—was $6,938,744. That sounds like a lot of money. But what I paid was only 17.4 percent of my taxable income—and that's actually a lower percentage than was paid by any of the other 20 people in our office. Their tax burdens ranged from 33 percent to 41 percent and averaged 36 percent."[41]

In many ways, the United States' tax system favors the rich. Wealthy Americans who make their money by buying and selling stocks and receiving dividends, for example, pay capital gains taxes instead of the traditionally higher income taxes. Social Security taxes, meanwhile, are only collected on a worker's first $118,500 in wages, allowing high earners to pay a much smaller share of their income into the program than those who earn less.

Because of these tax breaks and other reasons, "economic inequality has worsened significantly in the United States and some other countries. The richest 1 percent in the United States now own more wealth than the bottom 90 percent," columnist Nicholas Kristof wrote in the *New York Times*.[42]

But by increasing taxes on the wealthy, the government would give itself the flexibility to reduce taxes on middle-class Americans, providing them with more income to put back into the economy. "Higher taxes on the wealthy can finance more investments in infrastructure and education, which are vital for growth and the economic prospects of the middle class," said former Secretary of Labor Robert Reich. "Fairness isn't incompatible with growth. It's necessary for it."[43]

And for his part, Buffett denied the idea that higher taxes on wealthy Americans would harm economic investment and entrepreneurship. He said, "I have worked with investors for 60 years and I have yet to see anyone—not even when capital gains rates were 39.9 percent in 1976-77—shy away from a sensible investment because of the tax rate on the potential gain."[44]

## NO: Higher taxes discourage growth and feed wasteful government spending.

The American economy, which was founded on the principles of free-market capitalism, flourishes when taxes are low. Investors and entrepreneurs have the freedom and income to invest in new ventures, innovations, and businesses. But by hiking taxes on top earners, the government would be targeting the very investors and job creators who help the economy grow.

"Just what do we tax under our current system? Work, that's what," wrote Neal Boortz, coauthor of *FairTax: The Truth: Answering the Critics.* "The harder you work, the more you achieve. The more you achieve, the more you're taxed. To make matters worse, under our 'progressive' income tax system, the harder you work, the more severe the punishment actually is!"[45]

The truth is that wealthy Americans already pay a staggering share of the nation's taxes. In 2010, the top ten percent of taxpayers paid more than 70 percent of federal income taxes, according to the Tax Foundation. The remaining 90 percent of Americans paid a mere 30 percent of the federal tax burden.[46]

Therefore, to accuse the wealthy of failing to pay their fair share of taxes is merely stoking class warfare. "The notion, first of all, that in order for some people to do better, someone has to do worse, is just not true," said Senator Marco Rubio, R-Fla. "Raising taxes on people that are successful is not going to make people that are struggling more successful. The good news about free enterprise is that everyone can succeed without punishing anyone."[47]

Furthermore, as evidenced by the $2.9 trillion it collected in fiscal year 2013, the federal government is not suffering from a lack of tax revenue. "The American economy is going to create more tax revenue this year than any other year in our history. We don't have a revenue problem. We have a spending problem," said Speaker Boehner. "How much more money do we want to steal from the American people to fund more government? I'm for no more."[48]

"Consider the 'Buffett Rule' that the president spent many months promoting," wrote Arthur Brooks, president of the American Enterprise Institute, and Edwin Feulner, former president of the Heritage Foundation. "According to the Joint Committee on Taxation, it would raise about $47 billion over a decade. The federal government currently spends about $4 billion more per day than it takes in. The Buffett Rule, then, would raise about enough next year to cover 28 hours of government overspending."[49]

# CONCLUSION

Raising the federal minimum wage and increasing taxes on top earners are only two examples of the economic policy debates Americans have engaged in for centuries. And although the fate of these two policy options remains far from certain, American policymakers, business owners, workers, and consumers will undoubtedly continue to debate the goals, priorities, and means of economic development—and which government policies best reflect and achieve them.

---

[1] Abdullah, Halimah, and Joe Van Canel. "Economy tops voter concerns in exit polls." CNN. 6 Nov. 2012. Web. 6 Mar. 2015.

[2] U.S. Bureau of Economic Analysis. *National Income and Product Accounts, Gross Domestic Product: Fourth Quarter and Annual 2014* (Second Estimate). 27 Feb. 2015. Web. 6 Mar. 2015.

[3] "Action, and Action Now: FDR's First 100 Days." Special exhibit at the Franklin D. Roosevelt Presidential Library and Museum, Hyde Park. Web. 6 Mar. 2015.

[4] Grossman, Jonathan. "Fair Labor Standards Act of 1938: Maximum Struggle for a Minimum Wage." *Monthly Labor Review*. 1978. Web. 6 Mar. 2015.

[5] "Questions and Answers About the Minimum Wage." U.S. Department of Labor. Wage and Hour Division. Web. 6 Mar. 2015.

[6] Elwell, Craig K. *Inflation and the Real Minimum Wage: A Fact Sheet.* Congressional Research Service. 8 Jan. 2014. Web. 6 Mar. 2015.

[7] U.S. Department of Labor, Bureau of Labor Statistics. *Characteristics of Minimum Wage Workers: 2012.* 26 Feb. 2013. Web. 6 Mar. 2015.

[8] "Overtime Pay." U.S. Department of Labor, Wage and Hour Division. Web. 6 Mar. 2015.

[9] "Child Labor." U.S. Department of Labor, Wage and Hour Division. Web. 6 Mar. 2015.

[10] Miller, Zeke J. "Barack Obama Minimum Wage Order Affects Only About 200,000 Workers." *Time.* 30 Jan. 2014. Web. 6 Mar. 2015.

[11] The White House. *Fact Sheet—Opportunity For All: Rewarding Hard Work.* 12 Feb. 2014. Web. 6 Mar. 2015.

[12] Cooper, David. "The Minimum Wage Used to Be Enough to Keep Workers Out of Poverty—It's Not Anymore." Economic Policy Institute. 4 Dec. 2013. Web. 6 Mar. 2015.

[13] "2014 Poverty Guidelines." U.S. Department of Health and Human Services, Office of the Assistant Secretary for Planning and Evaluation. Web. 6 Mar. 2015.

[14] Harkin, Tom. Remarks Introducing the Fair Minimum Wage Act of 2013. 5 Mar. 2013. House Committee on Education and the Workforce, Democrats. Web. 6 Mar. 2015.

[15] Arnold, Althea, Sheila Crowley, Elina Bravve, Sarah Brundage, and Christine Biddlecombe. "Out of Reach 2014." National Low Income Housing Coalition. 2014. Web. 6 Mar. 2015.

[16] Congressional Budget Office. *The Effects of a Minimum-Wage Increase on Employment and Family Income.* 18 Feb. 2014. Web. 6 Mar. 2015.

[17] Miller, George. Remarks Introducing the Fair Minimum Wage Act of 2013. 5 Mar. 2013. House Committee on Education and the Workforce, Democrats. Web. 6 Mar. 2015.

[18] Obama, Barack. State of the Union Address. 20 Jan. 2015. White House Transcript. Web. 6 Mar. 2015.

[19] Delreal, Jose. "20 quotes: Politicians on minimum wage." *Politico.* 12 Dec. 2013. Web. 6 Mar. 2015.

[20] U.S. Department of Labor, Bureau of Labor Statistics. *Employment Situation Summary.* 6 Mar. 2015. Web. 6 Mar. 2015.

[21] Congressional Budget Office. *The Effects of a Minimum-Wage Increase on Employment and Family Income.* 18 Feb. 2014. Web. 6 Mar. 2015.

[22] Greenhouse, Steven. "Raising the Floor on Pay." *New York Times.* 9 Apr. 2012. Web. 6 Mar. 2015.

[23] U.S. Small Business Administration, Office of Advocacy. "Frequently Asked Questions." Sep. 2012. Web. 6 Mar. 2015.

[24] Dugan, Andrew. "U.S. Small-Business Owners Split on Raising Minimum Wage." Gallup. 22 Nov. 2013. Web. 6 Mar. 2015.

[25] U.S. Department of Labor, Bureau of Labor Statistics. *Characteristics of Minimum Wage Workers: 2012.* 26 Feb. 2013. Web. 6 Mar. 2015.

[26] Ryan, Paul. Remarks at a town hall meeting. Elkhorn, Wisconsin. 20 Mar. 2014. ThinkProgress. Web. 6 Mar. 2015.

[27] *U.S. Constitution.* Article I, Section 8.

[28] U.S. Department of the Treasury, Internal Revenue Service. *Data Book 2013.* Web. 6 Mar. 2015.

[29] Sherlock, Molly F., and Donald J. Marples. *Overview of the Federal Tax System.* Congressional Research Service. 21 Nov. 2014. Web. 6 Mar. 2015.

[30] Sherlock, Molly F., and Donald J. Marples. *Overview of the Federal Tax System.* Congressional Research Service. 21 Nov. 2014. Web. 6 Mar. 2015.

[31] Sherlock, Molly F., and Donald J. Marples. *Overview of the Federal Tax System.* Congressional Research Service. 21 Nov. 2014. Web. 6 Mar. 2015.

[32] Sherlock, Molly F., and Donald J. Marples. *Overview of the Federal Tax System.* Congressional Research Service. 21 Nov. 2014. Web. 6 Mar. 2015.

[33] Sherlock, Molly F., and Donald J. Marples. *Overview of the Federal Tax System.* Congressional Research Service. 21 Nov. 2014. Web. 6 Mar. 2015.

[34] "Individual Federal Income Tax Rates by Tax Year." eFile.com. Web. 6 Mar. 2015.

[35] "Policy Basics: The 2001 and 2003 Tax Cuts." Center on Budget and Policy Priorities. 5 Mar. 2009. Web. 6 Mar. 2015.

[36] Goldfarb, Zachary. "The legacy of the Bush tax cuts, in four charts." *Washington Post.* 2 Jan. 2013. Web. 6 Mar. 2015.

[37] McKinnon, John. "New Taxes Would Hit Wealthy, Companies." *Wall Street Journal.* 2 Feb. 2015. Web. 6 Mar. 2015.

[38] Sahadi, Jeanne. "The Buffett Rule is back." CNN Money. 2 Feb. 2015. Web. 6 Mar. 2015.

[39] U.S. National Debt Clock. Brillig. Web. 6 Mar. 2015.

[40] Bailey, Holly. "Cory Booker: Raising taxes on the rich is about 'patriotism,' not 'class warfare.'" Yahoo News. 4 Sep. 2012. Web. 6 Mar. 2015.

[41] Buffett, Warren. "Stop Coddling the Super-Rich." *New York Times.* 14 Aug. 2011. Web. 6 Mar. 2015.

[42] Kristof, Nicholas. "An idiot's guide to inequality." *New York Times.* 23 July 2014. Web. 12 Mar. 2015

[43] Reich, Robert. "Taxing the rich is good for the economy." Marketplace. 18 Apr. 2012. Web. 6 Mar. 2015.

[44] Buffett, Warren. "Stop Coddling the Super-Rich." *New York Times.* 14 Aug. 2011. Web. 6 Mar. 2015.

[45] Boortz, Neal, John Linder, and Bob Woodall. *FairTax: The Truth: Answering the Critics.* William Morrow Paperbacks. 12 Feb. 2008.

[46] Hargreaves, Steve. "The rich pay majority of U.S. income taxes." CNN Money. 12 Mar. 2013. Web. 6 Mar. 2015.

[47] Rubio, Marco. Interview. "Face the Nation." CBS. 18 Jan. 2015. Web. 6 Mar. 2015.

[48] Boehner, John. Remarks at a press conference. Washington, D.C. 28 Feb. 2013. Web. 6 Mar. 2015.

[49] Brooks, Arthur, and Edwin Feulner. "Column: Why tax increases don't work." *USA Today.* 5 Dec. 2012. Web. 6 Mar. 2015.

# EDUCATION

## CURRENT CONTROVERSIES

- Should Congress pass legislation to use federal funds on school choice programs in various states?

- Should governments fund universal preschool?

# INTRODUCTION

> *"Laws for the liberal education of youth, especially of the lower class of people, are so extremely wise and useful, that, to a humane and generous mind, no expense for this purpose would be thought extravagant."*
>
> —John Adams

> *"In large states public education will always be mediocre, for the same reason that in large kitchens the cooking is usually bad."*
>
> —Friedrich Nietzsche

The debate over education policy in the United States is as old as the nation itself. For centuries, Americans have sought to clarify what role the government should assume in educating its citizens and which specific policies should be implemented and prioritized. In this chapter, we will consider several enduring tensions in American education policy and examine two current controversial issues:

- Should Congress pass legislation to use federal funds on school choice programs in various states?

- Should governments fund universal preschool?

**Why Is Education Policy Controversial?** Each and every American citizen is guaranteed access to a free public education, from the first day of kindergarten until high school graduation. In the fall of 2014, 49.8 million American students began the academic year at more than 98,800 public elementary and secondary schools—schools that employed 3.1 million full-time-equivalent teachers.

At the same time, local, state, and federal governments were expected to spend $619 billion—or more than $12,000 per student—on books, materials, salaries, benefits, and transportation during the 2014–2015 academic year.[1] And that money is not spent without controversy, as American policymakers, educators, parents, and students have struggled for years to reconcile competing goals, priorities, and means of public education.

- *Competing Goals.* What should be the most important goals of public schools? To prepare students for the workforce by teaching them important skills? To help students reach college? To create responsible citizens?

- *Competing Priorities.* What should be the priorities of the public education system? To be lean and thrifty by cutting inefficient programs and targeting needed resources? To boost spending and focus on student enrichment? To provide additional resources to disadvantaged schools and students?

- *Competing Means.* What means and methods should we employ to best educate students? Are charter schools necessary to compete with traditional public schools? Should students have the option of attending private schools with government vouchers? Should we support existing public schools and construct new ones when necessary? And how do we best measure student and teacher achievement?

Secretary of Education Arne Duncan speaks at an elementary school in Washington, D.C., about federal education priorities.

**Why Is Education Policy So Complicated?** In a nation comprising 50 states and more than 14,000 school districts, education policy is far from uniform.[2] In certain states, district and local officials are empowered to make big decisions about schools and curriculum; in others, the most important school-related policies are crafted by the state government. Large school districts, such as the Los Angeles Unified School District, often have more authority than smaller districts in the same state. And charter schools, while regulated by their districts, states, and authorizers, are exempt from many state and local regulations.

As the states work to tailor their public education systems to meet the needs of their populations, the role of the federal government is not always clear. While schools are subject to federal laws regarding discrimination and equal access, the Department of Education does not have true authority over the United States' decentralized public school system. As a result, the Department of Education instead incentivizes schools, districts, and states to make certain reforms by awarding grants and funding.

## THE ONGOING DEBATE

### Should the government pursue market-based education reforms or seek to strengthen existing public schools?

The school reform movement largely began in 1983, when the National Commission on Excellence in Education—a panel of educators, administrators, and policymakers formed by Secretary of Education Terrel Bell—issued a blistering critique of American public education in a report titled "A Nation at Risk." This watershed document spoke of a "rising tide of mediocrity" in the nation's schools—one that "threatens our very future as a Nation and a people."[3]

In the decades that followed the release of "A Nation at Risk," presidents, governors, legislators, and school boards began pushing for a wide variety of public education reforms. Some of these policies—such as school choice and vouchers, charter schools, merit pay for teachers, and virtual schools—became known as "market-based reforms," because they encourage free-market competition in public education.

# MARKET-BASED REFORMS IN EDUCATION

**School Choice and Vouchers.** The public school system was traditionally structured to only allow students to attend the elementary and secondary schools in their neighborhoods. But as some policymakers and reformers began arguing that the system confined certain unlucky students to failing neighborhood schools, they pushed for a change in policy. Some school districts experimented with busing programs, which shuttled students to different schools in an effort to combat residential inequalities and the effects of historic segregation. But as busing largely failed to take hold, some reformers turned to school choice programs, in which parents receive a government grant—or voucher—to help pay for their child to attend an approved private school of their choosing.

As of 2014, voucher programs existed in 13 states and the District of Columbia, according to the National Conference of State Legislatures. Eight states offered vouchers to students with special needs; four states and the District of Columbia offered vouchers to low-income students and students who attended failing schools; and two states offered vouchers to rural students. Two states—Louisiana and Ohio—provided vouchers for both low-income students and students with special needs.[4]

**Charter Schools.** In 1992, a new reform movement was born when City Academy in St. Paul, Minnesota, opened its doors as the nation's first charter school. Charter schools are publicly funded schools designed to meet specific educational goals, created by an organization under a contract—or charter— with a state or jurisdiction. Charter schools must abide by federal laws regarding equal rights and access, but they are exempt from many state and local regulations. Students attend charter schools tuition-free and by the choice of their parents; if there is an overflow of applicants, a lottery determines enrollment.

According to the National Alliance for Public Charter Schools, there were 6,440 charter schools operating in the United States during the 2013–2014 academic year, serving more than 2.5 million students.[5] And as of early 2015, every state except eight—Alabama, Kentucky, Montana, Nebraska, North Dakota, South Dakota, Vermont, and West Virginia—had enacted charter school laws.[6]

**Merit Pay for Teachers.** Traditionally, teachers have been compensated on a salary scale, collectively negotiated though a union, based on their number of years of experience, their graduate degrees, and their professional development. In the last several decades, however, some school districts have begun experimenting with merit pay, or teacher compensation based on classroom performance.

As of 2011, the National Center on Performance Initiatives had documented teacher merit pay systems in 500—or 3.5 percent—of the nation's 14,000 school districts.[7] And these systems vary greatly from district to district and state to state. Some school districts base teachers' salaries primarily on peer or administrator evaluations; others take students' standardized test scores into greater account.

**Virtual Schools.** Virtual K-12 schools—or online schools—allow students to learn from their homes or from learning centers, as all instruction is done through electronic communication. In a 2013 report, the National Education Policy Center found a total of 311 full-time virtual schools operating in the United States during the 2011–2012 academic year, serving nearly 200,000 students.[8]

Students rally at the New York State Capitol to support their charter school education.

While these policies represent only a few of the major ideas put forward in the American education reform discussion, recent congressional proposals have reignited the debate over certain types of market-based reforms.

## THE CURRENT CONTROVERSY

### Should Congress pass legislation to use federal funds on school choice programs in various states?

In January 2014, Senator and former Secretary of Education Lamar Alexander, R-Tenn., brought the debate over market-based reforms to the forefront when he proposed the Scholarships for Kids Act. If enacted, the bill would annually redirect $24 billion—or 41 percent— of existing federal K-12 funding, allowing states with school choice programs to provide $2,100 vouchers for children living in poverty to use toward any accredited public or private school their parents choose.[9]

Supporters of the bill believe the free market would rapidly improve schools in a way that new state or federal government policies never could. Proponents argue that if schools are forced to compete for funding, they will improve more rapidly than if they are merely pressured by policymakers and education officials. And as underperforming schools begin to close their doors, ineffective teachers would be forced from the workforce. Supporters of the bill also believe it would encourage innovation in education, as schools would be pushed to seek advantages over their competitors. Furthermore, proponents note that students from low-income families would be afforded valuable opportunities to leave failing schools.

Opponents of the Scholarships for Kids Act, however, believe it would only increase inequality. Critics of the bill say it would deprive struggling public schools—the schools most in need of assistance—of vital public funding. Detractors also argue that the poorest students would not be able to afford transportation to better schools in other neighborhoods, thus limiting their ability to take advantage of the program. Furthermore, private schools are not accountable to public standards, including those set by states or the Common Core State Standards. As a result, poor students who end up in private schools may not be as well-tracked and supported as those in public schools.

### Should Congress pass legislation to use federal funds on school choice programs in various states?

---

**YES: Let parents choose how to educate their children.**

The most powerful way to improve any product is to offer a choice to consumers—a lesson that economic history has taught us time and again. So why do we continue to force students and parents to accept the school to which they are arbitrarily assigned?

Senator Alexander is attempting to put the force of the federal government behind the idea that students and families are free to choose. When he announced his new legislation, Senator Alexander said, "Allowing federal dollars to follow students has been a successful strategy in American education for 70 years. Last year, $33 billion in federal Pell grants and $106 billion in loans followed students to public and private colleges. Since the GI Bill began in 1944, these vouchers have helped create a marketplace of 6,000 autonomous higher education institutions—the best in the world.

"Our elementary and secondary education system is not the best in the world. American 15-year-olds rank 28th in science and 36th in math. I believe one reason for this is that while more than 93 percent of federal dollars spent for higher education follow students to colleges of their choice, federal dollars do not automatically follow K-12 students to schools of their choice."[10]

Michael McShane, a fellow at the American Enterprise Institute, argued that consumer choice will foster school improvement. "Put simply, schools haven't had to evolve like enterprises in competitive markets. If auto manufacturers made the same cars they made in 1974, they'd be out of business. If computer companies still charged thousands of dollars for computers with 64 megabytes of hard drive space, they'd be out of business. But our education system keeps plodding along, year after year, making some improvements in some places at some times, to be sure, but not rising in quality at the same rate as almost any other good or service in our economy."[11]

Representative Luke Messer, R-Ind., who introduced the Scholarships for Kids Act in the House of Representatives in February 2014, added, "Too many families live in neighborhoods with bad schools. They can't afford to move, and they can't afford tuition to go to a better school either. There is another way. Imagine a system not limited by zip code, where education dollars follow the child, and every family in America can afford to send their child to the school of their choice."[12]

## NO: Support our public schools.

For more than a decade, conservatives have waged war against public schools by supporting voucher programs and diverting funds and students into charter schools. But despite their push for greater rigor and testing, these conservatives have few accomplishments to show for their efforts. Instead, public schools are in worse shape than they were before the passage of No Child Left Behind.

There is little evidence suggesting that charter schools do a better job educating students than public schools, and the same is true of lower-cost private schools. In fact, researchers at the Harvard Graduate School of Education concluded in nine studies of school choice programs that such initiatives actually deepen educational inequality and fail to yield consistent learning gains.

The voucher system that this bill creates would ultimately do harm to the public school system. It would remove funding from important K-12 programs that support low-income students, education research, and professional development for teachers, and put it toward an untested, unproven school choice system.

Diane Ravitch, the author of *Death and Life of the Great American School System* and the former assistant secretary of education under the bill's author, Senator Alexander, said, "Do not be fooled: this is not a conservative plan. This is a radical plan. It will send public dollars to backwoods churches and ambitious entrepreneurs. No high-performing nation in the world has vouchers."[13]

Senator Patty Murray, D-Wash., the ranking Democrat on the Senate Committee on Health, Education, Labor, and Pensions, argued in 2001, "Vouchers do not offer true choice for students. While parents may remove their children from public schools, no voucher system guarantees them admission to the school of their 'choice.' Private schools will still choose which students they will admit. So while vouchers drain money from the public schools to help a few students, they leave other students at a public school with fewer resources. That won't help all kids succeed."[14]

Garrison Keillor, an author and radio host, also weighed in on the school choice debate. "When you wage war on the public schools, you're attacking the mortar that holds the community together," Keillor said. "You're not a conservative, you're a vandal."[15]

# THE ONGOING DEBATE

## What level of education should the government guarantee to American citizens?

The framers of the Constitution made no mention of education in the founding document, thus leaving the responsibility of educating American citizens to the states. Under the Tenth Amendment, "The powers not delegated to the United States by the Constitution, nor prohibited by it to the states, are reserved to the states respectively, or to the people."[16] This American belief in locally controlled public education dates back to 1647, when the Massachusetts Bay Colony laid the cornerstone of the nation's public education system by requiring its towns to establish and support schools.

As a result, the United States does not have one federally controlled system of public education. Instead, each state in its constitution has outlined the state's responsibilities to educate its citizens. State legislatures exercise varying degrees of authority over education, depending on their constitutional powers; many have delegated responsibilities to appointed or elected state boards of education. Therefore, it is in the hands of state and local officials to establish schools, develop curriculum standards, determine teacher qualifications, and establish enrollment and graduation requirements. For example, some states—Connecticut, New Mexico, Oklahoma, and Virginia—require children to attend school between the ages of five and 18, while other states—Alaska, Idaho, Indiana, Minnesota, Missouri, Montana, North Carolina, North Dakota, and Wyoming—only require school attendance by children between the ages of seven and 16.[17]

In each state, however, American citizens are guaranteed access to a free public K-12 education. Beyond that, the level of education promised to each citizen depends on the state in which they reside. In Tennessee, for example, residents can attend community college tuition-free, regardless of their income level. And in Oregon, state lawmakers were considering a bill in early 2015 to require community college students to pay only $50 per course—but only if students first apply for federal and state financial aid. In his 2015 State of the Union

address, President Barack Obama said, "Tennessee, a state with Republican leadership, and Chicago, a city with Democratic leadership, are showing that free community college is possible. I want to spread that idea all across America, so that two years of college becomes as free and universal in America as high school is today."[18]

Some states have also worked to increase access to early childhood education. As of the 2012–2013 academic year, the National Institute for Early Education Research had documented state-supported preschool programs in 40 states and the District of Columbia—31 of which had income requirements. These programs served more than 1.3 million children, or four percent of three-year-olds and 28 percent of four-year-olds in the United States. The District of Columbia had the highest percentage—93.9 percent—of its four-year-olds enrolled in state-supported preschool programs that year, followed by Florida (78.5 percent) and Oklahoma (74.1 percent). At the same time, ten states—Hawaii, Idaho, Indiana, Mississippi, Montana, New Hampshire, North Dakota, South Dakota, Utah, and Wyoming—had not implemented state-supported preschool programs in 2012–2013.[19]

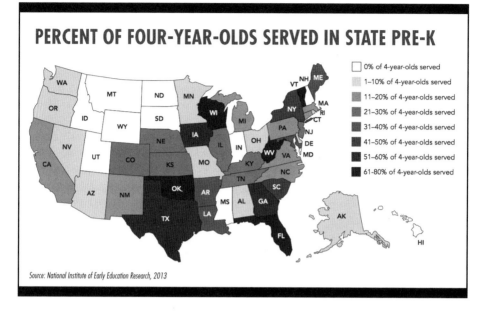

# PERCENT OF FOUR-YEAR-OLDS SERVED IN STATE PRE-K

- 0% of 4-year-olds served
- 1–10% of 4-year-olds served
- 11–20% of 4-year-olds served
- 21–30% of 4-year-olds served
- 31–40% of 4-year-olds served
- 41–50% of 4-year-olds served
- 51–60% of 4-year-olds served
- 61–80% of 4-year-olds served

Source: National Institute of Early Education Research, 2013

On the federal level, Head Start was established in 1965 to provide educational, nutritional, health, and social services for young children from low-income families to help prepare them for school. The Department of Health and Human Services awards Head Start grants to approximately 1,700 public and private organizations across the country, which, in turn, offer locally tailored programs in centers and schools. In fiscal year 2013, Head Start programs served 932,164 children and their families.[20]

The debate over expanding educational guarantees has spread to communities across the country, as several states and cities were considering or implementing universal preschool programs in 2015. And on the federal level, at the urging of President Obama, there was some movement to expand Head Start programs or to provide universal preschool.

# THE CURRENT CONTROVERSERY

## Should governments fund universal preschool?

In early 2015, policymakers were debating government-supported universal preschool programs in Massachusetts, Minnesota, and New York. And in New York City, where Mayor Bill de Blasio, a Democrat, made the issue a centerpiece of his 2013 campaign, a universal pre-school initiative was launched in September 2014, enrolling 53,230 four-year-olds in programs across the city—nearly three times the 19,303 slots available the year before. [21]

Supporters of universal preschool argue that such programs provide children of all backgrounds with vital cognitive and social skills, giving them an upper hand in their future education. These children learn how to relate with one another, as well as how to behave in a class-room setting. Furthermore, proponents believe that public money spent on universal preschool creates even larger economic returns, as preschool-educated children are more likely to boost their lifetime earnings, and less likely to require welfare, remedial education, or special education.

But critics of universal preschool disagree. They argue that these costly government programs do not automatically create better, more engaged students. When governments focus on increasing access to broad, one-size-fits-all preschool programs, the quality of these pro-grams can suffer. By expanding preschool access instead of targeting resources for low-income students, critics believe these programs leave poor children behind—and provide unnecessary services for middle- and high-income families.

## Should governments fund universal preschool?

### YES: Early education creates success and equality.

"If you want to build a strong house, you've got to build a strong foundation first," Mayor de Blasio said in August 2014. "I sat with a group of kindergarten and first grade teachers ... and I said, 'What can you tell me about the impact that pre-K has?' And they said, literally, like in the first hour of the school year, they can tell you which kids went to pre-K and which kids didn't, because they're so much more engaged. Those who did are so much more engaged, so much more comfortable. The foundational skills are there and they're ready to go and they're on grade-level and they're advancing. That's what we need for every child."[22]

Universal preschool programs provide children with vital cognitive and social skills that give them an upper hand in their future education. And universal preschool is not just good education policy—it is good economic policy. According to James Heckman, winner of the Nobel Prize in Economics, investments made in early education have a higher payoff than investments made later in life. The Rand Corporation, a federally funded research center, also concluded, "Well-designed early childhood interventions have been found to generate a return to society ranging from $1.80 to $17.07 for each dollar spent on the program." [23]

But equally important to the return on investment is the promise of educational equality. Right now, parents with money are able to give their children a massive advantage over children from low-income families by sending them to private preschools and daycare centers. Wealthier children begin their K-12 education with larger vocabularies, better reading skills, and better social skills. David Deming, a Harvard University professor and a fellow at the National Bureau of Economic Research, wrote, "I estimate that the long-term impact of Head Start is [significant], with larger impacts for African Americans and relatively disadvantaged children."[24] In other words, early investments in low-income and minority children have meaningful educational and economic outcomes.

In the end, universal preschool is good policy. It saves governments money they would later spend on supporting low-income workers by ensuring a larger number of people find economic success. It narrows the gap between students from wealthy families and students from disadvantaged families. Raising standards and minimizing inequality are the nation's two top educational priorities—and universal preschool achieves both.

## NO: Governments cannot afford an unproven experiment.

In theory, universal preschool sounds like a tempting idea. But in practice, some experts believe its benefits have been grossly overstated.

"Preschool has been oversold. People too often speak as if it's a certainty that preschool has strong, lasting benefits," said Neal McCluskey, an education policy expert at the Cato Institute. "The reality is there isn't good research basis to say that pre-K is good." [25]

Ron Haskins, a preschool expert at the Brookings Institution Center on Children and Families, even called universal preschool "a very bad idea." "Universal pre-K is not a wise use of public resources," he said. "Invest [government dollars] where they're most needed and that's with low-income kids. [This] is going to waste a lot of money on families that don't need it." [26]

There is insufficient research to conclude whether preschools are effective—some show significant gains, some show small gains, and some seem to provide their students very little in the way of actual education. Alia Wong, author of *The Case Against Universal Preschool*, wrote, "[M]any of the country's existing private preschools are little more than glorified daycare centers. Their staffs often consist of unskilled, low-paid employees who work under the guise of classroom teachers. They don't use prepared lesson plans; they don't focus on developing the cognitive, physical, and social skills expected of today's kindergartners; they don't have the kinds of facilities a quality classroom needs."[27]

Chester E. Finn, Jr., a senior fellow at the Hoover Institution at Stanford University, said, "Thanks in part to that private sector, the vast majority of four-year-olds already have access to preschool—85 percent if we also count day-care—and it's not clear that many more parents want others to mind their children." He added, "As Berkeley sociologist Bruce Fuller and the University of Maryland's Douglas Besharov have each found, after exhaustively reviewing masses of studies, nearly all the gains—small to begin with—wash out within the first few grades."[28]

Local and state budgets have already been stretched to the breaking point. They cannot afford to provide funding for an educational experiment that has no guarantee of paying off.

# CONCLUSION

The Scholarships for Kids Act and local, state, and national universal preschool initiatives are only two examples of the debates that Americans have engaged in for centuries over public education policy. And although the fate of these programs remains far from certain, American policymakers, educators, parents, and students will undoubtedly continue to debate the goals, priorities, and means of public education—and which government policies best reflect and achieve them.

---

[1] "Back to School Statistics." National Center for Education Statistics. Web. 21 Feb. 2015.

[2] "School Districts." U.S. Census Bureau. Web. 21 Feb. 2015.

[3] National Commission on Excellence in Education. *A Nation at Risk: The Imperative for Educational Reform.* 26 Apr. 1983. Web. 21 Feb. 2015.

[4] "School Vouchers." National Conference of State Legislatures. Web. 21 Feb. 2015.

[5] "The Public Charter Schools Dashboard." National Alliance for Public Charter Schools. Web. 21 Feb. 2015.

[6] "Choice and Charter Schools, Laws & Legislation." Center for Education Reform. Web. 21 Feb. 2015.

[7] Buck, Stuart, and Jay Greene. "Blocked, Diluted, and Co-opted: Interest Groups Wage War Against Merit Pay." *EducationNext.* Vol. 11. 2011. Web. 21 Feb. 2015.

[8] Miron, Gary, Brian Horvitz, and Charisse Gulosino. *Virtual Schools in the U.S. 2013: Politics, Performance, Policy, and Research Evidence.* National Education Policy Center. May 2013. Web. 21 Feb. 2015.

[9] Alexander, Lamar. "Alexander Proposes 11 Million $2,100 'Scholarships for Kids.'" U.S. Senate Committee on Health, Education, Labor, and Pensions. 28 Jan. 2014. Web. 21 Feb. 2015.

[10] Alexander, Lamar. "11 Million $2,100 'Scholarships for Kids': A Real Answer to Inequality." *National Review.* 12 Feb. 2014. Print.

[11] McShane, Michael. "Why Should We Care about School Choice?" *Why Should We Care about School Choice?* 15 Jan. 2014. Web. 20 Feb. 2015.

[12] Messer, Luke. Floor speech. U.S. House of Representatives. 5 Feb. 2014.

[13] Ravitch, Diane. "Lamar Alexander Proposes Sweeping Voucher Legislation." *Diane Ravitch's Blog.* 28 Jan. 2014. Web. 20 Feb. 2015.

[14] Murray, Patty. Floor speech. U.S. Senate. 12 Jun. 2001.

[15] Hess, Frederick, and Jenna Schuette. "Private Schools, Public Ends." *The Daily Caller.* 14 Oct. 2010. Web. 20 Feb. 2015.

[16] *U.S. Constitution.* Amend. X.

[17] "Table 5.1: Compulsory school attendance laws, minimum and maximum age limits for required free education, by state: 2013." National Center for Education Statistics. Web. 21 Feb. 2015.

[18] Calvert, Kyla. "Obama: Community College Should Be 'as Free and Universal in America as High School'." PBS. Web. 20 Feb. 2015.

[19] Barnett, W.S., M.E. Carolan, J.H. Squires, K. Clarke Brown. *The State of Preschool 2013: State Preschool Yearbook*. National Institute for Early Education Research. 2013. Web. 21 Feb. 2015.

[20] "Head Start Services." Office of Head Start. Web. 21 Feb. 2015.

[21] Fermino, Jennifer, and Ben Chapman. "Univesal Pre-K exceeds first year enrollment target with 53,200 students." *New York Daily News*. 12 Nov. 2014. Web. 21 Feb. 2015.

[22] De Blasio, Bill. Remarks at the Preschool Nation Summit. New York City. 5 Aug. 2014. Web. 21 Feb. 2015.

[23] Karoly, Lynn, Rebecca Kilburn, and Jill Cannon. "Proven Benefits of Early Childhood Interventions." *Proven Benefits of Early Childhood Interventions*. Web. 20 Feb. 2015.

[24] Deming, David. "Early Childhood Intervention And Life-Cycle Skill Development: Evidence From Head Start." *American Economic Journal: Applied Economics* (2009): 111-34. Print.

[25] Wong, Alia. "The Case Against Universal Preschool." *The Atlantic*. 18 Nov. 2014. Print.

[26] Wong, Alia. "The Case Against Universal Preschool." *The Atlantic*. 18 Nov. 2014. Print.

[27] Wong, Alia. "The Case Against Universal Preschool." *The Atlantic*. 18 Nov. 2014. Print.

[28] Finn, Chester. "Preschool Can't Do It All." Hoover Institution. 9 Oct. 2009. Web. 20 Feb. 2015.

# ENERGY AND THE ENVIRONMENT

## CURRENT CONTROVERSIES

- Should the United States expand the practice of fracking?

- Should the development of renewable sources of energy be a federal government priority?

# INTRODUCTION

> "Plans to protect air and water, wilderness and wildlife, are in fact plans to protect man."
> —Stewart Udall

> "Oil is what this country runs on. You call it monopoly. I call it enterprise."
> —John D. Rockefeller

Ever since the American energy revolution took hold in the late 19th and early 20th centuries, the debate over energy policy—and its effects on the environment—has been a fierce one. Americans have long disagreed over what role the government should play in directing energy policy, and which goals and priorities those policies should reflect. In this chapter, we will consider several enduring tensions in American energy policy and examine two current controversial issues:

- Should the United States expand the practice of fracking?
- Should the development of renewable sources of energy be a federal government priority?

**Why Is Energy Policy Controversial?** Energy makes the world go—fueling cars, factories, and the lights that shine in homes and businesses—spurring economic development and increasing standards of living around the globe. In 2012, despite claiming only five percent of the world's population, the United States accounted for 18 percent of global energy consumption, according to the Energy Information Administration (EIA).[1] The United States is also among the world's leading energy producers, second only to China in 2012.[2]

Because the United States engages in such high levels of energy consumption and production, Americans in every state are affected by energy policies. Millions of American jobs are tied to the various energy industries, from oil and natural gas extraction to solar power and biofuel development, while the price of gasoline is felt by American companies and drivers each day. Americans require vast amounts of energy to build and support successful cities and industries—but these needs compete with efforts to preserve and protect the natural environment.

As a result, energy policy is not crafted without controversy, as American policymakers, energy producers, and environmentalists have struggled for years to reconcile competing goals, priorities, and means of energy development.

- *Competing Goals.* What should be the most important goals of American energy policy? To ensure that citizens and industries have access to low-cost sources of energy? To protect nature and reduce the human impact on the environment?

- *Competing Priorities.* What should be the priorities of American energy policy? To extract the United States' powerful reserves of fossil fuels? To invest in the development of renewable energy sources?

- *Competing Means.* What means and methods should we employ to harness our energy resources? Should the government expand the practice of fracking for oil and natural gas? Should the United States invest more in nuclear energy? Should the government work to spur the development of renewable energy?

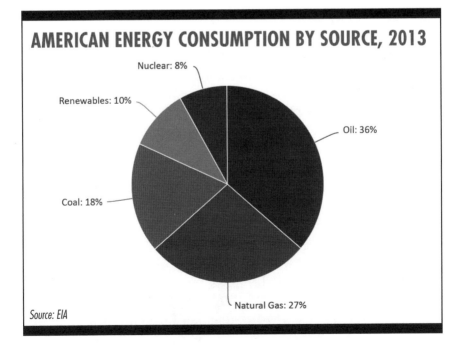

**AMERICAN ENERGY CONSUMPTION BY SOURCE, 2013**

Nuclear: 8%
Renewables: 10%
Oil: 36%
Coal: 18%
Natural Gas: 27%

*Source: EIA*

**Why Is Energy Policy So Complicated?** The United States' energy sources and needs are as diverse as the nation itself. Americans require energy for electricity, heat, transportation, and fuel for the industries that stimulate economic growth. Oil has been the primary source of domestic energy for decades, but it is only part of the American energy story.

The different sources of energy that Americans use each raise their own policy complications. Fossil fuels—non-renewable resources such as oil, natural gas, and coal that form from the remains of prehistoric plants and animals—provided 81 percent of power in the United States in 2013, but the burning of these fuels, namely oil and coal, pollutes the environment.[3] Renewable sources, such as biomass, geothermal, hydroelectric, solar, and wind, offer the promise of clean, long-lasting energy, but they can be expensive, inefficient, and unpredictable. And although nuclear energy is powerful and burns cleanly, it produces hazardous waste that must be stored safely for long periods of time. Therefore, policymakers are faced with a complicated energy landscape—one that must balance the availability, cost-effectiveness, and environmental impacts of various energy sources.

## THE ONGOING DEBATE

### Should the United States be more concerned with utilizing low-cost energy sources or protecting the environment?

The American energy revolution dates back to 1859, when Edwin Drake used a new drilling method to successfully extract crude oil—a material that can be refined into gasoline, diesel fuel, heating oil, and jet fuel—from a well near Titusville, Pennsylvania. By 1880, more major oil fields had been discovered in California, Oklahoma, and Texas, and the United States was responsible for producing and refining nearly 85 percent of the world's crude oil.[4]

But by the middle of the 20th century, the American energy landscape had begun to change. The 1948 discovery of Ghawar—the largest and most productive oil field in the world—helped Saudi Arabia become the world's largest oil exporter.[5] And by the 1980s, as the United States heightened restrictions on offshore oil drilling due to environmental concerns about spills, the gap between domestic energy production and consumption widened considerably, increasing Americans' dependence on foreign oil.

Yet new practices have rapidly pushed the United States back toward energy dominance. Technologies such as hydraulic fracturing, the drilling practice more commonly known as fracking, have dramatically increased the United States' output of oil and natural gas—a flammable gas burned to create electricity and generate heat. Developed throughout the course of the 20th century, fracking involves drilling into the ground; injecting water, sand, and chemicals into the rock at high pressure; and collecting any oil or natural gas that is trapped inside the rock. The process involves both vertical and horizontal drilling, allowing access to pockets of energy that were previously impossible to reach.

The use of fracking has surged in the United States since 2003, particularly in North Dakota, Texas, and other states with large formations of shale, a fine-grained sedimentary rock. By 2013, Americans had produced more oil than they imported for the first time since 1995[6] and had become the world leader in shale gas production.[7] And as domestic production has boomed, unemployment in shale-rich states has fallen and gasoline prices across the country have tumbled, saving American drivers roughly $14 billion in 2014, according to AAA.[8]

The fracking boom has also helped enshrine the significant role fossil fuels play in American energy production and usage.

- *Oil.* The United States—the largest oil producer and consumer in the world in 2015—had proven reserves of 44.2 billion barrels of oil in 2013, or 2.6 percent of the global total.[9]

- *Natural Gas.* The United States—the largest natural gas producer and consumer in the world in 2015—had proven reserves of 330 trillion cubic feet of gas in 2013, or five percent of the global total.[10]

- *Coal.* The United States is a distant second to China in the production and consumption of coal, accounting for 13 percent of global production and 12 percent of consumption in 2013.[11] But the United States has the largest proven coal reserves in the world, at 237 billion metric tons—or 27 percent of the global total in 2013.[12]

Oil, natural gas, and coal have provided Americans with powerful sources of energy, but the use of fossil fuels has not occurred without negative consequences. The burning of coal and oil releases dirt and smoke into the air, creating smog and contributing to acid rainfall. Natural gas burns more cleanly than oil and coal, but some experts have expressed concern about the effects of methane—its primary component—leaking from wells. And according to the Department of Energy, 75 percent of human-caused emissions over the last two decades have come from the burning of fossil fuels.[13]

Furthermore, as the air's concentration of carbon dioxide—a "greenhouse gas" that helps trap the Earth's heat in the atmosphere—has risen steadily over the past 150 years, many scientists have concluded that human activities, such as the burning of fossil fuels, are to blame. These scientists have predicted that the resulting increase in global temperatures could lead to drought, famine, the extinction of certain plants and animals, and the alteration of weather patterns around the world.

Protesters in California call on Governor Jerry Brown, D-Calif., to ban fracking.

Thus, Americans are at a crossroads. Should the nation continue to extract its fossil fuels to provide powerful low-cost energy? Or should the American people turn their focus to conservation and environmental protection?

## THE CURRENT CONTROVERSY

### Should the United States expand the practice of fracking?

In 2014, in the midst of the American fracking boom, the International Energy Agency determined that the United States had surpassed Saudi Arabia and Russia as the world's largest producer of oil and natural gas liquids.[14] And by January 2015, the surge in production led the average cost of one gallon of regular, unleaded gasoline in the United States to fall to $2.05—a decrease of more than $1.20 from the prior year, according to AAA.[15]

But the fracking revolution has also generated significant controversy. In recent years, activists and voters in California, Colorado, Maryland, Ohio, Pennsylvania, and other states have called for or passed local bans on fracking, while New York and Vermont have implemented statewide bans.

Supporters of fracking credit the practice for transforming the United States into the world's largest producer of oil and natural gas—reducing both energy costs and Americans' dangerous dependence on foreign oil. Proponents also argue that fracking has brought tens of thousands of construction and engineering jobs to the United States, helping many Americans recover from the 2008 global economic crisis. And the boom in shale gas production is leading more and more American factories to abandon coal in favor of cleaner and cheaper natural gas.

But many environmental advocates have criticized fracking for its high levels of water usage, its potential to contaminate groundwater, and its tendency to cause small earthquakes. Other critics have argued that an increase in the use of fracking will only encourage Americans' continued dependence on non-renewable, pollution-causing fossil fuels.

## Should the United States expand the practice of fracking?

### YES: Harness our powerful resources to create jobs and achieve energy independence.

For far too long, Americans have looked to other countries—Canada, Saudi Arabia, and less stable partners such as Russia and Venezuela—as valuable sources of the oil they consume. In the late 20th century, as the United States limited its own oil production, foreign imports grew from 25 percent of American consumption in the early 1970s to a dangerous 60 percent by 2005.[16] But by expanding the practice of fracking, Americans are once again on the road to energy dominance and independence.

"It is now within our reach to become energy independent in North America, if we simply develop the resources we already have," Governor Jack Dalrymple, R-N.D., said in 2012.[17] In his state, a sustained fracking boom at the Bakken Shale has helped virtually eliminate unemployment, which stood at a mere 2.7 percent in November 2014.[18] "In our part of the country, hydraulic fracturing takes place two miles below the surface of the Earth, and nowhere near any water supplies," Governor Dalrymple said.[19]

"We must take full advantage of energy innovations and resources here at home in order to end our dangerous dependency on foreign sources," former Senator Tom Coburn, R-Okla., said in 2013. "Hydraulic fracturing is safer and more efficient than traditional drilling techniques, and states already exercise extensive testing and regulation of the process."[20] Environmental engineer Radislav Vidic, who led a National Science Foundation study of the regional effects of fracking, reached a similar conclusion in 2013. "There is no irrefutable impact of this industry on surface or groundwater quality in Pennsylvania," Vidic said.[21]

Even Ernest Moniz, the current secretary of energy, argued in 2011 while he was a physicist at the Massachusetts Institute of Technology that fracked natural gas can serve as a valuable "bridge fuel" to a clean energy future. "In broad terms, we find that, given the large amounts of natural gas available in the U.S. at moderate cost (enabled to a large degree by the shale gas resource), natural gas can indeed play an important role over the next couple of decades (together with demand management) in economically advancing a clean energy system," he said.

In the end, fracking is helping the United States solidify its status as a leading energy producer—and providing Americans with long-lasting jobs and plentiful, affordable energy along the way.

## NO: Think of the future, and protect our citizens and environment.

"It's incredible that, despite real progress in reducing climate-disrupting carbon emissions, the United States is still charging ahead with a 'boom' in dirty fuels and extraction methods," Michael Brune, executive director of the Sierra Club, said in 2014. "It's like swallowing aspirin as you beat your head against a wall."[23]

Brune has a point. While the practice of fracking has surged in the United States, leading to a temporary reduction in gasoline prices, the fact remains that fossil fuels are harmful to the environment, limited in quantity, and non-renewable. And this invasive practice has only encouraged Americans to become more dependent on fossil fuels, which supplied an astounding 81 percent of domestic power in 2013. "This is not a bridge," climate activist and 350.org founder Bill McKibben said of fracked natural gas. "It's just a rickety pier stretching further out into the fossil fuel lake."[24]

But it is not only the fossil fuels themselves that damage the environment. The processes involved in fracking present their own risks: equipment failures, well blowouts, and wastewater pit leaks have already occurred in Colorado, Pennsylvania, and other states, leading to water contamination. In Pennsylvania, for example, an Associated Press review found more than 100 confirmed cases of drilling-related pollution in water wells between 2009 and 2014.[25] "As we pursue fracking with irrational exuberance, injecting chemicals into the groundwater of America, it seems that we may have taken leave of our senses," Governor Peter Shumlin, D-Vt., said in May 2012. "Human beings survived for thousands and thousands of years without oil and without natural gas. We have never known humanity or life on this planet to survive without clean water."[26]

Governor Shumlin is not alone in his negative view of fracking. In a 2014 Pew Research Center poll of members of the American Association for the Advancement of Science, only 31 percent of surveyed scientists said they favored the increased use of fracking, while 66 percent said they were opposed.[27]

And in December 2014, Dr. Howard Zucker, the acting health commissioner of New York, issued a report on the public health risks of fracking that convinced Governor Andrew Cuomo, D-N.Y., to ban the practice. "I cannot support high-volume hydraulic fracturing in the great state of New York," Zucker said. "I asked myself, 'Would I let my family live in a community with fracking?' The answer is no."[28]

# THE ONGOING DEBATE

## What is the appropriate role of government in directing the energy market?

The government has played a role in energy investment, development, and regulation for more than a century, and for equally as long, Americans have debated the appropriate scope of that role. Individuals and private enterprises have played a significant part in developing the United States' energy resources, but the government has provided measures of support as well.

So how exactly does the government involve itself in energy policy? Between 1950 and 2010, the federal government contributed an estimated $837 billion to energy developments, according to the Nuclear Energy Institute. And these incentives came in the form of tax policies (47 percent), federal regulations (19 percent), research and development funds (18 percent), market activities (ten percent), government services (seven percent), and grants and disbursements (less than one percent).[29]

**Tax Policies.** The federal tax code includes special exemptions, allowances, deductions, and credits related to energy production of all kinds. Oil and natural gas companies, for example, qualify for tax benefits that serve as incentives for exploration, development, and employment. These industries can deduct intangible drilling costs—such as ground clearing, labor wages, and supplies—from their tax liability, while small oil and natural gas companies can deduct a fixed percentage of their gross annual income to make up for the depletion of their finite resources.

**Regulations.** Throughout history, the government has issued rules and regulations to govern businesses in various energy industries. In June 2014, for example, the Environmental Protection Agency proposed a rule that would slash carbon dioxide emissions from existing coal-fired power plants by up to 30 percent by 2030—igniting a political battle in the process.

**Research and Development Funding.** The government often advances its energy interests by funding research, development, and demonstration programs. Between 1948 and 2010, the Congressional Research Service found that 50 percent of the Department of Energy's research and development spending went toward nuclear power, 25 percent went to fossil fuels, 12 percent went to renewable energy, and nine percent went to the study of energy efficiency.[30]

**Market Activities.** The government has, at times, directly intervened in the energy market. On the larger scale, Congress in 1933 created the Tennessee Valley Authority (TVA), a government-owned corporation formed to provide low-cost electricity to Americans during the Great Depression. As of 2015, the TVA was the nation's largest public power provider, serving more than nine million people.[31]

On the smaller scale, the government has provided loans and loan guarantees to assist energy companies and projects. The Hoover Dam, which brought electricity to much of the southwestern United States in 1935, was partially financed by federal government loans. And in May 2013, Tesla Motors Inc. repaid a $465 million government loan nine years ahead of schedule. [32] By early

Former Governor Mitt Romney, R-Mass., campaigns in front of the failed energy firm, Solyndra. The Obama administration financially supported the firm with $535 million in loan guarantees. Solyndra went bankrupt in 2011.

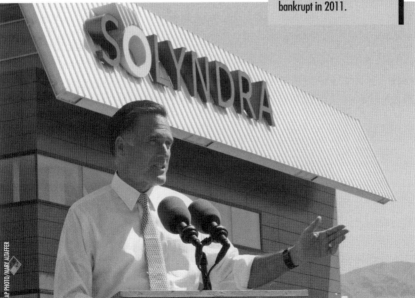

2014, the electric car company exceeded $30 billion in market value.[33] But government market interventions have also attracted controversy. In 2011, the solar panel start-up Solyndra filed for bankruptcy after receiving $535 million in loan guarantees from the federal government, leaving taxpayers largely on the hook.[34] And in 2013, American taxpayers lost $139 million in loans when the electric car company Fisker Automotive Inc. filed for bankruptcy.[35]

**Government Services.** Over the years, the government has provided services to energy industries—such as the use of ports and waterways—without charge.

**Grants and Disbursements.** The government also awards direct financial grants to energy industries, such as subsidies for the construction and operation of oil tankers and contributions to various waste disposal and energy safety funds.

As the United States has grown and diversified, so too have its sources of power. As a result, the focus of the energy incentives provided by the federal government has changed over the years. Timber and coal gained prominence in the 19th century, while oil, natural gas, and nuclear power were largely developed in the 20th century. And in the early years of the 21st century, some energy developers and policymakers began calling on the government to focus its attention on renewable energy.

## THE CURRENT CONTROVERSY

### Should the development of renewable sources of energy be a federal government priority?

Certain energy sources—such as biomass, geothermal, hydroelectric, solar, and wind power—are known as renewables, because they are self-generating and cannot be depleted. These energy sources accounted for ten percent of the energy consumed by Americans in 2013, while generating 13 percent of the nation's electricity, according to the EIA.[36] Worldwide, renewables accounted for approximately 11 percent of energy consumption in 2011, while generating 21 percent of electricity.[37]

The creation of a viable renewable energy sector has been a cornerstone of President Barack Obama's energy policy, which has allocated billions of dollars in loans and tax benefits to renewable energy development. And in his 2016 budget plan, President Obama called on Congress to appropriate $7.4 billion for clean energy programs—an increase of 13.8 percent from 2015.[38]

Supporters of increased government involvement in renewable energy note that the United States has a long history of government support for emerging industries—from oil and natural gas to nuclear power. Advocates also argue that Americans must work quickly to reduce their dependence on fossil fuels, which are non-renewable and limited in supply. They believe the renewable energy sector has the potential to create millions of jobs while protecting the environment and playing a role in combating climate change for future generations.

But critics of increased government intervention disagree. They argue that for the foreseeable future, renewable energy cannot realistically meet more than a small fraction of the country's energy needs. Detractors note that renewable sources of energy are less efficient, less consistent, and far less cost-effective than fossil fuels. And they believe that funneling billions of taxpayer dollars into such uncompetitive industries is a wasteful use of scarce government resources—and a responsibility that should be left to the private sector.

## Should the creation of renewable sources of energy be a federal government priority?

### YES: The government must intervene now to protect the planet and our future.

"No challenge poses a greater threat to future generations than climate change," President Obama said in his 2015 State of the Union address. "If we do not act forcefully, we'll continue to see rising oceans, longer, hotter heat waves, dangerous droughts and floods, and massive disruptions that can trigger greater migration, conflict, and hunger around the globe. The Pentagon says that climate change poses immediate risks to our national security. We should act like it."[39]

Americans have reached a point of dangerous dependence on non-renewable, pollution-causing fossil fuels. And if the government does not immediately encourage the development of renewable technologies, Americans will soon face an energy crisis of epic proportions—once fossil fuels have been mined into extinction.

"This year, BrightSource Energy Inc. will begin generating power from a new solar plant, the largest of its type in the world," wrote Richard Caperton, managing director of energy at the Center for American Progress, in 2013. "During the first half of 2013, electric-car maker Tesla Motors Inc. brought in nearly $1 billion in revenue, the first step in revolutionizing U.S. transportation. What do these milestones have in common? They each came about because of government investment in clean-energy startups."

Throughout the history of the United States, the federal government has played a significant role in supporting American energy development. "Businesses like BrightSource, Tesla, and Project Amp ... needed government support because banks won't lend millions of dollars to innovative technologies," Caperton said. "Yet billions of dollars is what it takes to bring these technologies to market. And the government is uniquely able to provide this capital."[40]

Not only is the government uniquely qualified to assist emerging renewable energy companies, it has a positive track record. Despite the high-profile bankruptcies of Fisker Automotive and Solyndra, the Department of Energy reported in November 2014 that its Loan Programs Office had begun to turn a $30 million profit on its energy investments.[41]

"It is not about whether government is picking winners and losers, because clearly government has been doing just that for years, with the fossil fuel and nuclear industries being the big winners," Senator Bernie Sanders, I-Vt., said in 2012. "What is necessary to reverse global warming and create jobs is that we pick the right winners—the technologies that will transform our energy system and protect the environment."[42]

## NO: Do not waste taxpayer dollars on overblown threats and ineffective technologies.

For years, environmentalists have sounded the alarm about the so-called "crisis" of climate change. But in reality, some scientists continue to question whether the Earth is warming in a dangerous manner, or whether warming trends are mere natural patterns.

However, a very real crisis does exist in the United States—a national debt of more than $18 trillion in early 2015, or nearly $57,000 per citizen.[43] And at a time when the government must reduce its spending for the sake of future Americans, federal investments in costly, ineffective renewable energy technologies are little more than a waste of taxpayer dollars.

Much of the problem lies in the methods the government has used to assist emerging renewable energy companies. "Yes, the government ought to invest in research, as it does with [the National Institutes of Health], for example," syndicated columnist Charles Krauthammer said in 2012. "But the role is not to subsidize infant industries like [Solyndra] which are clearly not economical and are miles away from being economical."[44]

The fact remains that many renewable energy industries are untested, ineffective, inconsistent, and expensive. And until more research is completed to ensure that these technologies can survive in the energy marketplace, the government should leave risky investments to the private sector.

"If the government were effective at promoting alternative energy sources, today you'd have driven your hydrogen car (having recently traded in your cellulosic ethanol-fueled model) from your all-electric home powered by a breeder reactor to your office lighted by Carter-era synfuels," said Douglas Holtz-Eakin, president of the American Action Forum, in 2013. "The government is just not a good venture capitalist. Venture capitalists provide funds, discipline, and replace weak management. They pull the plug on losers. That is hardly the way the government operates."[45]

Representative Mike Pompeo, R-Kan., who introduced a bill in 2012 to repeal all federal tax credits for energy companies, argued that the merits of renewables must be judged by the market—not the government. "It's time for these industries to compete, to enter their products into the marketplace, and convince customers that the energy they provide is something that they can afford and they want," he said.[46]

Even if renewables have a role to play in the United States' energy future, until alternative energy companies research, develop, and refine their products, the government has no business manipulating the marketplace.

# CONCLUSION

The expansion of fracking and government support for renewable energy are only two examples of the debates Americans have engaged in for decades over energy policy. And although the fate of these two policy options remains far from certain, American policymakers, energy producers, and consumers will undoubtedly continue to debate the goals, priorities, and means of energy development—and which government policies best reflect and achieve them.

---

[1] U.S. Energy Information Administration. "What Is the United States' Share of World Energy Consumption?" 10 Feb. 2015. Web. 24 Feb. 2015.

[2] U.S. Energy Information Administration. "International Energy Statistics." Web. 24 Feb. 2015.

[3] U.S. Energy Information Administration. *Monthly Energy Review.* Feb. 2015. Web. 24 Feb. 2015.

[4] Council on Foreign Relations. "Timeline: Oil Dependence and U.S. Foreign Policy." 2012. Web. 24 Feb. 2015.

[5] U.S. Energy Information Administration. "Saudi Arabia." 10 Sept. 2014. Web. 24 Feb. 2015.

[6] Mufson, Steven. "Improving U.S. Oil Production Reaches Milestone in October, Agency Says." *Washington Post.* 13 Nov. 2013. Web. 24 Nov. 2015.

[7] Koch, Wendy. "Fracking Puts U.S. First in Shale Gas Production." *USA Today.* 23 Oct. 2013. Web. 24 Feb 2015.

[8] Huddleston, Jr., Tom. "Gas Prices on Track to Tumble Below $2." *Fortune.* 21 Jan. 2015. Web. 24 Feb. 2015.

[9] British Petroleum. *BP Statistical Review of World Energy 2014.* June 2014. Web. 24 Feb. 2015.

[10] British Petroleum. *BP Statistical Review of World Energy 2014.* June 2014. Web. 24 Feb. 2015.

[11] Ayoub, Joseph. "China Produces and Consumes Almost As Much Coal As the Rest of the World Combined." U.S. Energy Information Administration. 14 May 2014. Web. 24 Feb. 2015.

[12] British Petroleum. *BP Statistical Review of World Energy 2014.* June 2014. Web. 24 Feb. 2015.

[13] U.S. Department of Energy. "Fossil." Web. 24 Feb. 2015.

[14] Institute for Energy Research. *"U.S. Overtakes Saudi Arabia and Russia as Largest Oil Producer."* 10 July 2014. Web. 24 Feb. 2015.

[15] Huddleston, Jr., Tom. "Gas Prices on Track to Tumble below $2." Fortune. 21 Jan. 2015. Web. 24 Feb. 2015.

[16] Ratner, Michael, and Carol Glover. *U.S. Energy: Overview and Key Statistics.* Congressional Research Service. 27 June 2014. Web. 24 Feb. 2015.

[17] Dalrymple, Jack. Weekly Republican Address. 10 Mar. 2012. Web. 24 Feb. 2015.

[18] U.S. Bureau of Labor Statistics. "Local Area Unemployment Statistics." 27 Jan. 2015. Web. 24 Feb. 2015.

[19] Dalrymple, Jack. Weekly Republican Address. 10 Mar. 2012. Web. 24 Feb. 2015.

[20] Senator James Inhofe. "Senators Reject Department of Interior's Federal Hydraulic Fracturing Regulation with Introduction of FRESH Act." Official website. 26 June 2013. Web. 24 Feb. 2015.

[21] Biello, David. "Fracking Can Be Done Safely, but Will It Be?" *Scientific American.* 17 May 2013. Web. 24 Feb. 2015.

[22] Moniz, Dr. Ernest. Testimony before the U.S. Senate Committee on Energy and Natural Resources. Washington, D.C. 19 July 2011.

23  Brune, Michael. "Fracking 101: Two Steps Back." Coming Clean: The blog of Executive Director Michael Brune. 8 Dec. 2014. Web. 24 Feb. 2015.

24  McKibben, Bill. "The Climate Movement Takes on Fracking: Interview with Bill McKibben." *Truthout.* 17 Apr. 2012. Web. 24 Feb. 2015.

25  Begos, Kevin. "4 States Confirm Water Pollution from Drilling." Associated Press. 5 Jan. 2014. Web. 24 Feb. 2015.

26  Shumlin, Peter. Statement at the signing of H. 464. 16 May 2012. Web. 24 Feb. 2015.

27  Cusick, Marie. "Survey: Majority of Scientists Oppose Expanded Use of Fracking." NPR State Impact. 30 Jan. 2015. Web. 24 Feb. 2015.

28  St. Fleur, Nicholas. "The Alarming Research behind New York's Fracking Ban." *The Atlantic.* 19 Dec. 2014. Web. 24 Feb. 2015.

29  Management Information Services, Inc. *60 Years of Energy Incentives: Analysis of Federal Expenditures for Energy Development.* Nuclear Energy Institute. Oct. 2011. Web. 24 Feb. 2015.

30  Pfund, Nancy, and Ben Healy. *What Would Jefferson Do? The Historical Role of Federal Subsidies in Shaping America's Energy Future.* Sept. 2011. Web. 24 Feb. 2015.

31  Tennessee Valley Authority. "From the New Deal to a New Century." Web. 24 Feb. 2015.

32  Isidore, Chris. "Tesla Repays Federal Loan Nearly 10 Years Early." CNN Money. 22 May 2013. Web. 24 Feb. 2015.

33  Ohnsman, Alan. "Tesla Tops $30 Billion as Morgan Stanley Boosts Outlook." Bloomberg Business. 25 Feb. 2014. Web. 24 Feb. 2015.

34  Brady, Jeff. "After Solyndra Loss, U.S. Energy Loan Program Turning a Profit." NPR. 13 Nov. 2014. Web. 24 Feb. 2015.

35  Greiling Keane, Angela. "Fisker to Sell Assets in Bankruptcy at $139 Million Loss." Bloomberg Business. 22 Nov. 2013. Web. 24 Feb. 2015.

36  U.S. Energy Information Administration. "How Much U.S. Energy Consumption and Electricity Generation Comes from Renewable Sources?" 26 June 2014. Web. 24 Feb. 2015.

37  U.S. Energy Information Administration. "How Much of World Energy Consumption and Electricity Generation Is from Renewable Energy?" 18 Dec. 2014. Web. 24 Feb. 2015.

38  Harder, Amy. "Obama Budget Would Pour Funds into Climate, Renewable Energy." *Wall Street Journal.* 3 Feb. 2015. Web. 24 Feb. 2015.

39  Obama, Barack. State of the Union Address. 20 Jan. 2015. CNN Transcript. Web. 24 Feb. 2015.

40  Caperton, Richard. "Yes: The Government Must Help Change the Country's Energy Mix." *Wall Street Journal.* 22 Sept. 2013. Web. 24 Feb. 2015.

41  Brady, Jeff. "After Solyndra Loss, U.S. Energy Loan Program Turning a Profit." NPR. 13 Nov. 2014. Web. 24 Feb. 2015.

42  Sanders, Bernie. "Senator Bernie Sanders: To Battle Global Warming, We Must Pick Clean Energy as a 'Winner.'" Climate Progress. 15 Oct. 2012. Web. 24 Feb. 2015.

43  U.S. National Debt Clock. Brillig. Web. 24 Feb. 2015.

44  Krauthammer, Charles. "Should the Government Invest in Alternative Energy?" *Special Report with Bret Baier.* Fox News Channel. 16 May 2012. Web. 24 Feb. 2015.

45  Holtz-Eakin, Douglas. "No: Politicians Simply Do Not Make Good Venture Capitalists." *Wall Street Journal.* 22 Sept. 2013. Web. 24 Feb. 2015.

46  Burke, Patrick. "GOP Congressmen: Gov't Should Stop 'Picking Winners and Losers' in Energy Sector." CNS News. 2 Mar. 2012. Web. 24 Feb. 2015.

# IMMIGRATION

## CURRENT CONTROVERSIES

- Should Congress pass the Gang of Eight comprehensive immigration reform package?

- Should states offer in-state college tuition to "Dreamers"?

# INTRODUCTION

*"We didn't raise the Statue of Liberty with her back to the world, we did it with her light shining as a beacon to the world. And whether we were Irish or Italians or Germans crossing the Atlantic, or Japanese or Chinese crossing the Pacific; whether we crossed the Rio Grande or flew here from all over the world—generations of immigrants have made this country into what it is. It's what makes us special."*

—Barack Obama

*"Granting amnesty encourages the violation of our laws and perpetuates illegal immigration. America's a welcoming country. But citizenship must not be the automatic reward for violating the laws of America."*

—George W. Bush

The United States is a nation of immigrants—one that has attracted people from all over the world for reasons as diverse as the cultures they represent. But for generations, Americans have also struggled to determine how the government should best control and regulate levels of immigration. In this chapter, we will consider several enduring tensions in American immigration policy and examine two current controversial issues:

- Should Congress pass the Gang of Eight comprehensive immigration reform package?

- Should states offer in-state college tuition to "Dreamers"?

**Why Is Immigration Policy Controversial?** As of November 2014, more than 4.4 million people were on waiting lists to legally immigrate to the United States.[1] At the same time, there were an estimated 11.2 million undocumented immigrants living in the country, having reached the United States by sneaking over the border, using false documents, or overstaying the limits of their visas.[2] According to data compiled by the Department of Homeland Security (DHS), Mexico was the country of origin for approximately 59 percent of undocumented immigrants in 2011, followed by El Salvador at six percent, Guatemala at five percent, Honduras at three percent, and China at two percent. Once they arrived in the United States, 58 percent of undocumented immigrants lived in five states—California (25 percent), Texas (16 percent), Florida (six percent), New York (six percent), and Illinois (five percent).[3]

Despite laws forbidding employers from hiring undocumented workers, the Pew Research Center estimated that undocumented immigrants made up more than five percent of the American labor force in 2010.[4] These immigrants often possess few specialized skills and sometimes work for low wages, filling jobs that some business leaders say American citizens are reluctant to take. Their low-wage work helps companies keep production costs—and prices—low for many goods and services. But some policymakers worry that undocumented immigrants are taking jobs from American citizens at a time of fragile economic recovery, while also depressing wages by working for so little. Others believe undocumented workers pay too little in taxes to compensate for the burden they place on public services. And according to a 2014 Reuters poll, 70 percent of Americans said they believed undocumented immigrants threatened traditional American beliefs and customs.[5]

In the face of these varying pressures, the government spends millions of dollars each year to both cope with legal immigration and combat illegal immigration, leading many policymakers to call for reforms to the system. When considering their options, policymakers must weigh several competing goals, priorities, and means of reforming the American system of immigration.

- *Competing Goals.* What are the primary goals of American immigration policy? Securing the border to prevent illegal immigration? Making visas available to highly skilled workers? Creating a pathway to citizenship for undocumented immigrants already in the United States?

- *Competing Priorities.* What are the priorities of American immigration policy? Should the government overhaul the entire immigration system or should Congress focus on amending the least efficient and least successful policies and programs?

- *Competing Means.* What means and methods should the government employ to craft immigration policy? Which policies best discourage illegal immigration? What role should states play in forming their own policies and defending their borders? And what roles should Congress and the president assume?

Windows on the south side of the Great Hall at Ellis Island frame the Statue of Liberty.

## Why Is Immigration Policy So Complicated?

Immigration is a complex issue, and one that impacts a number of other policies, including education, health care, the economy, and national security. Immigration policy is also complicated by the fact that it directly affects the lives of millions of people, from the men, women, and children pursuing a better life in the United States to the hardworking taxpayers who foot the bills for increased spending on education, health care, and social safety net programs that support the immigrant population.

Adding to its complexity, immigration is also a deeply emotional issue. As the descendants of immigrants themselves, many American citizens sympathize with people who want to pursue new opportunities in the United States. At the same time, Americans are committed to the rule of law, and many decry the idea that undocumented immigrants could receive special protections for ignoring the rules.

Reforming immigration policy also presents several logistical issues for the government. With approximately 11.2 million undocumented immigrants already in the United States, policymakers must agree on a realistic policy to deal with this population, either through deportation or through the creation of a pathway to citizenship. Meanwhile, both state and federal governments craft immigration regulations, creating a patchwork of laws and priorities that, at times, conflict with one another. In recent years, President Barack Obama issued several executive orders relating to immigration, creating temporary policies that have left many undocumented immigrants in a state of flux.

Without permanent immigration reform policies in place, American citizens, immigrants, and government officials struggle to determine the best path forward. Should Congress enact sweeping reforms to the immigration system? Or is it more effective to tackle one issue at a time?

## THE ONGOING DEBATE

### How should the United States reform its immigration system?

Most modern immigration laws stem from the Immigration and Nationality Act of 1965, which created a system based largely on an immigrant's relationship with American citizens or employers. Under the current structure, legal immigrants enter the United States seeking to establish permanent residence. These lawful permanent residents (LPRs)—or "green card" recipients—can live and work in the United States, own property, attend public schools, and join the military; after five years, most LPRs are eligible to apply for citizenship upon completion of English language, civics, and American history exams.

Among those seeking LPR status, federal law gives priority to four categories of immigrants:

- *Family-sponsored preference* is given to the immediate relatives of American citizens and LPRs.

- *Employment-based preference* is given to professionals with advanced degrees, people with exceptional abilities, and needed unskilled workers.

- *Diversity immigrants* are from nations where fewer than 50,000 people have gained LPR status in the last five years.

- *Refugees and asylum seekers* are looking for protection from war, persecution, or natural disasters.[6]

But the fact that many individuals still enter the United States illegally has led elected officials to criticize the immigration system as woefully ineffective. Reformers face a great divide over how to best deal with both border security and the millions of undocumented immigrants already living in the United States. Meanwhile, business leaders and labor interests often disagree over whether to encourage the hiring of foreign workers.

In recent years, policymakers have made several attempts at immigration reform at the federal level, but they have struggled to achieve lasting results. Beginning in 2004, President George W. Bush advocated a major overhaul of the nation's immigration system. As part of his plan, President Bush called for the creation of a guest worker program—one in which temporary foreign workers would be encouraged to return to their home countries and apply for legal American citizenship. However, in the face of fierce opposition from conservatives who favored a border enforcement–only approach to immigration reform, the president's plan died in Congress.[7]

In 2006, President Bush appeased many conservatives by signing the Secure Fence Act, a law that authorized the construction of a fence along 700 miles of the 1,933-mile U.S. border with Mexico. But by 2007, President Bush had crafted a new compromise plan that contained a pathway to legal status for undocumented immigrants, as well as a guest worker program that was dependent on stricter enforcement of the border and of illegal hiring. Yet due to opposition from conservative Republicans and pro-labor Democrats, President Bush's legislation once again stalled in Congress.[8]

Frustrated at the lack of federal action, state governments have passed thousands of laws to address immigration during the last decade. In 2013 alone, lawmakers in 45 states and the District of Columbia enacted 184 laws and 253 resolutions related to immigration—a 64 percent increase from 2012.[9] Among the most controversial regulations was Arizona SB 1070, a 2010 state law signed by Governor Jan Brewer, R-Ariz., requiring immigrants to carry authorization documents at all times and mandating police to question people if there was reason to suspect they were in the United States illegally. After the federal government challenged the law, the Supreme Court struck down the provision regarding authorization documents, as well as another that allowed police to arrest suspected undocumented immigrants without a warrant. But the Court let stand the central provision allowing police to check the residency status of suspected undocumented immigrants while enforcing other laws.[10]

By late 2012, as a result of piecemeal state strategies and a lack of consensus at the federal level, the immigration landscape was deeply unsettled. But politicians received a wake-up call on Election Day, when Latino voters—making up ten percent of the electorate for the first time ever—overwhelmingly voted for President Obama over former Governor Mitt Romney, R-Mass., by a margin of 71 to 27 percent.[11]

## THE CURRENT CONTROVERSY

### Should Congress pass the Gang of Eight comprehensive immigration reform package?

In the wake of the 2012 election, a bipartisan group of senators formed what would become known as the Gang of Eight. Made up of four Republicans and four Democrats, the Gang of Eight met 24 times over several months to produce a comprehensive immigration reform proposal in April 2013.[12] The bill aimed to improve border security, reform the visa system, require employers to ensure the legal status of their employees, and provide a pathway to citizenship for undocumented immigrants who had arrived in the United States prior to 2012. These undocumented immigrants would have to pay fines and back taxes, learn English, remain employed, pass a criminal background check, apply for LPR status after ten years, and apply for citizenship three years later. The bill also mandated that DHS must monitor 100 percent of the U.S. border with Mexico within five years and maintain a 90 percent annual effectiveness rate in high-risk sectors. Additional visas would be made available for highly skilled immigrants, while fewer visas would be available for the relatives of American citizens.[13]

The Senate passed the Gang of Eight's bill 68-32 in June 2013, but the House Republican leadership declined to even consider it. As of 2015, the legislation had yet to be reintroduced in Congress, but it sparked a lasting debate over whether lawmakers would be capable of passing a comprehensive immigration reform package. Supporters of the bill believe it represents a true compromise that addresses many of the most pressing issues in the American immigration system. They argue that by simultaneously working to reduce illegal immigration while enhancing border security, the bill addresses all parties' priorities. Proponents also praise the Gang of Eight bill for reforming all facets of the immigration system—a far more effective approach than piecemeal reforms.

But critics of the bill disagree, believing it would provide amnesty for millions of people who have broken American laws. Opponents argue that if Congress abandons the rule of law and allows special protections for undocumented immigrants, it would only encourage more undocumented people to cross the United States' borders. Critics further note than in a time when the national debt is $18 trillion, American taxpayers simply cannot afford the additional strains this bill would place on public social safety net programs.[14]

## Should Congress pass the Gang of Eight comprehensive immigration reform package?

### YES: This bill will boost both the American economy and border security.

"We have a badly broken legal immigration system," said Senator Marco Rubio, R-Fla. "Not only does it not work, it actually encourages illegal immigration. We have a border with Mexico that, despite billions of dollars already spent, is still not secure. Every day, people, drugs, and guns are trafficked across that border. And we have 11 million people living in this country illegally in de facto amnesty. This is the way things are now. This is the status quo. And it is a terrible mess."[15]

If Congress passes the Gang of Eight comprehensive reform bill, it would allow more than 11 million undocumented immigrants to finally come out of the shadows and take part in the American dream. No longer would these people cost American taxpayers money—they would instead help the economy grow by working, paying taxes, and becoming contributing members of American society.[16]

And let us be clear—this bill does not make the path to citizenship easy. People who wish to become citizens of the United States must pay fines, pay back taxes, and prove they are adequately employed. Rather than amnesty, this is a difficult but fair process that offers a realistic solution to a very real problem. And because the bill offers citizenship only to those who were in the United States prior to 2012, future undocumented immigrants would have to follow the legal process for establishing residency and seeking citizenship.

"Those who are in our country illegally will be given a chance to earn their citizenship if they meet a number of conditions. That process will be tough, but fair," said Senator Richard Durbin, D-Ill. "Ours is a nation of immigrants and it's unacceptable that we've been without a coherent, fair, and humane immigration policy for so long."[17]

This comprehensive reform package would ensure the safety of Americans by enhancing border patrols and surveillance. It would also promote American competitiveness by allowing additional visas for highly skilled workers—the scientists, doctors, and entrepreneurs the United States must attract if it is going to compete on the global stage.

In addition, the Gang of Eight proposal includes countless safeguards to protect against future illegal immigration. "If you're serious about actually fixing the system, then this is the vehicle to do it," President Obama said. "This bill isn't perfect. No one is going to get everything that they want. But this is a bill that's largely consistent with the principles that I ... had laid out for common-sense reform."[18]

## NO: This bill will only hurt average Americans and encourage future illegal immigration.

"This Gang of Eight bill is a disaster. It is the exact same thing we saw in 1986," said Senator Ted Cruz, R-Texas. "The last big immigration reform was in 1986, and the federal government told the American people, 'We're gonna grant amnesty for the three million people who are here illegally. And in exchange for that, we're actually gonna secure the borders. We're gonna solve illegal immigration, and the problem is gonna go away.' Now, we saw what happened. The amnesty happened, the borders never got secured, and now three decades later, instead of three million people, it's 11 million people."[19]

As Senator Cruz correctly points out, the Gang of Eight bill would only make a broken immigration system worse. By promising a pathway to citizenship for undocumented immigrants before fully securing the nation's borders, Congress is practically inviting millions of people to show up at the United States' doors.

Although this bill poses as a comprehensive immigration reform package, it is, at its heart, a reward for immigrants who have chosen to disregard the law. The Gang of Eight is attempting to do too much, too quickly. Immigration is a vastly complex issue that requires precision and thoughtful deliberation. Therefore, instead of writing one prescription to heal countless individual policy problems, Congress should implement smaller changes that can be evaluated before a comprehensive overhaul of the entire system. "There's simply no legitimate reason why we have to pass a one-size-fits-all 1,200-page, take-it-or-leave-it immigration bill," said Senator Mike Lee, R-Utah.[20]

The Gang of Eight did not take into account the additional funds needed to cover welfare, unemployment insurance, and other social safety net programs that millions of new citizens would have access to—nor did it mention the millions of dollars needed to implement the new programs created by the bill.[21] In an era of $18 trillion in national debt, it is both irresponsible and shortsighted to pass a bill that would cost taxpayers so much money. Americans do not need a larger government—they need a more responsible government.

As many Americans continue to recover from the Great Recession of 2008, Congress has no business passing a bill that would increase the hiring of foreign workers and place American citizens' jobs at risk. "For American citizens, the legislation offered nothing except lower wages, higher unemployment, and a heavier tax burden," said Senator Jeff Sessions, R-Ala.[22]

# THE ONGOING DEBATE

### Should the government give special protections to undocumented immigrants brought to the United States as minors?

As Congress has debated immigration policies in recent years, lawmakers have often paid special attention to minors who were brought to the United States—often without their knowledge or consent—by their undocumented parents. In many cases, these young people have lived in the United States for an extended period of time and have little or no knowledge of life in their home countries. And over the last two decades, Congress and the president have enacted— or attempted to enact—policies to deal with this particular population of undocumented immigrants.

**The DREAM Act.** Perhaps the most well-known proposal is the Development, Relief, and Education for Alien Minors (DREAM) Act, first introduced in Congress in 2001 and repeatedly voted down in the years since then. If enacted, the DREAM Act would provide six-year conditional legal status to undocumented immigrants who were brought to the United States before the age of 16—but only if they had lived in the United States

Texas students wait to testify against repeal of the Texas Dream Act at an April 2015 hearing in Austin.

continuously for five years, had graduated from an American high school or obtained a GED, had demonstrated good character, and had not committed any crimes. If, during their conditional legal status, these "Dreamers" passed criminal background checks and attended college or served at least two years in the military, they would be eligible to apply for LPR status and eventually citizenship. If they failed to fulfill the requirements, they would be subject to deportation.[23]

**DACA.** As Congress failed to pass the DREAM Act, in 2012 President Obama launched the Deferred Action for Childhood Arrivals (DACA) program, which suspended deportation for many Dreamers. Immigrants were eligible for protection under DACA if they had lived in the United States continuously for at least five years; had never been convicted of a crime; were no older than 30; and had served in the military, completed a high school education, or were enrolled in school. Under DACA, these immigrants were eligible to apply for work authorization and to avoid deportation for two years, subject to renewal.[24] DHS approved 427,592 DACA cases—and denied 16,360—in fiscal year 2013.[25]

**Executive Actions.** In 2014, President Obama issued a series of executive actions that had enormous potential consequences for Dreamers and their parents. These actions expanded DACA work authorizations from two years to three years; extended DACA to undocumented immigrants of any age, as long as they were brought to the United States before the age of 16 and had lived in the United States continuously since 2010; and allowed the undocumented parents of American citizens and LPRs to request work authorization and deferred deportation for three years, as long as they passed background checks and had lived in the United States continuously since 2010.[26] According to the Migration Policy Institute, President Obama's executive actions could defer deportation for as many as 5.2 million people—or nearly half of the undocumented immigrants in the United States.[27]

But these actions also ignited fierce debates over the proper use and extent of executive power. "The American people want both parties to focus on solving problems together; they don't support unilateral action from a president who is more interested in partisan politics

than working with the people's elected representatives," Speaker of the House John Boehner, R-Ohio, said. "That is not how American democracy works."[28] In early 2015, U.S. District Judge Andrew Hanen agreed, and halted the implementation of the executive actions.[29]

## THE CURRENT CONTROVERSY

### Should states offer in-state college tuition to "Dreamers"?

DACA provided young undocumented immigrants with the ability to defer deportation and to seek work authorization, but they still face several challenges regarding their education. The Obama administration has explicitly stated that all children have a right to enroll in public schools, no matter their immigration status; however, undocumented students are subject to several restrictions in higher education.[30] As of 2015, for example, undocumented students were forbidden from receiving federal financial aid for college, while only five states—California, Minnesota, New Mexico, Texas, and

Washington—allowed them to receive state financial aid.[31] In addition, the 1996 Illegal Immigration Reform and Immigrant Responsibility Act prohibits state colleges and universities from providing in-state tuition rates based on residency to undocumented immigrants, unless the same rates are offered to all American citizens.[32]

However, because some states have made in-state tuition dependent on high school attendance rather than residency, 18 states had provisions extending in-state tuition to undocumented students as of 2014. Meanwhile, three states—Arizona, Georgia, and Indiana—have explicitly barred undocumented students from receiving in-state tuition rates.[33]

In the absence of consistent federal action, these state laws have sparked a nationwide debate over whether Dreamers should be eligible for in-state tuition at colleges and universities. Supporters argue that by helping undocumented students attend college, states would encourage more people to enter the workforce, creating a boost for the national economy. Proponents also note that the United States already invests in K-12 education for Dreamers; therefore it is illogical to bar them from higher education. But opponents argue that such a policy is an unfair and unnecessary burden on American taxpayers. Critics insist that tuition breaks are an improper and undeserved reward for those who have broken American laws—and that they are blatantly unfair to the millions of citizens forced to pay out-of-state tuition fees.

## Should states offer in-state college tuition to "Dreamers"?

### YES: Providing in-state tuition for Dreamers is good for students and good for the economy.

"Undocumented students are no different than their classmates," said Senator Patty Murray, D-Wash. "They live in the same towns, attend the same schools, and share the same dreams—and they deserve an equal chance to go to college and start successful careers in this country."[34]

A great many immigrants are hardworking, goal-oriented people. And Dreamers—the young men and women brought to the United States by their parents illegally—have worked hard to succeed in school and to make the most of their lives. Therefore, with so many futures at stake, it would be painfully unfair to punish these students for the mistakes of their parents and to deny them the opportunities they need to prosper.

In 2014–2015, the average in-state tuition and fees at a public four-year college in the United States amounted to $9,139 per year. But for out-of-state students, the average tuition and fees jumped to $22,958 per year—a price difference that most undocumented immigrant families simply cannot afford.[35]

By allowing undocumented students to receive in-state tuition, states would not only be expanding educational opportunities, they would be pursuing more cost-effective policies. In New Jersey, for example, the state government invests more than $240,000 per student when it comes to education.[36] "The most important thing is for these young men and women of our state, who we have invested hundreds of thousands of dollars in their K-12 education, we're now going to give them an opportunity in an affordable way to be able to continue their education," said Governor Chris Christie, R-N.J., who signed a bill in 2013 allowing Dreamers to pay in-state college tuition.[37] And thanks to this policy, striving students in New Jersey will be able to develop their skills, find higher-paying jobs, and start successful businesses.

"As an immigrant who came to this country at a young age, I know that education can be a great equalizer," Senator Mazie Hirono, D-Hawaii, said. "Students who were brought to this country as children deserve fair access to affordable higher education. I've had the privilege to meet many inspiring Dreamers who just want an opportunity to work hard and contribute to the country they call home."[38]

In the end, providing educational opportunities is smart—and compassionate—policy. Even the conservative Governor Rick Perry, R-Texas, says, "If you say that we should not educate children who come into our state for no other reason than that they've been brought there through no fault of their own, I don't think you have a heart."

## NO: Providing in-state tuition for Dreamers is too expensive and unfair to American citizens.

"The laws of the United States prohibit illegal aliens from residing in our country," the Federation for American Immigration Reform notes. "By their very presence, every day illegal aliens make a conscious decision to ignore these laws. Granting in-state tuition to illegal aliens undermines the rule of law and rewards illegal behavior."[39]

And it is as simple as that. When states offer in-state college tuition to undocumented immigrants, they inadvertently provide incentives for people to come to the United States illegally or to stay in the country beyond the limits of their visas. If the United States is a nation that values the rule of law, Americans cannot reward those who have broken the rules by providing college tuition discounts. In Florida, which passed a bill in 2014 to allow Dreamers to receive in-state tuition, state Senator Lizbeth Benacquisto, a Republican, noted, "I oppose forcing law-abiding Florida families to subsidize the tuition of those whose family's first act in the U.S. was breaking our immigration laws."[40]

At a time when many American citizens are still feeling the residual pain of the Great Recession, it is blatantly unfair to provide college tuition discounts to undocumented immigrants but withhold the same discounts from out-of-state American citizens. After all, why should people who have broken the law be entitled to public benefits that are denied to American citizens?

Furthermore, the idea of granting tuition assistance to undocumented immigrants is a poor policy solution for the future. For example, there is no guarantee that Dreamers will remain in the United States once they graduate from college. With federal immigration policy in a state of flux, these students could face deportation; they could also choose to return to their home countries once they have completed their discounted education. "I don't understand why they would take taxpayer dollars that could be going to U.S. citizens and instead subsidizing the education of non-citizens who could also be deported," said Kris Kobach, the Republican secretary of state in Kansas. "Why would you subsidize a workforce that may not be there tomorrow?"[41]

Americans would be wise to remember that post-secondary public education is heavily subsidized by taxpayer money; therefore, it is taxpayer dollars that help pay for undocumented immigrants to attend college. And at a time when educational institutions are already affected by a weakened economy, policies that grant in-state tuition to undocumented immigrants would only further threaten the American education system.

# CONCLUSION

The Gang of Eight bill and tuition discounts for Dreamers are only two examples of the debates Americans have engaged in as they contemplate reforming the immigration system. And although the fates of these two specific policies remain far from certain, American policymakers, immigrants, and citizens will undoubtedly continue to debate the goals and priorities of the immigration system—and which government policies best reflect and achieve them.

[1] U.S. State Department. *Annual Report of Immigrant Visa Applicants in the Family-Sponsored and Employment-Based Preferences Registered at the National Visa Center as of November 1, 2014.* Web. 15 Mar. 2015.

[2] Pew Research Center. "5 Facts about Illegal Immigration in the U.S." Web. 15 Mar. 2015.

[3] Hoefer, Michael, Nancy Rytina, and Bryan Baker. Estimates of the Unauthorized Immigrant Population Residing in the United States: January 2011. U.S. Department of Homeland Security, Office of Immigration Statistics. Mar. 2012. Web. 14 Apr. 2015.

[4] Passel, Jeffrey, and D'Vera Cohn. *"Unauthorized Immigrant Population: National and State Trends, 2010."* Pew Research Center. 1 Feb. 2011. Web. 14 Apr. 2015.

[5] Reuters. "Americans Worry That Illegal Migrants Threaten Way of Life, Economy." Web. 9 Apr. 2015.

[6] Monger, Randall, and James Yankay. *U.S. Legal Permanent Residents: 2012.* U.S. Department of Homeland Security, Office of Immigration Statistics. Mar. 2013. Web. 14 Apr. 2015.

[7] Weiner, Rachel. "How Immigration Reform Failed, Over and Over." *Washington Post.* 30 Jan. 2013. Web. 14 Apr. 2015.

[8] Ibid.

[9] National Conference of State Legislatures. "State Laws Related to Immigration and Immigrants." 7 Jan. 2015. Web. 14 Apr. 2015.

[10] Cohen, Tom, and Bill Mears. "Supreme Court Mostly Rejects Arizona Immigration Law; Governor Says 'Heart' Remains." CNN. 26 Jun. 2012.

[11] Rodriguez, Cindy. "Latino Vote Key to Obama's Re-election." CNN. 9 Nov. 2012. Web. 14 Apr. 2014.

[12] Avila, Jim, and Serena Marshall. "Bipartisan Senators Roll Out Historic Immigration Bill." ABC News. 18 Apr. 2013. Web. 14 Apr. 2015.

[13] *Washington Post.* "Key Provisions in 'Gang of Eight' Senate Proposal." 15 Apr. 2013. Web. 14 Apr. 2015.

[14] Brillig. U.S. National Debt Clock. Web. 6 Mar. 2015.

[15] Rubio, Marco. Floor Speech. U.S. Senate. 26 Jun. 2013.

[16] Vallejo, Jody Agius. "Giving Immigrants a Path to Citizenship is Key to US Economic Growth" *The Guardian.* 17 April 2013. Web. 9 April 2015.

[17] Senator Richard Durbin. "Durbin, Bipartisan Group of Senators Unveil Immigration Reform Principles." Official Website. 28 Jan. 2013. Web. 14 Apr. 2015.

18  Gomez, Alan, and Susan Davis. "'Gang of Eight' Immigration Bill Clears Senate Hurdle." *USA Today*. 11 Jun. 2013. Web. 14 Apr. 2015.

19  Real Clear Politics. "Cruz: Gang of Eight Bill Offers 'Same Empty Promises' as 1986 Reform." 19 Jun. 2013. Web. 14 Apr. 2015.

20  Lee, Mike. Floor Speech. U.S. Senate. 27 Jun. 2013.

21  Fox News. "Cost of Giving Illegal Immigrants Path to Citizenship Could Outweigh Fiscal Benefits." 29 Jan. 2013. Web. 15 Mar. 2015.

22  Sessions, Jeff. "The Immigration Handbook for the New Republic Majority." Jan. 2015. Print.

23  Immigration Policy Center. "The DREAM Act." 18 May 2011. Web. 14 Apr. 2015.

24  U.S. Department of Homeland Security. "Secretary Napolitano Announces Deferred Action Process for Young People Who are Low Enforcement Priorities." 15 Jun. 2012. Web. 14 Apr. 2015.

25  U.S. Citizenship and Immigration Services. "Requests by Intake, Biometrics and Case Status." Jun. 2014. Web. 14 Apr. 2015.

26  U.S. Citizenship and Immigration Services. "Executive Actions on Immigration." Web. 14 Apr. 2014.

27  Migration Policy Institute. "MPI: As Many as 3.7 Million Unauthorized Immigrants Could Get Relief from Deportation under Anticipated New Deferred Action Program." 19 Nov. 2014. Web. 14 Apr. 2015.

28  Epstein, Jennifer. "'Come Out of the Shadows.'" *Politico*. 20 Nov. 2014. Web. 14 Apr. 2015.

29  Chappell, Bill. "Federal Judge Blocks Obama's Executive Actions on Immigration." NPR. 17 Feb. 2015. Web. 14 Apr. 2015.

30  Emma, Caitlin. "Feds: Schools Can't Shut Out Undocumented Immigrants." *Politico*. 8 May 2014. Web. 14 Apr. 2015.

31  National Conference of State Legislatures. "Undocumented Student Tuition: Overview." 10 Feb. 2015. Web. 14 Apr. 2015.

32  Von Spakovsky, Hans A., and Charles Stimson. "Providing In-State Tuition for Illegal Aliens: A Violation of Federal Law." Heritage Foundation. Web. 15 Mar. 2015.

33  National Conference of State Legislatures. "Undocumented Student Tuition: State Action." 12 Jun. 2014. Web. 14 Apr. 2015.

34  Senator Patty Murray. "Murray, Polis Introduce Bill to Provide In-State Tuition for Dreamer Students." Official Website. 16 Jan. 2014. Web. 14 Apr. 2015.

35  College Board. "Average Published Undergraduate Charges by Sector, 2014-2015." Web. 14 Apr. 2015.

36  Nava, Erika J. "Issue Brief: It's Time for Tuition Equity." *New Jersey Policy Perspective*. 17 Jun. 2013. Web. 15 Mar. 2015.

37  Jacobsen, Katherine. "Chris Christie Reaches Deal on In-State Tuition for Illegal Immigrants." *Christian Science Monitor*. 20 Dec. 2013. Web. 14 Apr. 2015.

38  Senator Patty Murray. "Murray, Polis Introduce Bill to Provide In-State Tuition for Dreamer Students." Official Website. 16 Jan. 2014. Web. 14 Apr. 2015.

39  Federation for American Immigration Reform. "In-State Tuition for Illegal Aliens: Talking Points." Web. 14 Apr. 2015.

40  Buzzacco-Foerster, Jenna. "Committee Advances In-State Tuition Rates for Illegal Immigrants." *Tampa Tribune*. 18 Mar. 2014. Web. 9 Apr. 2015.

41  Fox News. "More States Grant In-State Tuition to Immigrants." 1 Feb. 2014. Web. 14 Apr. 2015.

# LAW AND ORDER

## CURRENT CONTROVERSIES

- Should the federal government impose universal background checks on gun purchases?

- Should "three strikes" laws be abolished?

# INTRODUCTION

> "The end of law is not to abolish or restrain, but to preserve and enlarge freedom. For in all the states of created beings capable of law, where there is no law, there is no freedom."
>
> —John Locke

> "When injustice becomes law, resistance becomes duty."
>
> —Thomas Jefferson

The United States is a nation of laws—laws that are intended to apply equally to each and every citizen, no matter their background, race, or position in society. But Americans have long debated which laws most fairly and effectively maintain order and security in the United States, and how those laws should be interpreted and enforced. In this chapter, we will consider several enduring tensions in American law and order and examine two current controversial issues:

- Should the federal government impose universal background checks on gun purchases?

- Should "three strikes" laws be abolished?

**Why Is This Issue Controversial?** Ever since a group of armed colonists rebelled against Great Britain and founded the United States, Americans have placed great value on the principles of freedom and individual liberty. Yet to maintain order and safety in American society, these ideals must be delicately—and often controversially—balanced with laws that limit what individuals are permitted to do.

In order to discourage and combat crime, the government—at the local, state, and federal levels—passes and enforces criminal laws, brings charges against Americans accused of committing crimes, oversees the judicial process, and establishes sentencing guidelines for prisoners. However, policymakers do not always agree on what causes crime—nor do they agree on which policies most effectively prevent it. Over the last several decades, the rate of violent crime has dropped significantly in the United States, from 713.6 violent crimes per 100,000 inhabitants in 1994 to 367.9 violent crimes per 100,000 inhabitants in 2013.[1]

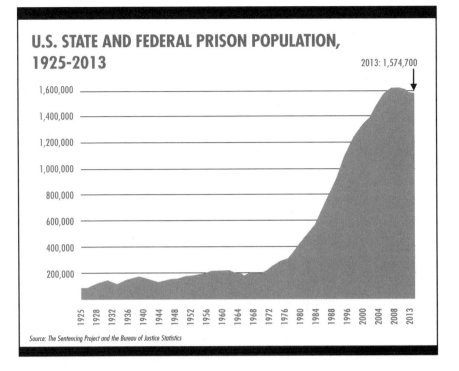

## U.S. STATE AND FEDERAL PRISON POPULATION, 1925-2013

2013: 1,574,700

Source: The Sentencing Project and the Bureau of Justice Statistics

Criminologists have cited a number of potential reasons for the trend, including proactive policing and surveillance practices, an increase in community outreach programs, a boost in government welfare programs, and increased rates of incarceration. In fact, the United States is the global leader in incarceration, with nearly 2.2 million people behind bars in 2015, according to The Sentencing Project.[2]

Some of the United States' most fiercely debated law and order policies are those that govern the use and regulation of weapons, such as firearms. The Second Amendment to the Constitution reads, "A well regulated Militia, being necessary to the security of a free State, the right of the people to keep and bear Arms, shall not be infringed."[3] Like much of the vague language in the Constitution, the Second Amendment has proven to be enormously controversial. Some Americans believe "the right of the people to keep and bear Arms" establishes an individual constitutional right to own firearms, making it unconstitutional for the government to restrict or prohibit gun possession. But others point to the language regarding "a well regulated Militia" and insist the framers' intent was to prevent Congress from revoking a state's right to self-defense. Under this collective rights theory, legislators have the authority to regulate firearms without violating an individual's constitutional rights.

Gun-related policies remain controversial because of the high number of Americans personally affected by the use or regulation of firearms. In 2013, the Institute of Medicine and the National Research Council concluded that handguns were used in 87 percent of American violent crimes, and the rate of gun-related homicide in the United States was 19.5 times higher than that of other high-income nations.[4] At the same time, an October 2014 Gallup poll revealed that 42 percent of Americans—or roughly 134 million people—kept a gun inside their home, whether for self-defense, hunting, recreation, or other reasons.[5]

**Why Is This Issue So Complicated?** Criminal laws exist at the local, state, and federal levels, creating a complicated patchwork of legal and sentencing guidelines across the country. Criminal penalties, for example, often vary by state. While 32 states allowed the death penalty

## PERCENTAGE OF AMERICANS WHO HAVE A GUN IN THEIR HOME BY DEMOGRAPHIC GROUP

| | %YES | %NO |
|---|---|---|
| Men | 47 | 48 |
| Women | 38 | 59 |
| Whites | 49 | 46 |
| Nonwhites | 28 | 70 |
| East | 31 | 66 |
| Midwest | 44 | 49 |
| South | 51 | 45 |
| West | 39 | 57 |
| Republicans | 55 | 38 |
| Independents | 43 | 53 |
| Democrats | 27 | 72 |

Source: Gallup, October 2014

in early 2015, 18 states and the District of Columbia had abolished the practice.[6] Meanwhile, only 28 states have passed laws requiring heavier sentences for repeat criminal offenders.[7]

The regulation of firearms also presents its own web of complications for law enforcement officials. Although only a minority of Americans own guns, there were, by various estimates, between 270 million and 310 million civilian-owned guns in the United States in 2013.[8] And in 2007, the global Small Arms Survey concluded that the United States had the highest rate of gun ownership per capita in the world, with an average of 89 civilian-owned firearms for every 100 people. Distantly in second and third place were Yemen, which reported 55 guns for every 100 people, and Switzerland, which reported 46 guns per 100 people.[9] Given these figures, it is difficult for the government to fully control and monitor who has access to firearms in the United States.

Americans also largely disagree on the chief causes of crime and gun violence in the United States. While some point to the proliferation of guns and believe it is too easy for criminals to obtain weapons, others cast the blame on cyclical poverty, the illegal drug trade, the inadequate assessment and treatment of people with severe mental illnesses, poor enforcement of established gun and criminal laws, and a culture that celebrates violent forms of entertainment.

## THE ONGOING DEBATE

### What is the appropriate role of government in regulating gun ownership?

The Supreme Court has weighed several Second Amendment cases in recent years—most notably, *District of Columbia v. Heller* in 2008. In its decision, the Court ruled that the Second Amendment grants an individual the right to possess a firearm for traditionally lawful purposes, such as self-defense. According to the Court's majority decision, the Second Amendment's "well regulated Militia" clause merely establishes the individual right to bear arms—but it does not limit it. The Court, however, also ruled that the individual right to bear arms is still subject to regulation, such as limits on concealed weapons or on the rights of felons and the mentally ill.[10]

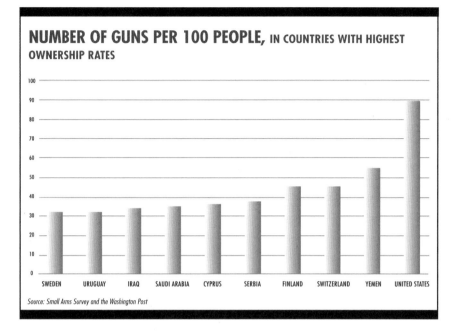

**NUMBER OF GUNS PER 100 PEOPLE,** IN COUNTRIES WITH HIGHEST OWNERSHIP RATES

Source: Small Arms Survey and the Washington Post

Just as guns have been a part of the American legal landscape for years, so too have gun regulations. Spurred by the assassinations of President John F. Kennedy, Senator Robert Kennedy, D-N.Y., and Dr. Martin Luther King, Jr., Congress passed the Omnibus Crime Control and Safe Streets Act and the Gun Control Act (GCA) in 1968. Among its provisions, the GCA required gun dealers to obtain federal licenses; restricted the interstate transportation of guns; and prohibited the transfer of guns to certain groups of people which, as of 2015, included the following:

- Convicted felons
- Fugitives from justice
- People under restraining orders
- People who have been convicted of domestic violence charges
- Unlawful drug users or addicts
- People who have been committed to mental institutions
- Undocumented immigrants or people who have renounced their American citizenship
- Dishonorably discharged U.S. servicemen[11]

Congress eased several GCA restrictions in 1986 by passing the Firearm Owners' Protection Act, which aimed to decrease undue restrictions on law-abiding citizens by exempting "hobbyists" and collectors from obtaining federal licenses to sell guns. The law also prohibited the Bureau of Alcohol, Tobacco, Firearms, and Explosives from creating a national gun purchase registry and from conducting more than one warrantless inspection of a gun dealer in a given year.[12]

The failed assassination attempt on President Ronald Reagan in 1981 launched a movement for stronger restrictions on the purchase, sale, and ownership of guns. By 1993, President Bill Clinton signed the Brady Handgun Violence Protection Act—a law named after White House press secretary James Brady, who had been partially paralyzed by a gunshot wound during the attack on President Reagan. The so-called Brady Law mandated federal background checks of gun buyers at licensed dealers, in order to prevent sales to people restricted under the GCA. The National Instant Criminal Background Check System (NICS) was established in 1998 to support this initiative and is currently maintained by the Federal Bureau of Investigation (FBI).[13]

Prior to finalizing a gun sale, licensed firearm dealers use NICS to reference records from three databases: the National Crime Information Center, which contains information on wanted persons and protection orders; the Interstate Identification Index, which contains criminal history records; and the NICS Index, which contains information submitted by local, state, and federal agencies, mental health institutions, and other sources.[14] But private sales— transactions by unlicensed collectors or hobbyists to buyers from the same state—do not require an NICS background check.

In 1994, Congress passed the Violent Crime Control and Law Enforcement Act, which placed a ten-year federal ban on the manufacture or sale of semiautomatic assault weapons, several of which had become popular with violent criminal gangs. The law also limited high-capacity ammunition magazines to ten rounds.[15] In response, many gun rights supporters, led by the National Rifle Association (NRA), expressed their displeasure with the Brady Law and the assault weapons ban through the political process. Two

Representative Gabby Giffords, D-Ariz., shot in the head during a rampage in 2011, returned to the Capitol to advocate on behalf of gun regulations.

months after Congress passed the ban, Democrats lost control of both the House of Representatives and the Senate in the 1994 midterm elections—a loss some analysts attributed to members' recent gun-related votes. Perceiving the outcome as an example of the political perils of gun control, many legislators have attempted to avoid addressing the issue. And in 2004, the federal ban on assault weapons expired when no congressional action was taken to renew it.

## THE CURRENT CONTROVERSY

### Should the federal government impose universal background checks on gun purchases?

On December 14, 2012, a young man with a history of mental illness shot and killed his mother as she lay in her bed in Newtown, Connecticut. He then drove to Sandy Hook Elementary School, armed with several of his mother's legally purchased semiautomatic weapons, and within minutes had killed six adults and 20 children, all of them six or seven years old.[16]

In the aftermath of the Sandy Hook shooting, Americans engaged in a forceful new debate over gun control—highlighting how the nation remains deeply divided over the issue. By January 2013, President Barack Obama unveiled a plan to make sweeping changes to the nation's gun laws. Among its provisions, the president's proposal called for new laws requiring criminal background checks for all gun sales, including those by private collectors and hobbyists; reinstating the federal ban on assault weapons; limiting ammunition magazines to ten rounds; banning the possession of armor-piercing bullets by anyone other than military or law enforcement; and expanding mental health programs for young people.[17]

However, the president's advocacy was matched by an intense lobbying effort by the NRA and gun rights supporters. By April, several proposals—including legislation to expand background checks—had been voted down in the Senate, reigniting the debate over whether universal background checks would reduce gun violence. Gun control advocates insist such a policy is the most effective way to ensure guns do not fall into the hands of dangerous people. They also believe a universal system would not violate the rights of law-abiding citizens; it would merely ask them to help enhance public safety.

But opponents of universal background checks believe the current system does little to keep Americans safe from gun violence—and expanding it would not help. Several of the most notorious mass shooters in history passed background checks despite their records of mental instability. Therefore, many gun rights advocates believe it would be more productive for the government to better enforce existing laws so criminals cannot easily sidestep the process.

## Should the federal government impose universal background checks on gun purchases?

### YES: Background checks are common sense and can help stop the epidemic of gun violence.

People in the United States are nearly 20 times as likely to be killed by guns as people who reside in other developed countries. According to the United Nations, the United States experiences four times as many gun-related homicides per capita as Switzerland and Turkey, which are tied for third place among developed countries.[18] And between 2006 and early 2015, there were 36 public mass shootings in the United States in which at least four people were killed.[19]

In the face of such an indisputable epidemic of gun violence, the federal government must move to impose universal background checks on gun purchases. "If you want to buy a gun—whether it's from a licensed dealer or a private seller—you should at least have to show you are not a felon or somebody legally prohibited from buying one," President Obama said in 2013. "This is common sense."[20]

Between 1994 and 2012, nearly 148 million applications for gun sales or permits were subject to background checks, resulting in 2.4 million denials.[21] Therefore, in 2.4 million instances, the federal background check system ensured that deadly firearms did not fall into the hands of felons, fugitives, drug addicts, and the severely mentally ill. But federal background checks cover only a portion of gun transactions, allowing private buyers to bypass the system.

"Take Zina Daniel, a victim of domestic violence who procured a restraining order against her estranged husband, making him unable to pass a background check. He bought a semiautomatic handgun from a private seller online, where he didn't need a background check. He used that gun to kill Zina and two others and wound four more at a nail salon," wrote Sarah Brady, the wife of the late gun control advocate. "Imagine if Zina's husband were on the 'no fly' list and was one of 40 percent of airline passengers the Transportation Security Administration allowed to fly without undergoing a security screening. Would Americans feel safe in the air in this scenario? Not likely."[22]

There is a reason why 92 percent of Americans support universal background checks for gun purchases, according to a June 2014 Quinnipiac University poll.[23] Background checks work. In 2007, after the repeal of a Missouri law that required universal background checks for handgun purchases, the statewide murder rate jumped 16 percent.[24]

In sum, the government simply cannot afford not to act. Senator Chris Murphy, D-Conn., said, "It is beyond comprehension that Congress is watching this epidemic of school shootings and chooses to do nothing."[25]

## NO: Expanded background checks are ineffective and a dangerous invasion of privacy.

As tragic and senseless as gun violence is, Americans should not be fooled into believing universal background checks offer a simple solution. The federal system, NICS, has already cost American taxpayers $650 million to maintain—yet it has largely failed to keep guns out of the hands of dangerous criminals and the severely mentally ill.[26]

Universal background checks would not have prevented Adam Lanza, for example, from brutally murdering 26 people at Sandy Hook Elementary School in 2012. "The weapons were legally purchased by his mother," Senator Dianne Feinstein, D-Calif., a supporter of background checks, conceded. "And while he was disturbed, he had no criminal record or record of mental illness and would not have been subject to a background check because his mother gave him these weapons."[27]

The sad truth is that the federal background check system is full of holes, and expanding it would only ignore the serious problem at hand. Under the current system, states are not required to submit mental health records to NICS, and as of 2012, only 30 percent of the estimated 4.4 million mental health records from the previous two decades could be found in the system. This broken structure led the gun control organization Everytown for Gun Safety to conclude that each of the public mass shooters who murdered innocent Americans between 2009 and 2014 could have slipped through NICS.[28]

"The fact is, we could dramatically cut crime in this country with guns and save lives all over this country if we would start enforcing the 9,000 federal laws we have on the books," said Wayne LaPierre, executive vice president of the NRA.[29] Congress could start by enhancing NICS reporting requirements, improving the mental health care system, prosecuting violent criminals, and improving security in schools.

In the end, universal background checks are a policy too easily sidestepped by criminals, as well as a dangerous invasion of privacy by the government. "You cannot track all gun sales without tracking all gun owners," wrote Senator Mike Lee, R-Utah. "But the government has no business monitoring a constitutionally protected activity, like gun ownership, any more than it has any business tracking what books Americans read or how often they attend church."[30]

"This so-called universal background check that you're hearing about is aimed at one thing," added LaPierre. "It's aimed at registering your guns and, when another tragic opportunity presents itself, that registry will be used to confiscate your guns."[31]

# THE ONGOING DEBATE

## Should the government pursue mandatory minimum sentencing policies?

The Constitution offers few specific guidelines when it comes to the punishment of Americans who are convicted of crimes. The Eighth Amendment reads, "Excessive bail shall not be required, nor excessive fines imposed, nor cruel and unusual punishments inflicted."[32] But the framers left it to the American people and the Supreme Court to determine what exactly constitutes "excessive bail," "excessive fines," and "cruel and unusual punishment."

Over the years, local, state, and federal governments have often used the promise of strict sentencing to deter criminal activity. In the mid-1980s, for example, crack—a potent, smokable form of cocaine—spread rapidly throughout Los Angeles, New York City, and other urban areas in the United States, thanks to its low cost and powerfully addictive qualities. As Americans grew more concerned about the violent international drug trade, Congress passed the Anti-Drug Abuse Act of 1986, which appropriated $1.7 billion to fight the drug crisis.[33] But the law's most significant component was the creation of mandatory minimum penalties for drug offenses. The law mandated a minimum five-year prison sentence for possession of 500 grams of powder cocaine or five grams of crack; it also mandated a ten-year sentence for five kilograms of powder cocaine or 50 grams of crack. Between 1980 and 2011, the number of drug offenders in American jails and prisons rose from approximately 41,000 to 501,500, according to The Sentencing Project.[34]

In addition to the new mandatory minimum sentences of the 1980s, the early 1990s saw the first of the "three strikes" laws passed in the United States. Also known as habitual offender laws, three strikes laws are state laws that require a heavier penalty—often a life sentence—the third time a person commits a felony. By 2015, 28 states had adopted some form of a habitual offender law, but few attracted as much attention as Proposition 184 in California.[35] Overwhelmingly enacted by state voters in 1994, California's three strikes law earned widespread support from voters who believed it would help keep murderers, rapists, child molesters, and repeat offenders behind bars.

RECEIVING & RELEASE

California prisoners await transfer from state to county prisons because of overcrowding in the state system.

Under the law, criminals who had one prior violent or serious felony received double the prison time for a second felony—and offenders with two violent or serious prior felonies faced 25 years to life in prison for a third felony. But in California, unlike many other states, the third felony did not have to be violent or serious to qualify for a life sentence—a provision that allowed life sentences to be handed down for crimes such as drug possession or theft.

California voters reformed the three strikes law in 2012 by passing Proposition 36. The amended law allows third-strikers to receive sentences of 25 years to life in prison only if their third felonies are serious or violent, or if they have certain disqualifying prior crimes, such as sex offenses. All other third felonies are sentenced to twice the normal time in prison. The new California law also permitted inmates already serving life sentences for non-serious, nonviolent felonies to petition for new sentences.[36] Yet, California is not the only state with a strict habitual offender law. In Georgia, for example, a felon convicted of only two serious or violent crimes—such as murder, rape, or armed robbery—receives a life sentence without the possibility of parole.[37]

By the 2000s, the tide had begun to turn against some federal sentencing guidelines—chief among them, the provision of the Anti-Drug Abuse Act mandating that possession of an amount of crack carry the same sentence as possession of an amount of powder cocaine 100 times greater. In 2009, the Sentencing Commission found that 53 percent of powder cocaine offenders were Hispanic, 28 percent were African American, and 17 percent were Caucasian. But among crack offenders, the data were more racially skewed—79 percent were African American, ten percent were Caucasian, and ten percent were Hispanic.[38] And with a disproportionate number of African Americans facing tougher crack-related sentences, many policymakers believed it was time to amend the law. In 2010, a bipartisan majority of Congress passed the Fair Sentencing Act, which reduced the disparity between the amount of powder cocaine and crack needed to trigger minimum penalties, from a 100:1 ratio to 18:1.

The rise of mandatory minimum sentences and three strikes laws coincided with a precipitous decrease in violent crime in the United States, seeming to support arguments that strict sentencing guidelines deter criminal activity. "There is a reason that stiff sentencing came about," said Bill Otis, a former federal prosecutor. "It was an answer to the crime wave during the '60s and '70s. And the answer has been successful. People are safer now than they were at any time since the baby boomers were in grade school."[39] But opponents of these policies fear they have contributed to an American culture of incarceration, in which the punishment does not always fit the crime. "Mandatory minimums, to some degree, sometimes entirely, take judging out of the mix," said U.S. District Judge John Gleeson. "That's a bad thing for our system."[40]

# THE CURRENT CONTROVERSY
## Should "three strikes" laws be abolished?

California's three strikes law is perhaps the most well known in the nation, and as a result, policymakers will closely watch and analyze the effects of the 2012 policy reform. The new law has already ignited a nationwide debate on the wisdom of such laws and could, in turn, inspire other states to change their three strikes policies.

Proponents of three strikes policies insist they are a powerful deterrent for both violent and drug-related crime in states across the country. Recidivism—the relapse by prior offenders into criminal behavior—is all too common in the American justice system, and three strikes laws are the only way to reduce this trend. But opponents of three strikes laws believe they punish non-serious and nonviolent offenders with disproportionately harsh sentences. Critics also argue that they do little more than increase prison populations and budgets—while offering few tangible crime-reducing results in return.

## Should "three strikes" laws be abolished?

### YES: This expensive and ineffective policy disproportionately punishes nonviolent criminals.

As of June 2013, there were 42,417 second- and third-strikers imprisoned in California. Of these men and women, 48 percent were incarcerated for committing serious or violent crimes against people, such as murder, assault, or kidnapping. But an alarming 41 percent of these second- and third-strikers—17,195 people in just one state—were serving lengthened prison sentences for drug or property crimes, such as burglary or the sale of marijuana.[41]

In an open letter to Washington state voters, a group of prosecutors outlined one of the greatest tragedies of three strikes laws—they have the potential to incur sentences disproportionate to the crimes in question. "An 18-year-old high school senior pushes a classmate down to steal his Michael Jordan $150 sneakers—Strike One," they wrote. "He gets out of jail and shoplifts a jacket from the Bon Marché, pushing aside the clerk as he runs out of the store—Strike Two; he gets out of jail, straightens out, and nine years later gets in a fight in a bar and intentionally hits someone, breaking his nose—criminal behavior, to be sure, but hardly the crime of the century, yet it is Strike Three. He is sent to prison for the rest of his life."[42]

And because African Americans are more likely than Caucasians to be arrested for drug charges—a "strike" under this system—three strikes laws disproportionately affect the black community. In California, for example, 46 percent of third-strikers in 2013 were African American,[43] even though African Americans made up only 29 percent of the total state prison population.[44]

Three strikes laws are also troubling because they promise to reduce crime, yet have produced few tangible results. A 2012 study by the University of California Riverside found that the violent crime rate actually began falling in California two years before the three strikes law was implemented—a trend that was largely due to decreased alcohol consumption and a healthy economy.[45] Meanwhile, a report by the California state auditor concluded that the men and women imprisoned under the three strikes law as of May 2010—53 percent of whom were serving sentences for nonviolent crimes—would cost the state a total of $19.2 billion.[46]

"If this very expensive policy isn't really impacting crime, what are we doing?" asked Robert Parker, the author of the University of California Riverside study. "Why are we spending all of this money, why are we cutting health, welfare, and education repeatedly to fund an expensive system that doesn't deliver on what its promises were?"[47]

## NO: Three strikes laws are the only way to keep violent repeat offenders behind bars.

In October 1993, Richard Allen Davis entered the bedroom of 12-year-old Polly Klaas in Petaluma, California, and kidnapped her from a slumber party at knifepoint. Davis, a convicted kidnapper with a long history of violence, later strangled the young girl and hid her body beneath a pile of scrap wood.[48]

The state of California sentenced Davis to death in 1996, but many Americans were horrified that a parolee with such a lengthy and violent criminal record—one that included grand theft, assault, and kidnapping—was out on the street, waiting to prey on a young girl.[49] As a result, the tragedy helped inspire Californians to pass a strict three strikes law to ensure habitual offenders receive the punishments they deserve.

"It's about stopping the victimization, about these guys understanding they face the possibility of 25-to-life if they continue to commit crimes," said Mark Klaas, Polly's father, in 2012. "The penalty enhancement is supposed to motivate these guys to do the right thing. And if they're not doing the right thing, then you want to get a hold of them and move them out before they rape somebody, before they murder somebody, before they commit assault and battery on somebody."[50]

It is a sad truth that people who commit crimes often strike more than once. In its most recent 30-state report, the Bureau of Justice Statistics found that more than two-thirds of prisoners released in 2005 were arrested for a new crime within three years. Three-quarters of released prisoners, meanwhile, were rearrested within five years, including a troubling 71 percent of violent offenders.[51] But three strikes laws provide innocent citizens with the peace of mind that they are less likely to be victimized by repeat offenders.

The Supreme Court, in the 2003 decision of *Ewing v. California,* also affirmed the right of a state to implement strict three strikes penalties against career criminals. "When the California Legislature enacted the three strikes law, it made a judgment that protecting the public safety requires incapacitating criminals who have already been convicted of at least one serious or violent crime," former Justice Sandra Day O'Connor wrote in her opinion. "Nothing in the Eighth Amendment prohibits California from making that choice."[52]

"It does work," said Mike Reynolds, the author of the California law, whose daughter was murdered in 1992 by a recently released drug addict. "We have dropped the crime rate in half in California—not only reducing victims, but reducing the number of criminals."[53]

# CONCLUSION

Universal background checks for gun sales and the use of three strikes laws are only two examples of the debates Americans engage in when attempting to balance law and order and individual freedoms. While the fates of these two policies remain far from certain, American policymakers, law enforcement officers, gun owners, and gun control advocates will undoubtedly continue to debate the goals and priorities of the legal system—and which government policies best achieve them.

[1] Federal Bureau of Investigation. *Crime in the United States by Volume and Rate per 100,000 Inhabitants, 1994–2013*. Web. 13 Apr. 2015.

[2] The Sentencing Project. "Incarceration." Web. 13 Apr. 2015.

[3] *U.S. Constitution*. Amendment II.

[4] Leshner, Alan, Bruce Altevogt, Arlene Lee, Margaret McCoy, and Patrick Kelley. Priorities for Research to Reduce the Threat of Firearm-Related Violence. Institute of Medicine and National Research Council. 5 Jun. 2013. Web. 13 Apr. 2015.

[5] McCarthy, Justin. "More than Six in 10 Americans Say Guns Make Homes Safer." Gallup. 7 Nov. 2014. Web. 13 Apr. 2014.

[6] Death Penalty Information Center. "States With and Without the Death Penalty." 2015. Web. 13 Apr. 2015.

[7] Shoener, Nicole. "Three Strikes Laws in Different States." LegalMatch. 21 Jan. 2015. Web. 13 Apr. 2015.

[8] Desilver, Drew. "A Minority of Americans Own Guns, But Just How Many is Unclear." Pew Research Center. 4 Jun. 2013. Web. 13 Apr. 2015.

[9] Graduate Institute of International Studies. *Small Arms Survey 2007: Guns and the City*. New York: Cambridge University Press. 2007. Web. 13 Apr. 2015.

[10] The Law Library of Congress. "United States: Gun Ownership and the Supreme Court." Web. 13 Apr. 2015.

[11] U.S. Department of Justice. "Appendix C: History of Federal Firearms Laws in the United States." Web. 13 Apr. 2015.

[12] Ibid.

[13] Ibid.

[14] Federal Bureau of Investigation. "Brady Handgun Violence Protection Act of 1993." Web. 13 Apr. 2015.

[15] U.S. Department of Justice. "Appendix C: History of Federal Firearms Laws in the United States." Web. 13 Apr. 2015.

[16] CNN. "Connecticut Shootings Fast Facts." 26 Dec. 2014. Web. 13 Apr. 2015.

[17] Dann, Carrie. "Obama Unveils Sweeping New Gun Control Proposals." NBC News. 16 Jan. 2013. Web. 13 Apr. 2015.

[18] Fisher, Max. "The U.S. Has Far More Gun-Related Killings Than Any Other Developed Country." Chart. *Washington Post*. 14 Dec. 2012. Web. 13 Apr. 2015.

[19] *USA Today*. "Behind the Bloodshed: The Untold Story of America's Mass Killings." 2013. Web. 13 Apr. 2015.

[20] *Politico*. Cirilli, Kevin. "Background Checks: Do They Work?" 26 Jan. 2013. Web. 13 Apr. 2015.

[21] Durso, Joseph, Ronald Frandsen, Jennifer Karberg, and Alina Lee. *"Background Checks for Firearm Transfers 2012: Statistical Tables."* U.S. Bureau of Justice Statistics. 9 Dec. 2014. Web. 13 Apr. 2015.

22 Brady, Sarah. "Congress, Finish the Job on Brady Background Checks." CNN. 5 Aug. 2014. Web. 13 Apr. 2015.

23 Quinnipiac University. "Iraq — Getting In Was Wrong; Getting Out Was Right, U.S. Voters Tell Quinnipiac University National Poll; 92 Percent Back Background Checks for All Gun Buys." 3 Jul. 2014. Web. 13 Apr. 2015.

24 Caplan-Bricker, Nora. "The Strongest Evidence We Have That Background Checks Really Matter." *The New Republic*. 18 Feb. 2014. Web. 13 Apr. 2015.

25 Codianni, Ashley. "Sandy Hook Two Years Later: One Senator's Push for Gun Control." CNN. 12 Dec. 2014. Web. 13 Apr. 2015.

26 Ferris, Sarah. "Lack of Data Makes It Hard for Background Checks System to Work Properly." *Washington Post*. 28 Aug. 2014. Web. 13 Apr. 2015.

27 Real Clear Politics. "Feinstein: Background Checks 'Would Not Have Prevented Newtown.'" 17 Apr. 2013. Web. 13 Apr. 2015.

28 Ferris, Sarah. "Lack of Data Makes It Hard for Background Checks System to Work Properly." *Washington Post*. 28 Aug. 2014. Web. 13 Apr. 2015.

29 Good, Chris. "The Case Against Gun Background Checks." ABC News. 10 Apr. 2013. Web. 13 Apr. 2015.

30 Lee, Mike. "Mike Lee: Why I Voted Against Background Checks." *USA Today*. 17 Apr. 2013. Web. 13 Apr. 2015.

31 Ritz, Erica. "Wayne LaPierre's Bold Claim About Universal Background Checks: 'That Registry Will Be Used to Confiscate Your Guns.'" The Blaze. 23 Feb. 2013. Web. 13 Apr. 2015.

32 *U.S. Constitution*. Amendment VIII.

33 Frontline. "Thirty Years of America's Drug War: A Chronology." PBS. Web. 13 Apr. 2015.

34 The Sentencing Project. "Drug Policy." Web. 13 Apr. 2015.

35 Shoener, Nicole. "Three Strikes Laws in Different States." LegalMatch. 21 Jan. 2015. Web. 13 Apr. 2015.

36 California Courts, Judicial Branch of California. "California's Three Strikes Sentencing Law." Web. 13 Apr. 2015.

37 Heyer, Cole. "Comparing the Strike Zones of 'Three Strikes and You're Out' Laws for California and Georgia, the Nation's Two Heaviest Hitters." *Suffolk University Law Review*. 13 Nov. 2012. Web. 13 Apr. 2015.

38 Kurtzleben, Danielle. "Data Show Racial Disparity in Crack Sentencing." *U.S. News & World Report*. 3 Aug. 2010. Web. 13 Apr. 2015.

39 Johnson, Carrie, and Marisa Peñaloza. "Judge Regrets Harsh Human Toll of Mandatory Minimum Sentences." NPR. 16 Dec. 2014. Web. 13 Apr. 2015.

40 Ibid.

41 California Department of Corrections and Rehabilitation, Offender Information Services Branch, Estimates and Statistical Analysis Section, Data Analysis Unit. *Second and Third Striker Felons in the Adult Institution Population*. 30 Jun. 2013. Web. 13 Apr. 2015.

42 *American Civil Liberties Union*. "10 Reasons to Oppose '3 Strikes, You're Out.'" Web. 13 Apr. 2015.

43 California Department of Corrections and Rehabilitation, Offender Information Services Branch, Estimates and Statistical Analysis Section, Data Analysis Unit. *Second and Third Striker Felons in the Adult Institution Population*. 30 Jun. 2013. Web. 13 Apr. 2015.

44 Grattet, Ryken, and Joseph Hayes. "California's Changing Prison Population." Public Policy Institute of California. Jun. 2013. Web. 13 Apr. 2015.

45 Megerian, Chris. "On Politics in the Golden State." *Los Angeles Times*. 24 Feb. 2012. Web. 13 Apr. 2015.

46 Lagos, Marisa. "Rethinking California's 'Three Strikes' Law." *San Francisco Chronicle*. 3 Jul. 2011. Web. 13 Apr. 2015.

47 Megerian, Chris. "On Politics in the Golden State." *Los Angeles Times*. 24 Feb. 2012. Web. 13 Apr. 2015.

[48]  Fagan, Kevin. "20 Years After Polly Klaas Killing, Attitudes Change." *San Francisco Chronicle.* 2 Oct. 2013. Web. 13 Apr. 2015.

[49]  *San Francisco Chronicle.* "Richard Allen Davis' Life of Crime." 6 Aug. 1996. Web. 13 Apr. 2015.

[50]  Brooks, Jon. "Interview: Mark Klaas, Father of Murder Victim Polly Klaas, Speaks in Support of Death Penalty." KQED. 13 Jan. 2012. Web. 13 Apr. 2015.

[51]  Cooper, Alexia, Matthew Durose, and Howard Snyder. "Recidivism of Prisoners Released in 30 States in 2005: Patterns from 2005 to 2010." U.S. Bureau of Justice Statistics. 22 Apr. 2014. Web. 13 Apr. 2015.

[52]  O'Connor, Sandra Day. Opinion in *Ewing v. California.* 5 Mar. 2003. Web. 13 Apr. 2015.

[53]  Lagos, Marisa. "Rethinking California's 'Three Strikes' Law." *San Francisco Chronicle.* 3 Jul. 2011. Web. 13 Apr. 2015.

# WORK AND ECONOMIC SECURITY

## CURRENT CONTROVERSIES

- Should the government play a larger role in keeping people out of poverty?

- Should affirmative action be added to employee protection and workplace discrimination laws?

# INTRODUCTION

> "True individual freedom cannot exist without economic security and independence. People who are hungry and out of a job are the stuff of which dictatorships are made."
>
> —Franklin Delano Roosevelt

> "If we can but prevent the government from wasting the labours of the people, under the pretence of taking care of them, they must become happy."
>
> —Thomas Jefferson

What obligations does a government have to protect the economic security of its citizens? Who should foot the bills for assistance to the needy? What should the rules and requirements be? And how involved should the government be in protecting workers? For decades, these questions have been at the center of American political discourse. In this chapter, we will consider several enduring tensions in American policy and examine two current controversial issues:

- Should the government play a larger role in keeping people out of poverty?

- Should affirmative action be added to employee protection and workplace discrimination laws?

**Why Are Work and Economic Security Policies Controversial?** Employment and its many benefits play a central role in the lives of most Americans. Through their jobs, American workers earn wages to support themselves and their families; receive important benefits such as health care, dental care, life insurance, and retirement savings plans; and contribute their knowledge and skills to the production of goods and services, thus helping to boost the American economy. As of February 2015, 59.3 percent of the American working-age population was employed.[1]

However, the loss of a job, or the struggle to find or keep a job, can have equally momentous effects on the lives of Americans. Government officials have implemented a variety of policies over the last century in attempts to address these effects. The federal government has enacted laws to promote equal employment opportunities, to prevent employment discrimination, and to establish a social safety net—a system of programs aimed at promoting wage stability, employment security, and protection against poverty for Americans who are retired, unable to work, or unable to find work. Two examples of government programs that provide assistance to Americans are Social Security and Medicaid. Social Security provides benefits for retirees, disabled Americans, and the families of the retired, disabled, or deceased, while Medicaid is a health services program for low-income individuals and families. In 2011, the Census Bureau concluded that 49.1 percent of Americans lived in households in which at least one member received some type of government assistance—a significant increase from the 30 percent figure of the early 1980s.[2]

It is precisely because so many Americans depend on government programs that they are controversial. Ever since the founding of the United States, Americans have disagreed over the appropriate role of government in the lives of citizens—and the extent to which citizens should rely on the government. Programs such as Social Security, Medicare, Medicaid, unemployment insurance, food stamps, and welfare are funded by tax revenue, meaning they are financed by citizens who may or may not support their aims and methods. In an age when Americans are grappling with more than $18 trillion in national debt, these expensive social safety net programs must compete for funding with other priorities, such as education, infrastructure, and national security.[3]

**Why Are Work and Economic Security Policies So Complicated?** In 2012, the Pew Research Center found that 55 percent of Americans had received government benefits from at least one of the six largest social safety net programs. Nearly 27 percent of Americans had received unemployment benefits, followed by Social Security (26 percent), Medicare (22 percent), food stamps (18 percent), Medicaid (11 percent), and welfare (eight percent).[4] And these high usage patterns have, in turn, influenced government spending levels. The Congressional Budget Office found that mandatory government spending—nearly all of which goes toward social safety net programs—totaled $2 trillion in 2013, or 60 percent of federal spending; two-thirds of that mandatory spending went to Social Security and Medicare alone.[5]

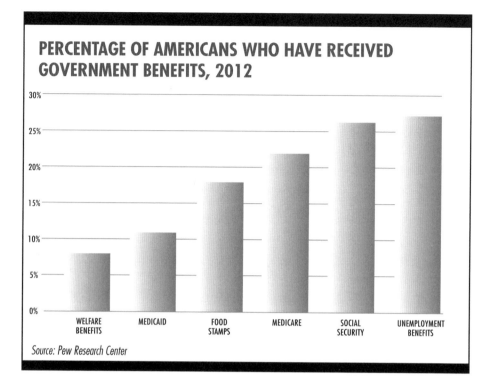

## PERCENTAGE OF AMERICANS WHO HAVE RECEIVED GOVERNMENT BENEFITS, 2012

Source: Pew Research Center

Policymakers often face resistance when they attempt to reform, curb, or cut social safety net programs precisely because so many Americans depend on them. Some of these growing programs, however, are predicted to face funding strains or crises in the future. In 2012, the Social Security Administration warned that approximately 10,000 "Baby Boomers" would retire each day for the next 20 years, dramatically boosting the demand for Social Security and Medicare benefits.[6] In addition, the Patient Protection and Affordable Care Act, the 2010 health care law more commonly known as Obamacare, gave states the option of expanding eligibility for Medicaid—a policy adopted by 28 states and the District of Columbia as of March 2015, thereby increasing future government expenses.[7]

On a broader level, work and economic security policies are complicated by the fact that there are many methods of fighting poverty and ensuring fairness in the workplace, and Americans often disagree on which are the most appropriate and effective. Traditionally, conservatives have favored a smaller government approach—one that keeps taxes low, eliminates business regulations, and seeks to reduce government dependency. Liberals tend to believe in a more expansive role for the government—one that bolsters federal and state assistance programs and increases government spending on behalf of Americans in need.

# THE ONGOING DEBATE

## What is the appropriate role of government in creating a social safety net?

Americans have debated government assistance programs since the nation's inception, but the Great Depression of the 1930s triggered massive and widespread need. Faced with an unemployment rate of nearly 25 percent when he took office in 1933, President Franklin Delano Roosevelt promised a "New Deal"—a series of government-led initiatives aimed at providing immediate relief, temporary work, and long-term economic reforms—for the American people.[8]

The New Deal era saw the establishment of several major social safety net programs and paved the way for others to come.

**Social Security.** Established in 1935, Social Security began as an old-age insurance program that provided monthly retirement benefits to workers, but it has since been expanded to include benefits for the disabled, as well as the families of the retired, disabled, or deceased. As of June 2014, Social Security had more than 58 million beneficiaries, nearly two-thirds of whom were retired workers.[9]

Social Security was designed as a pay-as-you-go program, in which current workers and their employers pay payroll taxes into the system, which then flow back out as monthly income to current retirees. Therefore, each generation's retirement benefits would, when the time came, be paid by the younger generation of workers. In 2015, workers and employers were each responsible for paying 6.2 percent of workers' first $118,500 in wages to Social Security.[10]

In 1983, as part of a comprehensive reform of the program, Congress raised Social Security payroll taxes to prepare for the impending retirement of the large Baby Boomer generation. As a result, Social Security took in more money than it paid out for years—a surplus that was invested in Treasury bonds, with interest credited to two trust funds. According to the 2014 Old Age, Survivors, and Disability Insurance Trustees Report, the trust funds held nearly $2.8 trillion at the end of 2013.[11] But the future funding of Social Security is in danger. In 2010—as Baby Boomers began retiring and many workers' wages stagnated—Social Security's payouts began to exceed its contributions, forcing the program to tap into its trust funds.[12] According to the trustees, Social Security's reserves will be fully depleted by 2033. After that point, the program will receive only enough tax revenue to pay 77 percent of scheduled benefits—unless Congress changes the benefits formula, raises the payroll tax, or raises the maximum taxable income.[13]

**Unemployment Insurance.** Enacted as part of the Social Security Act of 1935, unemployment insurance temporarily replaces a portion of workers' wages when they lose their jobs through no fault of their own. The program, which is overseen by the federal government but administered by the states, is financed largely by taxes collected from employers. In 2014, there were 7.4 million unemployment insurance beneficiaries, who received a total of $41.9 billion in benefits.[14]

In most states, the program provides up to 26 weeks of unemployment benefits, replacing approximately half of workers' previous wages. Extended benefits, however, are often available during times of heightened statewide unemployment. The federal government has also created temporary benefits programs during national economic crises and recessions.[15]

**Welfare.** The Social Security Act of 1935 created Aid to Families with Dependent Children (AFDC)—a federal cash assistance program, more commonly known as welfare, for low-income families who had one absent, disabled, or deceased parent. But by passing the Personal Responsibility and Work Opportunity Reconciliation Act of 1996, Congress replaced AFDC with Temporary Assistance for Needy Families (TANF), the current system of welfare benefits.

TANF programs are operated and maintained by the states, but they use federal block grants to offer a variety of services to low-income families, such as cash assistance, child care, education and job training, transportation, and aid to neglected or abused children. And although states set their own TANF eligibility rules, program recipients are subject to several federal regulations. For example, states are barred from using federal funds to provide cash assistance for more than five years to families with at least one adult. States must also maintain federal work participation rates among TANF recipients. In general, half of TANF families must be engaged in work activities for at least 30 hours per week, while 90 percent of two-parent TANF families must work at least 35 hours per week.[16] In fiscal year 2014, approximately 3.5 million American families received TANF assistance.[17]

**Food Stamps.** Under the original 1939 government food stamps program, needy Americans would purchase orange stamps equal to their food expenditures, and for every dollar of orange stamps purchased they would receive 50 cents in blue stamps. Orange stamps could be used to buy any food, while blue stamps could be used only to purchase food classified as surplus by the Department of Agriculture.[18]

The current incarnation of food stamps, the Supplemental Nutrition Assistance Program (SNAP), served more than 46 million people in 2014—nearly one in seven Americans—at a cost of more than $74 billion. In order to receive SNAP benefits—which averaged $125 per person each month in 2014—families must meet certain low-income requirements.[19] A University of Kentucky and Associated Press study found that working-age people, rather than children and the elderly, made up the majority of beneficiaries in American households that received SNAP benefits for the first time in 2014.[20]

**Medicare.** Signed into law in 1965, Medicare was a landmark program of "the Great Society," a series of progressive social programs pushed by President Lyndon Johnson. Under its current structure, Medicare is a federal health insurance program for Americans aged 65 or older, as well as Americans under the age of 65 with certain disabilities. In 2013, Medicare served 52.3 million people.[21]

Medicare is primarily funded by payroll taxes—2.9 percent of wages, split by workers and their employers—placed in a trust fund that the government uses to reimburse doctors, hospitals, and private insurance companies for health care services.[22] In 2014, the Board of Trustees for Medicare predicted that the trust fund would support the program through 2030.[23]

**Medicaid.** Signed into law with Medicare in 1965, Medicaid is a health and medical services program for low-income individuals and families which served more than 72 million Americans in 2013.[24] The federal government oversees Medicaid, but each state is responsible for establishing its own eligibility standards and determining the type and scope of health care services available. Under Medicaid, states make payments to health care providers and are reimbursed for a sizable share of their expenditures by the federal government. And in the wake of the Obamacare Medicaid expansion—adopted in 28 states and the District of Columbia as of March 2015—the federal government will pay all costs for newly eligible Medicaid recipients until 2016, as well as 90 percent of the costs thereafter.[25]

# THE CURRENT CONTROVERSY

## Should the government play a larger role in keeping people out of poverty?

For centuries, Americans have been deeply divided over the wisdom of social safety net programs—how these programs should be funded and which Americans, if any, should receive the benefits. In January 2014, for example, Congress allowed the expiration of the 2008 Emergency Unemployment Compensation program, a federal initiative that provided unemployment insurance to Americans who had been out of work for at least 27 weeks and thus had exhausted their state benefits.[26] The decision by Congress to end the program resurrected the debate over the positive and negative effects of unemployment insurance. But it also reignited a much broader question: Should the government play a larger role in keeping Americans out of poverty?

Supporters of a robust government role believe the social safety net prevents unnecessary suffering among the needy, the disabled, and the very young and elderly. Proponents argue that it is the responsibility of government to ensure the welfare, safety, and security of its citizens, and that by providing a base level of assistance, the government can place struggling people on the road to self-sufficiency and productivity.

But critics of a greater government role disagree. They argue that caring for the needy is a noble idea, but the current social safety net has created a dangerous cycle of poverty and government dependency—one that does little to promote personal responsibility and provides few incentives to work. And as the United States grapples with more than $18 trillion in national debt, Americans simply cannot afford to expand these enormous programs, which already support an unacceptable number of government dependents.

## Should the government play a larger role in keeping people out of poverty?

### YES: The government has a responsibility to protect its most vulnerable citizens.

In 2013, a total of 45.3 million Americans—a stunning 14.5 percent of the U.S. population—were living in poverty.[27] "In the richest nation on Earth, far too many children are still born into poverty," President Barack Obama said in 2014. "Far too few have a fair shot to escape it, and Americans of all races and backgrounds experience wages and incomes that aren't rising, making it harder to share in the opportunities a growing economy provides."[28]

The United States may have rebounded from the Great Recession of 2007–2009, but many Americans are still feeling economic pain. In February 2015, some 8.7 million Americans remained unemployed, while an additional 2.2 million wanted work but had not searched for a job in the preceding month. Another 6.6 million were involuntarily employed part-time because their hours had been reduced or they were unable to find a full-time job.[29] And in 2013, the median household income in the United States was $51,939, only slightly higher than it was two decades before.[30]

In the face of such widespread need, it is the responsibility of the government to protect the welfare and security of its most vulnerable citizens. By expanding the reach of the social safety net—whether through enhanced welfare services or extended unemployment benefits—the government can provide more Americans with vital support.

And at a time of economic fragility, government assistance programs can help ensure that workers will continue to stimulate the economy. "Unemployment insurance is critically important not only because it keeps food on the table for millions of desperate families nationwide, but also because it is one of the best ways to generate economic demand and stimulate growth," said Senator Richard Durbin, D-Ill.[31] Senator Durbin also decried the idea that social safety net programs discourage Americans from working hard and supporting themselves and their families. "[Critics] feel that if people are not doing well economically, it's because they're lazy. I disagree," he said. "I think a lot of people are working very, very hard and can't keep up with the increased cost of living."[32]

"Without Social Security, nearly half of seniors would be living in poverty. Today, fewer than one in seven do. Before Medicare, only half of seniors had some form of health insurance. Today, virtually all do," said President Obama. "These endeavors didn't just make us a better country. They reaffirmed that we are a great country. They lived up to our best hopes as a people who value the dignity and potential of every human being."[33]

## NO: In the face of the debt crisis, too many Americans are dependent on the government.

"Liberals would replace opportunity with dependency on government largesse," said former Governor Mitt Romney, R-Mass. "They grow government and raise taxes to put more people on Medicaid, to take work requirements out of welfare, and to grow the ranks of those who pay no taxes at all. Dependency is death to initiative, risk-taking, and opportunity. It is time to stop the spread of government dependency, to fight it like the poison it is."[34]

A 2012 study showed that 55 percent of Americans had received government social safety net benefits at least once in their lives.[35] Many of these programs were born in an era of 25 percent unemployment, when many Americans could scarcely afford to feed their children. But in 2012, the unemployment rate hovered between 7.8 percent and 8.3 percent—yet more than half the country had depended on the government in some way.[36] "We don't want to turn the safety net into a hammock that lulls able-bodied people to lives of dependency and complacency, that drains them of their will and their incentive to make the most of their lives," Representative Paul Ryan, R-Wis., said.[37]

The social safety net does provide the poor, the elderly, the disabled, and the truly vulnerable with access to health care, financial assistance, food, and other vital needs. But these programs are rapidly growing too large and too involved in the lives of too many people. One in seven Americans should not have been relying on food stamps in 2014, for example, especially because working-age people made up the majority of SNAP households.

A social safety net that catches too many Americans can have dangerous effects on economic productivity and personal liberty. When Congress allowed the Emergency Unemployment Compensation program to expire in January 2014, for example, the National Bureau of Economic Research found that the benefit cut helped create 1.8 million jobs—one million of which were filled by people who would not have participated in the labor market had Congress passed the benefit extension.[38]

As the United States grapples with more than $18 trillion in national debt, now is not the time to expand the already massive social safety net. Instead, the government should refocus its anti-poverty programs on job training and education, while reducing its level of interference in the economy, thus making it easier for businesses to grow and hire. "Our current government programs offer, at best, only a partial solution," said Senator Marco Rubio, R-Fla. "They help people deal with poverty, but they do not help them escape it."[39]

# THE ONGOING DEBATE

## What is the appropriate role of government in preventing workplace discrimination?

Discrimination—the treatment of a person based on the group they belong to, rather than individual merit—has been part of the American conversation since the founding of the United States. The Constitution limits the power of the government to discriminate, both in the Fifth Amendment, which says citizens may not be "deprived of life, liberty, or property, without due process of law,"[40] and in the 14th Amendment, which forbids the government from denying "to any person within its jurisdiction the equal protection of the laws."[41]

The Constitution, however, does not explicitly limit the practice of discrimination in the private sector—an omission that has led American policymakers to pass a series of federal laws on the issue.

**Equal Pay Act of 1963.** This law prohibits employers from paying men and women different wages if they perform equal work in the same workplace.

**Title VII of the Civil Rights Act of 1964.** Title VII forbids employment-related discrimination on the basis of race, color, religion, national origin, sex, pregnancy, or childbirth. The law applies to labor organizations, employment agencies, and most employers engaged in interstate commerce that have more than 15 employees.

**Age Discrimination in Employment Act of 1967.** This law forbids workplace discrimination against people aged 40 or older because of their age.

**Rehabilitation Act of 1973.** This law outlawed discrimination within the federal government against qualified people with disabilities.

**Title I of the Americans with Disabilities Act of 1990.** This law prohibits discrimination against qualified people with disabilities both in the private sector and in state and local governments.

**Civil Rights Act of 1991.** This law allows jury trials and the awarding of monetary damages in cases of intentional employment discrimination.

**Genetic Information Nondiscrimination Act of 2008.** This law prohibits employment discrimination based on genetic information about an applicant, employee, or former employee.[42]

These federal laws protect Americans from various employment-related discriminatory practices, but states have also passed their own laws, which vary in scope. As of April 2015, for example, 21 states and the District of Columbia had passed state laws outlawing workplace discrimination based on sexual orientation—a provision that Congress had not explicitly passed.[43]

Efforts to combat workplace discrimination also brought forward the idea of affirmative action. In 1965, President Johnson issued Executive Order 11246, which mandated that federal government contractors "take affirmative action to ensure that applicants are employed, and that employees are treated during employment, without regard to their race, color, religion, sex, or national origin."[44] Modern affirmative action policies actively seek to improve opportunities for historically disadvantaged or excluded groups in order to overcome the effects of past discrimination. These policies may take the form of outreach, recruitment, or training programs aimed at minority populations. But these programs have also sparked a nationwide debate in the United States, as Americans disagree over whether they alleviate—or further contribute to—discriminatory practices.

# THE CURRENT CONTROVERSY

## Should affirmative action be added to employee protection and workplace discrimination laws?

As of 2015, the federal government required its contractors and subcontractors to use affirmative action policies to "recruit and advance qualified minorities, women, persons with disabilities, and covered veterans," according to the Department of Labor.[45] And while certain private companies across the country voluntarily implement affirmative action programs, there is no federal law that requires employers to use affirmative action when recruiting or hiring employees.

Demonstrators with By Any Means Necessary protest near the University of Michigan admissions offices in Ann Arbor. The pro-affirmative action group began their protest by temporarily shutting down the Board of Regents meeting.

Over the years, the use of affirmative action in the workplace has become a controversial idea. Supporters of such policies believe they are a vital answer to centuries of racial segregation and economic inequality in the United States. Proponents believe affirmative action not only encourages a valuable diversity

of background and thought in the workplace but also helps level the playing field for American workers who have not had the same opportunities as more privileged Americans.

But opponents of affirmative action programs in the workplace vehemently disagree. Critics argue that instead of ending discrimination, affirmative action encourages it—by favoring the members of one group over the members of another. Opponents insist that such policies only breed resentment, while doing little to address the root causes of inequality in the United States.

### Should affirmative action be added to employee protection and workplace discrimination laws?

## YES: Affirmative action helps historically disadvantaged people, as well as the entire workplace.

"You do not take a person who, for years, has been hobbled by chains and liberate him, bring him up to the starting line of a race and then say, 'You are free to compete with all the others,' and still justly believe that you have been completely fair."[46] It has been half a century since President Johnson said those words at Howard University in 1965, but they remain as true as ever.

The United States has made great strides toward eliminating workplace discrimination based on race, religion, sex, national origin, and disabilities, but vast inequalities still remain. "This refusal to accept the stark reality that race matters is regrettable," Justice Sonia Sotomayor wrote in her 2014 dissent in *Schuette v. Coalition to Defend Affirmative Action,* a case that upheld a Michigan law banning the use of racial criteria in college admissions. "The way to stop discrimination on the basis of race is to speak openly and candidly on the subject of race, and to apply the Constitution with eyes open to the unfortunate effects of centuries of racial discrimination."[47]

In March 2015, the national unemployment rate stood at 4.7 percent among white Americans—but it jumped to 10.1 percent among African Americans.[48] In 2013, the Pew Research Center found the median wealth of white households to be 13 times the median wealth of black households, and ten times the median wealth of Hispanic households.[49] And in June 2014, the share of female CEOs of Fortune 500 companies hit a "historic high" of 4.8 percent.[50]

In the face of such deeply rooted inequalities, the federal government must require employers to implement affirmative action policies. "According to an American Society of News Editors study, minorities make up 12.3 percent of newspaper staffs and 16.4 percent of online-only news staffs despite being a third of the general population," journalist LZ Granderson wrote. "So I ask you, if the so-called liberal media struggles to employ diversity that's representative of the people—and it has affirmative action policies in place—what makes us think completely removing such initiatives is going to improve the situation?"[51]

The workplace diversity promoted by affirmative action is not only fair—it has vast potential to boost productivity. "Management training sessions are designed to help managers bridge communication gaps they might not even realize exist," said Deborah Dagit of Silicon Graphics Inc., a technology company that embraced affirmative action and diversity initiatives. "Having a more diverse team leads to greater innovation and creativity as well as opening up the possibilities of different perspectives."[52]

## NO: Affirmative action only furthers discrimination and ignores the root causes of inequality.

"The way to stop discrimination on the basis of race is to stop discriminating on the basis of race."[53] Chief Justice John Roberts wrote these words in 2007, when the Supreme Court ruled in *Parents Involved in Community Schools v. Seattle School District No. 1* that public school systems cannot seek to achieve integration through rules that take explicit account of a student's race. And Justice Roberts' words are just as relevant to affirmative action in the workplace—a policy that discriminates against majority populations as a method of countering past discrimination against minority populations.

Discrimination is defined as the treatment of a person based on the group they belong to, rather than individual merit. And that is exactly what affirmative action policies do, no matter their good intentions. Under an affirmative action policy, employers could be compelled to select a qualified applicant over a highly qualified applicant, simply because the qualified applicant represents a minority population. "I believe our nation is at its best when people are evaluated as individuals," Governor Romney said.[54]

As of April 2014, the injustices of affirmative action policies had inspired seven states—Arizona, California, Florida, Michigan, New Hampshire, Oklahoma, and Washington—to outlaw preferential treatment based on race, sex, or national origin in government hiring.[55] "There was a time when we had done such terrible things in our country that there really needed to be special protections," Senator Rand Paul, R-Ky., said. "We've come a long way, and I think really that the time in which justice can be colorblind is now."[56]

Furthermore, workplace affirmative action policies largely fail to address and heal the inequalities that remain in society. "The nature of affirmative action is that it skims. It elevates the best and the brightest of a disadvantaged group while doing nothing to eliminate the root causes of that group's disadvantage," author Tanner Colby wrote. "Affirmative action treats workplace discrimination like a bureaucratic, process-based problem. In reality, workplace discrimination stems from a very nebulous social and cultural problem. The government claims it can regulate the racial composition of our professional lives, but too much of what we call 'work' is actually rooted in the messy, socially segregated realm of our personal lives. How many affirmative action compliance officers were stationed in Steve Jobs' garage while he and his buddy Steve Wozniak assembled the first Apple? Zero."[57]

It is critically important to encourage diversity and to create opportunities for the historically disadvantaged. But the government will never achieve this goal with policies that promote more discrimination.

# CONCLUSION

The expansion of the social safety net and the use of affirmative action are only two examples of the work and economic security policy debates Americans have engaged in for years. And although the fate of these two policies remains far from certain, policymakers, employers, and workers will undoubtedly continue to debate the goals and priorities of the American labor system—and which government policies best reflect and achieve them.

[1] U.S. Department of Labor, Bureau of Labor Statistics. *Employment Situation Summary.* 6 Mar. 2015. Web. 6 Mar. 2015.

[2] Izzo, Phil. "Number of the Week: Half of U.S. Lives in Household Getting Benefits." *Wall Street Journal.* 26 May 2012. Web. 8 Apr. 2015.

[3] U.S. National Debt Clock. Brillig. Web. 8 Apr. 2015.

[4] Kurtz, Annalyn. "Majority of Americans have received government aid." CNN Money. 18 Dec. 2012. Web. 8 Apr. 2015.

[5] Congressional Budget Office. "Mandatory Spending Options." Web. 8 Apr. 2015.

[6] Social Security Administration. *Annual Performance Plan for FY 2012 and Revised Final Performance Plan for FY 2011.* 2012. Web. 8 Apr 2015.

[7] Kaiser Family Foundation. "Status of State Action on the Medicaid Expansion Decision." 6 Mar. 2015. Web. 8 Apr. 2015.

[8] "Action, and Action Now: FDR's First 100 Days." Special exhibit at the Franklin D. Roosevelt Presidential Library and Museum, Hyde Park. Web. 6 Mar. 2015.

[9] Social Security Administration, Office of the Chief Actuary. *Fact Sheet on the Old-Age, Survivors, and Disability Insurance Program.* 17 Jul. 2014. Web. 8 Apr. 2015.

[10] Sherlock, Molly F., and Donald J. Marples. *Overview of the Federal Tax System.* Congressional Research Service. 21 Nov. 2014. Web. 6 Mar. 2015.

[11] Board of Trustees of the Federal Old-Age and Survivors Insurance and Federal Disability Insurance Trust Funds. *2014 Annual Report of the Board of Trustees of the Federal Old-Age and Survivors Insurance and Federal Disability Insurance Trust Funds.* 28 Jul. 2014. Web. 8 Apr. 2015.

[12] Kessler, Glenn. "Social Security: a Guide to Critical Questions." *Washington Post.* 8 Jan. 2014. Web. 8 Apr. 2015.

[13] Board of Trustees of the Federal Old-Age and Survivors Insurance and Federal Disability Insurance Trust Funds. *2014 Annual Report of the Board of Trustees of the Federal Old-Age and Survivors Insurance and Federal Disability Insurance Trust Funds.* 28 Jul. 2014. Web. 8 Apr. 2015.

[14] U.S. Department of Labor, Employment and Training Administration. "Unemployment Insurance Data." Web. 8 Apr. 2015.

[15] U.S. Department of Labor, Employment and Training Administration. *Unemployment Insurance 75th Anniversary Fact Sheet.* Web. 8 Apr. 2015.

[16] Schott, Liz. "Policy Basics: An Introduction to TANF." Center on Budget and Policy Priorities. 4 Dec. 2012. Web. 8 Apr. 2015.

17  U.S. Department of Health and Human Services, Office of Family Assistance. *TANF: Total Number of Recipients. Fiscal and Calendar Year 2014 Average Monthly Number Families: October 2013 through December 2014.* 26 Jan. 2015. Web. 8 Apr. 2015.

18  *New York Times.* "A History of Food Stamps Use and Policy." 11 Feb. 2010. Web. 8 Apr. 2015.

19  U.S. Department of Agriculture. *Supplemental Nutrition Assistance Program Participation and Costs.* 6 Mar. 2015. Web. 8 Apr. 2015.

20  Associated Press. "One in 7 Americans on Food Stamps." 26 Jan. 2014. Web. 8 Apr. 2015.

21  Board of Trustees of the Federal Hospital Insurance and Federal Supplementary Medical Insurance Trust Funds. *2014 Annual Report of the Board of Trustees of the Federal Hospital Insurance and Federal Supplementary Medical Insurance Trust Funds.* 28 Jul. 2014. Web. 8 Apr. 2015.

22  Sherlock, Molly F., and Donald J. Marples. *Overview of the Federal Tax System.* Congressional Research Service. 21 Nov. 2014. Web. 6 Mar. 2015.

23  Board of Trustees of the Federal Hospital Insurance and Federal Supplementary Medical Insurance Trust Funds. *2014 Annual Report of the Board of Trustees of the Federal Hospital Insurance and Federal Supplementary Medical Insurance Trust Funds.* 28 Jul. 2014. Web. 8 Apr. 2015.

24  Congressional Budget Office. "Detail of Spending and Enrollment for Medicaid for CBO's April 2014 Baseline." Web. 8 Apr. 2015.

25  Mann, Cindy. "Medicaid and CHIP Enrollment Grows by 8.7 Million Additional Americans." Centers for Medicaid and CHIP Services. 17 Oct. 2014. Web. 8 Apr. 2015.

26  U.S. Department of Labor, Employment and Training Administration. "Emergency Unemployment Compensation (EUC) Expired on January 1, 2014." 13 Jan. 2014. Web. 8 Apr. 2015.

27  Luhbi, Tami. "U.S. Poverty Rate Drops for the First Time since 2006." CNN Money. 16 Sep. 2014. Web. 8 Apr. 2015.

28  Jackson, David. "Obama: More Work Remains in 'War on Poverty.'" *USA Today.* 8 Jan. 2014. Web. 8 Apr. 2015.

29  U.S. Department of Labor, Bureau of Labor Statistics. *Employment Situation Summary.* 6 Mar. 2015. Web. 6 Mar. 2015.

30  Luhbi, Tami. "U.S. Poverty Rate Drops for the First Time since 2006." CNN Money. 16 Sep. 2014. Web. 8 Apr. 2015.

31  Senator Richard Durbin. "Durbin Demands Federal Extension of Unemployment Insurance." Official website. 18 Jul. 2010. Web. 8 Apr. 2015.

32  Mackey, Brian. "Senator Durbin Continues Push for an Extension of Unemployment Benefits." Peoria Public Radio. 20 Jan. 2014. Web. 8 Apr. 2015.

33  Jackson, David. "Obama: More Work Remains in 'War on Poverty.'" *USA Today.* 8 Jan. 2014. Web. 8 Apr. 2015.

34  "Romney: Throw Out the Big-Government Liberals." CNN. 3 Sep. 2008. Web. 8 Apr. 2015.

35  Kurtz, Annalyn. "Majority of Americans Have Received Government Aid." CNN Money. 18 Dec. 2012. Web. 8 Apr. 2015.

36  U.S. Department of Labor, Bureau of Labor Statistics. "Labor Force Statistics from the Current Population Survey." 8 Apr. 2015. Web. 8 Apr. 2015.

37  Krugman, Paul. "The Hammock Fallacy." *New York Times.* 6 Mar. 2014. Web. 8 Apr. 2015.

38  Hagedorn, Marcus, Iourii Manovskii, and Kurt Mitman. *The Impact of Unemployment Benefit Extensions on Employment: The 2014 Employment Miracle?* National Bureau of Economic Research. Jan. 2015. Web. 8 Apr. 2015.

39  Senator Marco Rubio. "Excerpts of Marco Rubio's Address on 50th Anniversary of the 'War on Poverty.'" Official website. 8 Jan. 2014. Web. 8 Apr. 2015.

40  *U.S. Constitution.* Amendment V.

41  *U.S. Constitution.* Amendment XIV.

42  U.S. Equal Employment Opportunity Commission. "Laws Enforced by EEOC." Web. 8 Apr. 2015.

43  American Civil Liberties Union. "Non-Discrimination Laws: State-by-State Information — Map." Web. 8 Apr. 2015.

44  U.S. Department of Labor, Office of Federal Contract Compliance Programs. "Executive Order 11246." Web. 8 Apr. 2015.

45  U.S. Department of Labor. "Affirmative Action." Web. 8 Apr. 2015.

46  Johnson, Lyndon. Commencement address at Howard University, 4 Jun. 1965. LBJ Presidential Library. Web. 8 Apr. 2015.

47  Mears, Bill. "Michigan's Ban on Affirmative Action Upheld by Supreme Court." CNN. 23 Apr. 2014. Web. 8 Apr. 2015.

48  U.S. Department of Labor, Bureau of Labor Statistics. "Economic News Release." Table A-2. Employment status of the civilian population by race, sex, and age. Web. 8 Apr. 2015.

49  Kochhar, Rakesh, and Richard Fry. "Wealth Inequality Has Widened along Racial, Ethnic Lines Since End of Great Recession." Pew Research Center. 12 Dec. 2014. Web. 8 Apr. 2015.

50  Fairchild, Caroline. "Number of Fortune 500 Women CEOs Reaches Historic High." *Fortune.* 3 Jun. 2014. Web. 8 Apr. 2015.

51  Granderson, LZ. "What's Wrong with Affirmative Action — and Why We Need It." CNN. 13 Oct. 2012. Web. 8 Apr. 2015.

52  Leporini, Christopher. "Affirmative Action in the Workplace." *Focus on Law Studies.* Vol. XIII. No. 2. American Bar Association. 1998. Web. 8 Apr. 2015.

53  Roberts, John. Opinion in *Parents Involved in Community Schools v. Seattle School Dist.* No. 1. 28 Jun. 2007. Web. 8 Apr. 2015.

54  Miga, Andrew. "Mitt Romney's Record of Affirmative Action in Massachusetts." Associated Press. 2 Jun. 2012. Web. 8 Apr. 2015.

55  National Conference of State Legislatures. "Affirmative Action: State Action." Apr. 2014. Web. 8 Apr. 2015.

56  McCormick, John. "Rand Paul Appeals to Democratic Base in Obama's Hometown." Bloomberg Business. 22 Apr. 2014. Web. 8 Apr. 2015.

57  Colby, Tanner. "The Massive Liberal Failure on Race." *Slate.* 10 Feb. 2014. Web. 8 Apr. 2015.

# FOREIGN POLICY:
## KEY PRINCIPLES AND PRACTICES

# INTRODUCTION

> "International politics, like all politics, is a struggle for power."
> —Hans J. Morgenthau

> "Human rights is the soul of our foreign policy, because human rights is the very soul of our sense of nationhood."
> —Jimmy Carter

Today it is difficult for the United States, or any nation, to accomplish goals and important tasks on its own. Countries have to work together on issues such as terrorism, the economy, the environment, and the spread of disease, to name just a few. It is becoming so difficult for nations to make decisions entirely on their own that the world now is sometimes referred to as the global community.

How the United States gets what it wants in this global community is complicated; how the United States decides what it wants can be even more so. What are the goals of the United States in the global community? What issues and objectives are the most important? Should economic interests outweigh security interests? And what role should ideological interests play?

For the United States, answering these questions is not always easy. Many different groups work to influence foreign policy. In Congress, both the House of Representatives and the Senate have several committees that work on foreign relations, national security, trade, and defense issues. In the executive branch, there are more competing agencies, although the president has the final say. International groups, such as the United Nations (UN), the World Bank, and the International Monetary Fund (IMF) influence U.S. foreign policy as well.

With all of these groups trying to influence the foreign policy agenda, international relations can be a complex undertaking. Further complicating the creation of foreign policy is the difficulty of enforcement, as countries cannot impose their ideas on one another. If one nation succeeds, another nation may lose out. As the world becomes more intricately linked, it is important to understand how nations like the United States develop and implement foreign policy.

# RECENT HISTORY

**The United States in the World.** Since the end of World War II, the United States has been a dominant force in world politics. The instability that persisted from the beginning of World War I until the end of World War II caused the international community to look to a stabilizing force—a vacuum that, at first, only the United States was able to fill.

Several international institutions were created during the post-war period and were headquartered in the United States. The UN was established with the aim of maintaining and promoting international peace and order. The major Allied victors of the war—the United States, China, Russia, France, and the United Kingdom—gave themselves the most control over the UN, including granting each country veto power over all Security Council initiatives. The Allied nations also came together to create rules regarding trade and monetary policy that became known as the Bretton Woods system. This system recognized the primacy of the United States and of the dollar and also created the World Bank and the IMF to provide loans to war-shattered and developing countries.

This brief era of international cooperation was darkened by the onset of the Cold War, which became a long-standing conflict between the United States and the Soviet Union. The Cold War was a standoff between a communist bloc in the East, led by the Soviet Union, and a capitalist bloc in the West, led by the United States. The two blocs in this conflict engaged in a power struggle, each seeking to spread its ideology and to bolster its economy.

At times during this standoff, there were wars, like the Korean and Vietnam Wars; at other times, there were threats of war, such as the Cuban Missile Crisis of 1962. Other battles were waged in the field of technology, such as the nuclear arms race and the space race. However, much of the Cold War happened behind the scenes in the world of covert agencies, such as the Central Intelligence Agency (CIA). Ultimately, the Cold War never became the full-scale global conflict that many feared; instead, it ended quietly. The Soviet Union collapsed from within and its satellite states, such as East Germany and Poland, pushed for their own independence.

**The Post–Cold War World.** With the end of the Cold War, the United States was again perceived as the only true world power. This image was reinforced by the U.S. military's resounding victory in the Persian Gulf War of 1990–1991. Although there were bombings and acts of terrorism committed against U.S. government personnel abroad, such as the embassy bombings in Tanzania and Kenya in 1998 and the bombing of the *USS Cole* in Yemen in 2000, the 1990s were a time of relative peace and prosperity for the United States.

This peace was shattered on September 11, 2001, when terrorists hijacked four American commercial airliners and crashed them into the World Trade Center in New York City, the Pentagon outside the District of Colombia, and a field in rural Pennsylvania. The terrorist group al-Qaeda, led by Saudi national Osama bin Laden, executed the attacks. Al-Qaeda is a terrorist network based in Afghanistan and Pakistan that is supported by the Taliban, an Islamic fundamentalist group of warlords.

The United States invaded Afghanistan in 2001 to root out al-Qaeda and to dismantle the Taliban. Since then, the United States has been significantly more active abroad than at any time since the end of the Cold War. In 2003, the United States invaded Iraq over fears that it may have had weapons of mass destruction and that its government may have been sponsoring terrorism. Although there is still some dispute about whether these concerns were justified, the United States remains engaged in the rebuilding and protection of Iraq, although U.S. troop levels there are now very low.

Since 2003, much has changed in Iraq and in the United States' efforts to combat terrorism. Al-Qaeda has been significantly weakened by U.S. military and covert operations in Afghanistan, Pakistan, and Yemen. However, turmoil in countries such as Syria, Somalia, and Nigeria have made space for the rise of new regional terrorist organizations such as the Islamic State of Iraq and the Levant (ISIL), al-Shabab, and Boko Haram. These terrorist organizations pose different levels of threat to the United States, but each plays a significant role in destabilizing its base country and region. Of these, ISIL is considered the greatest threat to the United States and its interests, largely because it is causing instability in Iraq and is engaged in Syria's civil war.

When crafting its foreign policy, President Barack Obama's administration has placed greater emphasis on cooperating with other nations. For example, during the civil war in Libya, which removed long-time dictator Moammar Gaddafi from power in 2011, the United States joined many European nations in assisting the forces opposed to Gaddafi. However, the United States did not take a leading position, instead choosing to allow rebel forces and European nations to take the lead role. This represented a shift in U.S. policy and angered some observers, particularly those who believed the United States should play a more robust role in global affairs.

The world of international relations is a complex one; countries are constantly trying to figure out what they want while weighing their goals against the needs and desires of other nations. The tangled web created by competing interests, competing countries, different agencies, and different branches of government working to define and protect national interests makes for intricate work.

## SETTING FOREIGN POLICY

National interests, loosely defined, are what a country wants or needs to survive and to improve its situation. Just as any individual makes decisions by balancing self-interest and personal values, nations operate in the world based on national interests and beliefs. Most of these interests and beliefs can be divided into three broad categories: economic, security, and ideological interests.

**Economic Interests.** Trade policy, contracts, taxes and tariffs, and monetary policy all fall within the realm of economic interests. Governments do their best to make sure that their export products make it to retail shelves in other countries; they also try to protect their domestic industries through the use of import tariffs and subsidies.

The category of economic interests is difficult to navigate because governments have different levels of control over the economy in different countries. China, for instance, has a planned economy in which the government is in charge of most aspects of the marketplace, including the value of its currency. Other countries, such as many in Western Europe, have a mixed economy in which the government

# WHO SETS U.S. FOREIGN POLICY?

According to the Constitution, both the legislative and executive branches have a say in the creation of foreign policy. Congress controls spending, declares war, approves treaties and presidential nominations to diplomatic posts, and can pass laws or resolutions stating specific policies.

The executive branch conducts war and commands military personnel, negotiates treaties and other international agreements, and has the power to appoint ambassadors and other diplomats. Within the executive branch, many individuals and groups create and enact U.S. foreign policy.

**The President.** The president ultimately has the power to make all foreign policy decisions within the realm of the executive branch. The president is also the commander-in-chief of the military and the country's head of state.

**Secretary of State.** The secretary of state advises the president and acts as the nation's chief diplomat. The secretary also implements policy decisions, oversees the embassies, and administers foreign aid.

**Secretary of Defense.** Along with the Joint Chiefs of Staff, the secretary of defense advises the president on military matters. The secretary also implements military orders and policy decisions, and oversees military aid to other countries.

**National Security Council.** The National Security Council conducts policy studies, advises the president, and coordinates policymaking and implementation. The council includes the president, vice president, the secretaries of state and defense, and the national security advisor.

Other departments, such as the Departments of Agriculture, Commerce, and the Treasury, and agencies such as the Arms Control and Disarmament Agency, play a role in the creation of U.S. foreign policy.

has some control over large industries, such as health care, banking, and air travel, but leaves much of the economy uncontrolled. In the United States, almost all companies and industries are susceptible to free-market forces, although the government has moved to protect agriculture, transportation, and finance, among other industries.

In the past several years, many countries have worked to find common ground to deal with the worldwide economic downturn. Nations with different market philosophies have debated the proper level of government stimulus in the economy. Some countries and international organizations are also considering the regulation of international trade and debating how much oversight is needed in the arena of world trade.

**Security Interests.** Of vital importance to every country is its safety. Any threats, or potential threats, fall into the realm of security interests. All countries do their best to keep their homelands safe, but security interests can also be about threats less obvious than military attacks.

Because the U.S. military is spread out, with bases and installations in more than 120 countries, threats and instabilities in these countries can have security implications for the United States. For example, the U.S. embassy in Beirut, Lebanon, was bombed in 1983 by the terrorist group Hezbollah. In 1998, groups linked to Osama bin Laden simultaneously bombed U.S. embassies in Kenya and Tanzania. And in 2011, the U.S. consulate in Benghazi, Libya, was bombed, killing four Americans, including Ambassador Christopher Stevens.

The rise in international terrorism has left its mark in Madrid, London, New York City, and Washington, D.C., and in countries and communities across the Muslim world. As a result, many nations feel the need to work together on matters of security. Countries now work in concert to defuse threats and share intelligence, and to protect themselves, their friends, and their neighbors.

**Ideological Interests.** Ideological interests are those that relate to a country's way of life and ideals. All countries have their own worldviews; some are in direct conflict with one another. Often these views are about forms of government, civil rights, or religion.

The United States has been regarded as a world leader since the end of World War II. Because of this status and the allure and influence of American cultural products, the United States has had a strong impact on world ideologies. However, it has also come into conflict with other countries because of ideological concerns—the chief example being the Cold War, in which the United States believed it was fighting international communism.

# AN INTERSECTION OF INTERESTS

Some national objectives defy categorization. For example, the United States commits a great deal of energy and money to protect international shipping routes in order to keep the global economy functioning smoothly. Of course, the United States has economic motivations to do so—international trade is a major driver of the American economy. But there are also security reasons to do this work; it protects major harbors and keeps the crews of ships safe. Finally, the American belief in free trade provides an ideological reason to do this work as well.

Some, including former Vice President Dick Cheney, have argued that the sole reason terrorist groups such as Hezbollah and al-Qaeda do not like the United States is ideological. Vice President Cheney and others have declared that these terrorist groups hate American freedoms. President George W. Bush made the argument that one reason the United States went into Iraq in 2003 was to liberate the Iraqi people from a horrible dictator; this reason had no security or economic implications for the United States and is an example of an ideological interest.

Advocates of humanitarian intervention in Sudan have used ideological interests to argue that the United States should use its military power to stop or to prevent humanitarian crises. Pro-democracy advocates have also argued that the United States should have intervened more forcefully in the various uprisings of the 2011 Arab Spring.

**Which Interest is Most Important?** Sometimes an international interest fits into only one category; more often there is much overlap between the categories. The Iraq War, according to some, could be justified by all three types of interests. There were security concerns that Saddam Hussein was stockpiling weapons and harboring terrorists; there were economic concerns that oil supplies could be cut off by instability in the region; and the Bush administration had an ideological goal of bringing democracy to the Middle East through Iraq.

So what happens when these interests do not align? For example, it is in the United States' economic interests to trade with China, but China's human rights practices violate the American ideals of individual liberty and due process. It is also in American security interests to support and work with the regime in Pakistan, but doing so is expensive and, because of the way the regime treats its own citizens, counter to the United States' ideological interests.

When conflicts arise, the competing interests must be worked out, and inevitably some citizens and decision-makers are unhappy with the resolution. And between Congress and the many executive agencies that deal with the international community, finding any resolution can be quite a challenge.

## NAVIGATING THE GLOBAL STAGE

Although the work of setting foreign policy is difficult, given the many players in the game and the many priorities and interests the United States has, setting policy is actually the easiest part of the job. Implementing foreign policy is more difficult. When a country finally decides what it wants in the realm of international relations, achieving its goals can prove to be the more challenging part of the job.

For a long time in world history, the use of military force was the primary way to achieve international goals. In fact, humorist Will Rogers once quipped, "Diplomacy is the art of saying 'nice doggie!' until you can find a rock." However, with the emergence of international institutions, alliances, and global trade, there are now more subtle means of approaching the world than with President Theodore Roosevelt's "big stick."

**Diplomacy and Cooperation.** Nations work together through their embassies and other government agencies to negotiate and enforce treaties, to build goodwill through cultural exchanges, and to enhance trade relationships. Some countries are "integrated," meaning they are connected and sensitive to the global community. Other countries are more isolated, while some, such as North Korea, are isolated by the international community rather than by choice.

The United States is economically and diplomatically connected to the world at large. It is a member of many large international organizations, such as the North Atlantic Treaty Organization (NATO), the UN Security

Council, the World Bank, the IMF, and the Group of Eight developed nations with large economies (G8). These organizations are very influential in international relations.

In addition, the United States is a signatory of many trade agreements. The North American Free Trade Agreement (NAFTA) is a far-reaching partnership between Canada, Mexico, and the United States that has had significant impacts on the economies of all three countries. The Dominican Republic–Central America Free Trade Agreement (CAFTA-DR) is a similarly expansive trade agreement between the United States, Costa Rica, the Dominican Republic, El Salvador, Guatemala, Honduras, and Nicaragua. As of 2015, the United States was negotiating two additional large-scale trade agreements: the Trans-Pacific Partnership (TPP), which would tighten trade relations with Australia, Brunei, Canada, Chile, Japan, Malaysia, Mexico, New Zealand, Peru, Singapore, and Vietnam; and the Transatlantic Trade and Investment Partnership (T-TIP), which would tighten relations between the United States and the European Union (EU).

Whereas trade agreements bring two or more countries closer together, economic sanctions and embargoes can be used to punish or to isolate countries. The American economy is the largest in the world; the United States has the ability to seriously influence the economy of any other nation through its trade policy. However, embargoes and sanctions can be more effective if other countries join them. As of 2015, the United States, the EU, and their allies were imposing economic sanctions on Iran to curb its nuclear ambitions. However, because of energy needs, the EU was less eager to participate in the economic sanctions the United States has placed on Russia.

**Economic and Military Aid.** Countries can give money, food, medicines, and loans to other countries or choose to withhold those items. Nations can also choose to extend or withhold military aid in the form of weapons, training, technology, equipment, ammunitions, and personnel. Nations do this to build partnerships with other nations, to promote stability and security in key regions, and to help other nations in times of turmoil and crisis.

According to the Center for Global Development, in 2013, the United States ranked 20th in foreign aid to other nations as a percentage of gross national product (GNP), a rough estimate of the size of a nation's economy. In terms of total giving, the United States gave more money than any other nation. In 2012, four nations received the bulk of American foreign aid: Israel ($3.07 billion); Afghanistan ($2.3 billion); Pakistan ($2.1 billion); and Iraq ($1.7 billion).

Some foreign aid is given with restrictions or conditions. For example, when nations give loans to other nations, they often include provisions that benefit the lending country. This may mean that a guarantee of a certain amount of trade is built into the loan, or it could mean that a particular company is allowed to mine for minerals in the nation receiving the loan. Some foreign aid is not given in the form of money at all. Much of the U.S. aid given to Israel, Afghanistan, Pakistan, and Iraq, for example, has been in the form of military aid.

**Multilateralism vs. Unilateralism.** In the past, states frequently aimed to create foreign policy without entanglements and alliances. This policy, unilateralism, calls for states to rely on their own resources and abilities to carry out their foreign affairs. Many leaders prefer unilateralism because it enables each government to retain a maximum amount of sovereignty and to act without the approval or support of another country. States pursue unilateralism when cooperation to achieve a goal is unnecessary or when a country decides it has enough power to impose a desired policy. Recently, countries have used unilateralism to set an example and to demonstrate their resolve to follow a certain course of action. South Africa did this when it unilaterally committed to nuclear disarmament in the early 1990s. And although the use of this approach continues to have supporters, there is increasing pressure for countries to work together to create and execute international policies in the face of growing global interdependence.

In today's global community, the actions of one state often directly or indirectly affect other states. In the face of this reality, many states have turned toward international cooperation and the policy of multilateralism. Multilateralism engages at least three countries, and often seeks to bring as many states into agreement as possible to achieve mutual goals. Multilateralism is usually the preferred option when dealing with issues that require communication and cooperation between numerous states. Within multilateral accords, states must compromise with others in order to achieve a cohesive policy. This requires ceding sovereignty in return for an assurance of alliance and concerted action. Advocates point to the Montreal Protocol, ratified by 196 countries and the EU, as a successful multilateral action aimed at preserving the Earth's ozone layer.

In the disorganized global arena, where states may pursue any number of means to implement policy, intergovernmental organizations promote multilateralism and provide a forum for governments to talk through solutions. Foremost among these is the UN, which claims almost every state in the world as a member. There is widespread disagreement over the benefits and influence of these organizations, in which membership is voluntary and policy enforcement is difficult. Believers in international organizations argue that they provide a model as we move toward global governance and away from the importance of sovereign states. Challengers dismiss this view, and regard these organizations as an ineffective façade for states that actually act unilaterally through them.

## CONCLUSION

All nations face significant challenges when they enter the arena of global affairs. Countries compete for scarce resources, seek to impose order and security in dangerous places, cooperate with some nations and come into conflict with others, and take any available actions to advance their national agendas. Navigating the chaos of global affairs will be one of the United States' most important challenges in the 21st century.

# ROADMAP FOR PEACE?: THE ARAB-ISRAELI CONFLICT

## CURRENT CONTROVERSIES

- Should the United States halt aid to Israel if it continues building settlements in disputed territories?

- Should the United States engage a Palestinian Authority government that includes Hamas?

# INTRODUCTION

> "This is my homeland; no one can kick me out."
>
> —Yasser Arafat

> "If the Arabs put down their weapons today, there would be no more violence. If the Jews put down their weapons today, there would be no more Israel."
>
> —Benjamin Netanyahu

Over the course of the last century, few regions have captured Americans' interest more than the Middle East. This complex and diverse intersection of Africa, Asia, and Europe has long been critical to the United States, as the source of nearly half of the proven crude oil reserves in the world, the home of several important American allies, and the site of many cultural, ethnic, and religious conflicts.[1] One conflict in particular—the territorial dispute between Israelis and Palestinians—showed few signs of resolution in 2015, despite years of efforts by several American presidents acting as brokers for a lasting peace agreement. In this chapter, we will consider several enduring tensions in American policy toward Israel and the Palestinian Authority, and examine two current controversial issues:

- Should the United States halt aid to Israel if it continues building settlements in disputed territories?
- Should the United States engage a Palestinian Authority government that includes Hamas?

**What Are the Origins of the Arab-Israeli Conflict?** As the birthplace of Judaism, Christianity, and Islam, the Middle East is home to a diverse group of migrating peoples, creating a population with many ethnicities, languages, cultures, and religious traditions. Although the Middle East is predominately Arab—a reference to those who speak Arabic as their first language—it comprises other smaller cultural and ethnic groups as well, such as Persians, Turks, Jews, and Kurds.

The shape of many modern-day Middle Eastern countries emerged after World War I, as the Ottoman Empire dissolved and the victorious Allied powers assumed control of several former Ottoman territories. In 1920, Allied leaders gathered at the San Remo Conference in Italy, where they created two mandates—commissions for territorial administration—in the Middle East:

1. The Mandate for Syria and Lebanon gave France control of Syria and Lebanon.

2. The Mandate for Palestine assigned administration of Iraq and Palestine to Great Britain.

As part of the second mandate, Transjordan—which became Jordan in 1949—was created from Palestine in 1921. The British mandate also called for the creation of "a national home for the Jewish people" in Palestine, their historic holy land, to counteract a wave of anti-Semitism that had taken hold of Europe in the 19th century.[2]

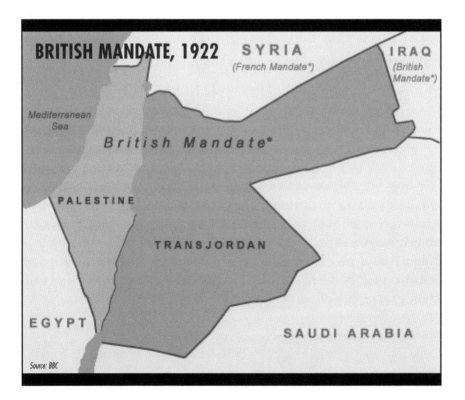

© 2015 Close Up Foundation

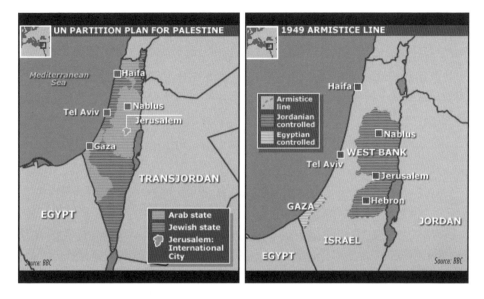

This declaration spurred hundreds of thousands of Jews to immigrate to Palestine, sparking a three-year revolt in the Palestinian Arab community beginning in 1936.[3] Jewish immigration continued nonetheless, especially as the horrors of the Holocaust inspired many Jewish survivors of World War II to seek new lives in their religious homeland.[4]

The mandate system began to break down in the 1930s, as independence was declared or restored in Iraq (1932), Lebanon (1943), Transjordan (1946), and Syria (1946). As a result, Great Britain announced that it would terminate its mandatory rule in the aftermath of World War II, leaving the United Nations (UN) to forge a territory-sharing agreement between Palestinian Arabs and Jews. In 1947, the UN adopted Resolution 181, which divided Palestine into Arab and Jewish states of roughly equal size while keeping Jerusalem and its surrounding sites of religious significance under UN control. The proposal was approved by Palestinian Jews and the UN General Assembly but it was rejected by Palestinian Arabs.[5]

Thus, with no partition plan in place, Palestinian Jews declared their independence and founded the state of Israel on May 14, 1948—the same day the British mandate expired. Within days, the United States had officially recognized Israel, while the neighboring Arab nations of Egypt, Iraq, Lebanon, Syria, and Transjordan declared war on the Israelis. By the time formal armistice lines were drawn in 1949, Israel had gained some of the territory that would have been designated for Palestinian Arabs under UN Resolution 181. The remaining Palestinian territory was absorbed by Egypt, which assumed control of the Gaza Strip, and Transjordan, which annexed East Jerusalem and the West Bank.[6] As their territory was appropriated by neighboring nations, approximately 750,000 Palestinian Arabs became refugees without a state.[7]

The borders of Israel and its neighbors, however, would be redrawn in the aftermath of the Six-Day War of 1967. In June of that year, after weeks of growing tensions, Israel responded to an Egyptian troop build-up on its border by launching a preemptive strike—and within six days, it defeated forces from Egypt, Jordan, and Syria. By the time the two sides agreed to a ceasefire, Israel had won additional territory from its Arab neighbors, annexing the Gaza Strip and Sinai Peninsula from Egypt, East Jerusalem and the West Bank from Jordan, and the Golan Heights from Syria.[8]

Yet the wars of 1948 and 1967 were only the beginnings of a conflict that would rage into the 21st century—resulting in additional territorial exchanges, diplomatic negotiations, armed uprisings,

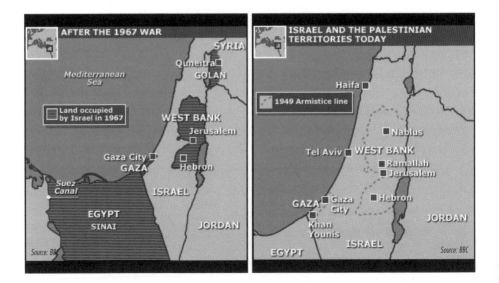

acts of terrorism, and full-scale wars. The next five decades would see Israelis return the Sinai Peninsula to Egypt as part of a 1979 peace treaty;[9] Israelis and Palestinians recognize a new Palestinian Authority in 1993 to temporarily govern the Gaza Strip and the West Bank; and Israelis complete a full withdrawal from the Gaza Strip in 2005.[10] Despite these changes, as of 2015, much of the central Arab-Israeli conflict remained unresolved.

In general, Palestinians have called for (1) Israel to withdraw to its pre-1967 borders; (2) the creation of a viable Palestinian state that includes East Jerusalem, the Gaza Strip, and the West Bank; and (3) Israel to recognize the "right of return"—the right of Palestinian refugees and their descendants to return to present-day Israel and reclaim the land they left behind as a result of the 1948 or 1967 wars. More militant Palestinians have gone so far as to call for the complete destruction of Israel. But Israelis believe the land they possess is rightfully theirs—inhabited thousands of years ago by their ancestors, promised by the international community, and secured while fighting wars instigated by their Arab neighbors.[11] Although a June 2014 Dialog Institute poll suggested that 60 percent of Israelis supported a separate Palestinian state, many also believe the right of return would effectively destroy Israel.[12]

Therefore, policymakers seeking a permanent solution to the Arab-Israeli conflict must answer several complicated and controversial questions. What are the rightful borders of Israel? Are Palestinians entitled to a state of their own? How and where should that state be created? How can Israelis and Palestinians share or relinquish territory that has been occupied by civilians for decades, or that holds vital religious or strategic significance? How can Israelis and Palestinians best protect the safety, security, and human rights of their people? What role, if any, should the United States play in encouraging a permanent peace agreement?

# THE ONGOING DEBATE

## How much aid should the United States give to Israel?

Ever since the United States became the first country to officially recognize the state of Israel in 1948, Americans and Israelis have enjoyed an extraordinarily close relationship.[13] Israel—a democratic nation in a tumultuous and unpredictable region—has been a reliable American ally, while the United States has provided Israel with military aid, a vital trade relationship, and support in the Arab-Israeli conflict.

**Military Aid.** Israel has been the largest cumulative recipient of American foreign assistance since World War II, having received a total of $121 billion—or approximately $3 billion of military financing per year—as of 2014.[14] Americans and Israelis also participate in joint military exercises, joint military research endeavors, and the joint development of weapons.[15]

At times, the United States has also used its own military to support Israel in the Arab-Israeli conflict. In October 1973, for example, Egypt and Syria launched an offensive against Israel in an attempt to regain the territories lost in 1967—a conflict that became known as the Yom Kippur War. But as the Soviet Union began supplying weapons to Egypt and Syria, the United States did the same for Israel while simultaneously making a diplomatic push for a ceasefire.[16] In 1982, Israel launched an invasion of Lebanon to drive out the Palestine Liberation Organization (PLO)—a group classified as a terrorist organization by the United States at the time—which had been using the country as a base to attack Israel. Fearing the conflict could erupt into regional warfare, the United States deployed a contingent of Marines to Lebanon to oversee the withdrawal of the PLO. But in 1983, 241 American servicemen were killed in an Iran-sponsored terrorist attack in Lebanon; one year later, a lack of diplomatic progress led President Ronald Reagan to withdraw American forces.[17]

**Trade.** The United States is Israel's single largest trading partner, and the two nations have had a free trade agreement in place since 1985.[18] In 2012 alone, the United States exported $18 billion in goods and services to Israel and imported $27 billion in goods and services.[19] Israel's top exports to the United States are diamonds, pharmaceutical products, machinery, medical instruments, and agricultural products. Similarly, the United States' top exports to Israel are diamonds, machinery, agricultural products, aircraft, and medical instruments.[20]

**Conflict Moderation.** The United States took its first steps in moderating the Arab-Israeli conflict in the 1970s, as Israel became the target of several high-profile acts of terrorism. In September 1970, for example, members of the Popular Front for the Liberation of Palestine (PFLP) hijacked four commercial airliners in protest of the Israeli occupation of the Gaza Strip and the West Bank. The PFLP evacuated passengers before blowing up the planes on the ground in Jordan, but it kept dozens of Jewish hostages for several weeks. Two years later, as worldwide attention focused on the 1972 Olympic Games in Munich, 11 Israeli athletes and coaches were kidnapped and murdered by a Palestinian terrorist group called Black September.

Peace activists organized by Code Pink protest outside a gathering of the American Israel Public Affairs Committee in March 2015.

As the Arab-Israeli conflict grew increasingly violent, the United States tried to act as a moderator between opposing parties. President Jimmy Carter helped bring about the Camp David Accords of 1978, a historic meeting between Israeli Prime Minister Menachem Begin and Egyptian President Anwar Sadat that led to the first peace agreement signed by Israel and one of its Arab neighbors. Under the treaty, signed in 1979, Egypt officially recognized Israel and established diplomatic relations with its government. In return, Egyptians regained control of the Sinai Peninsula. In the aftermath of the treaty, Egypt became the target of a boycott by other Arab states, and in 1981, Sadat was assassinated by radical Islamists.[21]

By the late 1980s, Palestinians had launched an uprising—or intifada—against the Israeli occupation of the Gaza Strip and the West Bank, sparking a six-year period of strikes, boycotts, vandalism, and mass demonstrations.[22] These developments helped usher in a period of frenzied peacemaking efforts, many of which were pushed by the United States. In September 1993, Israeli Prime Minister Yitzhak Rabin and PLO Chairman Yasser Arafat signed what came to be known as the Oslo Accords at the White House. Under the terms of the agreement, Israel accepted the PLO as the legitimate representative of Palestinians, while the PLO renounced terrorism and recognized Israel's right to exist in peace. The pact also established the Palestinian Authority, a subsidiary of the PLO, to assume governing responsibilities in the Gaza Strip and the West Bank for five years—at which point, permanent negotiations over borders, refugees, and the status of Jerusalem would begin.[23] These permanent negotiations, however, quickly stalled in the early 2000s under the weight of continued political conflict and armed violence.

Because the United States remains so heavily invested in supporting Israel through military, economic, and diplomatic means, American policymakers have a vested interest in ensuring that they agree with Israeli policies. But in recent years, some American officials have suggested the United States should rethink its promises of aid to Israel, especially as tensions have increased over Israeli construction in disputed territories.

# THE CURRENT CONTROVERSY

## Should the United States halt aid to Israel if it continues building settlements in disputed territories?

One of the most controversial outcomes of the 1967 Six-Day War was the fact that Israel gained several territories from its Arab neighbors—the Gaza Strip and Sinai Peninsula from Egypt, East Jerusalem and the West Bank from Jordan, and the Golan Heights from Syria. In 1979, Israel agreed to return the Sinai Peninsula to Egypt, and in 1993, it agreed to allow the Palestinian Authority to temporarily govern the Gaza Strip and the West Bank. In 2005, Israel completely evacuated the Gaza Strip.

But in recent years, policymakers have continued to feud over the status of East Jerusalem and the West Bank—two tracts of land that have become the site of Israeli settlements, or housing developments. The first of these settlements was established in the aftermath of the Six-Day War, as Jews began inhabiting their newly won territory for both economic and religious reasons. As of 2012, a total of 541,000 Israelis were living in settlements in the disputed territories—341,000 in the West Bank and 200,000 in East Jerusalem. At the same time, approximately 2.3 million Palestinians were living in the West Bank and another 300,000 in East Jerusalem.[24]

Israeli Prime Minister Benjamin Netanyahu, who won his fourth term in early 2015, has largely taken a hard-line stance, supporting the continued construction of settlements in East Jerusalem and the West Bank. Under his leadership between 2009 and 2014, for example, the population of Israeli settlers in the West Bank grew at more than twice the rate of the Israeli population as a whole.[25]

The UN, however, has classified the settlements as illegal, and President Barack Obama's administration has vocally opposed their continued construction. "This development will only draw condemnation from the international community, [and] distance Israel from even its closest allies," White House spokesperson Josh Earnest said in 2014.[26]

As President Obama disagreed with Netanyahu over the legitimacy of Israeli settlements, American policymakers began to debate whether the United States should suspend aid to Israel if it continues to build in the disputed territories. Supporters of freezing American aid argue that the Israeli settlements are a violation of international law and harmful to the prospects of a permanent peace agreement. Proponents note that only the United States—Israel's closest ally— has the necessary influence to convince the Israelis to change their behavior. But critics of such a policy insist that Israel has every right to construct homes for its citizens on its own land, and that the United States has no place interfering in Israel's domestic affairs. They argue that freezing settlement construction would only appease Palestinians who continue to question Israel's right to exist and would do little to achieve lasting peace.

## Should the United States halt aid to Israel if it continues building settlements in disputed territories?

### YES: This aggressive Israeli action is illegal and harms the prospects for a lasting peace.

In January 2014, the Israeli government announced plans to construct 1,400 new homes in East Jerusalem and the West Bank—disputed territories that Israel gained in the Six-Day War but Palestinians claim as part of their future state.[27] By December, Israeli authorities had given the green light to 623 additional settlements in the West Bank,[28] and by January 2015, had published plans for 450 more.[29]

Israel, in fact, authorized a stunning 4,485 tenders, or formal agreements, for settlement construction in 2014—a ten-year record and a dramatic increase from the 858 tenders issued in 2007. "[The Israelis] know they can do it," said Grant Rumley, a researcher at the Foundation for Defense of Democracies. "They know they can issue these tenders and there is very little pushback. The retaliation rarely extends past the rhetorical."[30]

In the face of such aggressive action by Israel, it is the responsibility of its closest ally, the United States, to take a stand by suspending foreign aid to the Israelis. Not only has the UN classified Israeli settlements as illegal under international law—they also harm Palestinians by creating crowded living conditions; limiting access to land, water, markets, and infrastructure; and creating conditions ripe for terrorism. "[The settlements are] a mesh of construction and infrastructure leading to a creeping annexation that prevents the establishment of a contiguous and viable Palestinian State and undermines the right of the Palestinian people to self-determination," the UN Human Rights Council concluded in 2013.[31]

By continuing to build homes on disputed land, Israel is only harming the prospects for a permanent peace agreement. "If Palestinians come to believe that the possibility of a contiguous sovereign Palestinian state is no longer within reach, then our ability to manage the international fallout is going to be limited," President Obama warned in March 2014.[32] And one month later, after peace talks between Israelis and Palestinians broke down, U.S. special envoy Martin Indyk said they had been partially "sabotaged" by Israeli settlement plans in East Jerusalem and the West Bank. "The expansion of settlements on land that the Palestinians believe is supposed to be part of their state and the prevention of their ability to build on the same land is a very problematic situation," Indyk said.[33]

"This has to stop," said Hanan Ashrawi, a member of the PLO executive committee. "Building is not just building, it's not something that is so benign. Building is the willful destruction of the two-state solution. It's a constant act of aggression. It's a war crime."[34]

## NO: Palestinians are using the settlements as a distraction, and Israel has a right to build on its land.

"The settlements are an important issue, but they are not the core of the problem," Netanyahu said in 2014. "This conflict has been going on for almost a century. During the first half of that century, there wasn't a single settlement. From 1920, when this conflict effectively began, until 1967, there wasn't a single Israeli settlement or a single Israeli soldier in the territories, and yet this conflict raged. What was that conflict about? It was about the persistent refusal to recognize a Jewish state, before it was established and after it was established."[35]

As Netanyahu so wisely points out, Israel's decision to build homes on the land it rightly won from hostile neighbors in 1967 is not the reason why the Arab-Israeli conflict persists. It persists because Palestinians refuse to recognize the legitimacy of the Jewish state, as well as the right of Israelis to live in peace.

In 2005, Israel made an enormous concession to the Palestinians by evacuating its settlements in the Gaza Strip. How were Israelis repaid? The next year, Palestinian voters gave Hamas—a radical Islamist group that has promised the destruction of Israel—a decisive majority in parliament. "They expect us to just leave, shut our eyes, tear out the settlements," Netanyahu said. "Well, been there, done that. We did it in Gaza. And what we got was not peace, but rocket fire." In 2010, Israel attempted to jump-start the peace process by freezing settlement construction for ten months. "And what has [Palestinian Authority President Mahmoud] Abbas done?" Netanyahu asked. "Nothing."[36]

In reality, the Israeli settlements in question are not settlements at all—they are vital, strategic, and historic regions of an independent nation. The Jewish people have lived in East Jerusalem and the West Bank for decades, and they have the right to build additional homes to accommodate their growing population. "The French build in Paris, the English build in London, and the Israelis build in Jerusalem," Netanyahu said.[37]

The question of whether and how Israel will expand the building of homes for its people is one that Israelis—not Americans—must answer. And by suspending foreign aid as punishment for a legitimate domestic policy, the United States would be risking its most vital alliance in a tumultuous Middle East. "My view is that the United States' role is to stand by our ally, to show not a dime's worth of distance diplomatically between us and Israel, to work to bring the parties together and to see progress," said former Governor Mitt Romney, R-Mass.[38]

# THE ONGOING DEBATE

## Is it ever appropriate for the United States to engage with terrorist organizations?

Terrorism has existed for centuries; in the late 1800s and early 1900s it was a tactic largely associated with high-profile political assassinations. The concept of modern terrorism—bombings, hijackings, kidnappings, and assassinations that gain immediate notoriety through international media exposure—originated in the 1960s and 1970s, as tensions flared in the Arab-Israeli conflict.

As the United States has attempted to combat terrorism over the course of the last several decades, policymakers have repeatedly declared that Americans will not recognize, or negotiate with, terrorist organizations. "Terror must be stopped," President George W. Bush said in 2002. "No nation can negotiate with terrorists. For there is no way to make peace with those whose only goal is death."[39]

In reality, however, there have been several instances in recent history when the United States has engaged or negotiated with terrorist organizations:

- During the 1960s and 1970s, the PLO waged a terrorist war against Israelis all over the world, using hijackings, bombings, and assassinations to fight on behalf of Palestinians. But under the Oslo Accords—signed at the White House in 1993—Israel accepted the PLO as the legitimate representative of Palestinians, while the PLO renounced terrorism and recognized Israel's right to exist in peace. The United States removed the PLO from its list of foreign terrorist organizations in 1994.

- Between 1985 and 1986, President Reagan approved the secret sale of arms to Iran, which agreed to use its influence to help release American hostages held by Iranian terrorists in Lebanon. The Iran-Contra affair violated a U.S. embargo on arms sales to Iran, which the Reagan administration had labeled as a state sponsor of terrorism.[40]

- In 1995, President Bill Clinton met with Gerry Adams, the political leader of the Irish Republican Army (IRA), at the White House, ignoring the United States' designation of the IRA as a terrorist organization. By 1998, the United States had helped facilitate the Good Friday Agreement, which forced the IRA and British loyalists to disarm.[41]

- In 2014, President Obama authorized the release of five Taliban detainees held by the United States in exchange for Sergeant Bowe Bergdahl, an American soldier who left his patrol base in Afghanistan in 2009 and was held captive by the Haqqani Network for five years. After Bergdahl returned home, the Army charged him with desertion and misbehaving before the enemy, charges which carry the possibility of life in prison.[42]

These events are just a small sample of notable instances when the United States engaged with terrorist organizations. "We have had very quiet negotiations, or discussions at least, with terrorist groups over the years on a whole host of things," said Charles Stimson, a senior fellow at the Heritage Foundation. "They just haven't usually come to light."[43]

# THE CURRENT CONTROVERSY

## Should the United States engage a Palestinian Authority government that includes Hamas?

In 1993, the Oslo Accords established the Palestinian Authority to govern the Gaza Strip and the West Bank until Israelis and Palestinians could reach a permanent peace agreement. Although Israel completed its withdrawal from the Gaza Strip in 2005, the peace process soon came to a grinding halt. In 2006, members of Hamas won a decisive majority in the Palestinian Authority parliament over the secular nationalist party, Fatah.

Hamas—labeled a terrorist organization by both the United States and Israel—has an extensive history of suicide bombings, rocket attacks, and armed violence against Israel. Its founding charter reads, "Israel will exist and will continue to exist until Islam will obliterate it."[44] When a fragile power-sharing agreement between Hamas and Fatah broke down in 2007, the Palestinian territories were divided—Abbas and Fatah controlled the West Bank, while Hamas assumed control of the Gaza Strip. As a result of Hamas' seizure of power, towns in southern Israel became the target of near-daily rocket attacks, prompting Israel to blockade the flow of people, commercial goods, weapons, and fuel into the Gaza Strip in an attempt to prevent future violence.[45]

As the Israeli blockade decimated the economy in the Gaza Strip, Hamas finally agreed in June 2014 to reunite with Fatah and the greater Palestinian Authority in a reconciliation government. As of early 2015, the unity government continued to struggle to take shape, after the 2014 murder of three young Israeli students ignited a war between Israel and Hamas in the Gaza Strip.[46]

The United States vowed to "judge any government based on its composition, policies and actions," but Americans were divided over whether they should engage a Palestinian Authority government that includes members of Hamas.[47] Supporters of engagement believe the isolation of Hamas during the last decade merely alienated the Palestinian people and produced few positive results in the permanent peace process. Proponents also note that a unity government would be composed of technocrats and academics—not Hamas militants. Opponents of engagement with Hamas believe such an action would be a betrayal of Israel and a violation of American ideals. They argue that Hamas, which has vowed to destroy Israel, can never be a legitimate partner in the quest for peace.

## Should the United States engage a Palestinian Authority government that includes Hamas?

### YES: Isolating Hamas would only do lasting harm to the permanent peace process.

In 2006, after Hamas candidates won a convincing majority in Palestinian elections, the United States and the European Union suspended hundreds of millions of dollars in aid to the Palestinian Authority.[48] Israel, meanwhile, reacted to Hamas' 2007 seizure of the Gaza Strip—and the regular rocket attacks that followed—by implementing a blockade, effectively strangling Hamas and the Palestinians who live in the Gaza Strip.

But what has been achieved by this attempt to isolate Hamas? As of September 2014, Oxfam reported that 1.7 million Palestinians remained trapped in the Gaza Strip, where the economy was in ruins and more than 40 percent of the population was unemployed.[49] Therefore, the effort to boycott Hamas only created a breeding ground for resentment of Israel and the United States, irrevocably damaging the prospects for a permanent peace agreement. "Today, Hamas has an unquestioned—and, in the eyes of most Gazans, largely legitimate—monopoly on the use of force in the Gaza Strip, and its political clout among Palestinians has grown at the expense of Fatah," author Daniel Byman wrote in 2010.[50]

"The fight to prevent others from talking to [Hamas] is childish," said Giora Eiland, a retired major general in the Israel Defense Forces and the former head of Israel's National Security Council. "The way to press Hamas on various fronts...is to talk to it, not to boycott it. A few weeks ago, Russia's president called for including Hamas in the diplomatic process. Israel quickly clashed with Russia and condemned the initiative, instead of lauding it and letting Hamas explain why it objects to a diplomatic agreement."[51]

In 2011, former President Carter noted, "Suspicions of Hamas stem from its charter, which calls for Israel's destruction. I find the charter repugnant. Yet it is worth remembering that Israel negotiated the Oslo Accords with the Palestine Liberation Organization while its charter had similar provisions."[52]

When the Palestinian Authority announced in 2014 that it was attempting to form a unity government, it sought a government of technocrats and academics—not Hamas hardliners. "[Abbas] made clear that this new technocratic government is committed to the principles of nonviolence, negotiations, recognizing the state of Israel, acceptance of the previous agreements and the Quartet principles," Secretary of State John Kerry said in June 2014. "Based on what we know now about the composition of this technocratic government, which has no minister affiliated to Hamas and is committed to the principles that I describe, we will work with it as we need to, as appropriate."[53]

## NO: Hamas wants only the destruction of Israel, not a lasting peace.

"Palestine is ours from the river to the sea and from the south to the north. There will be no concession on an inch of the land," Hamas leader Khaled Meshal told supporters in 2012. "We will never recognize the legitimacy of the Israeli occupation and therefore there is no legitimacy for Israel, no matter how long it will take."[54]

Meshal's alarming and uncompromising words demonstrate the futility of engaging a Palestinian Authority government that includes Hamas. Make no mistake: Hamas is a terrorist organization with a long history of armed violence against innocent Israeli civilians, not a legitimate representative of the Palestinian people. "Israel, Judaism, and Jews challenge Islam and the Moslem people," Hamas' founding charter reads. "May the cowards never sleep."[55]

In recent years, Hamas has demonstrated time and again that it is committed to waging war against Israel—not to forging a lasting peace. Between 2005, when Israel completed its withdrawal from the Gaza Strip, and 2014, more than five million Israelis were living under the near-constant threat of rocket attacks, as terrorists fired more than 11,000 rockets into Israel.[56] And in 2014, as war broke out between Israel and Hamas in the Gaza Strip, Israeli soldiers uncovered at least 36 tunnels that Hamas had dug into Israel—tunnels the Israeli military said were used to carry out "abductions of Israeli civilians and soldiers alike, infiltrations into Israeli communities, mass murders, and hostage-taking scenarios."[57]

As of 2014, the United States had committed more than $5 billion in bilateral assistance to the Palestinian Authority.[58] If the United States provides aid and engages a Palestinian government that includes Hamas, Americans will be violating their ideals by essentially financing terrorism. "President Abbas argues that the new government is composed of ministers without political affiliation, but this new government appears dependent upon Hamas, and Hamas continues to support terrorism in its quest to destroy the state of Israel," said former House Majority Leader Eric Cantor, R-Va.[59]

"They can call themselves 'ministers' if they want, but that won't change what they really are," Naftali Bennett, the Israeli leader of the Jewish Home party, noted in 2014. "This is a unity government of terrorists in suits."[60]

If the United States refuses to engage Hamas, it would be taking a stand in defense of one of its most loyal and important allies. It would also be sending a vital message to the Palestinian people that terrorism and violence only threaten and delegitimize their path to statehood.

# CONCLUSION

The legitimacy of Israeli settlements and the consequences of engagement with Hamas are only two examples of the Arab-Israeli debates that Americans have engaged in for decades. And although a permanent peace agreement remains far from assured, American policymakers will undoubtedly continue to debate how to best encourage a lasting peace—and which policies will best achieve that goal.

[1] British Petroleum. *BP Statistical Review of World Energy 2014.* Jun. 2014. Web. 24 Feb. 2015.

[2] "Global Connections: The Middle East." PBS. 2002. Web. 28 Apr. 2015.

[3] Council on Foreign Relations. "Crisis Guide: The Israeli-Palestinian Conflict." Web. 28 Apr. 2015.

[4] "Jewish Population of Europe in 1945." U.S. Holocaust Memorial Museum. 20 Jun. 2014. Web. 28 Apr. 2015.

[5] "Global Connections: The Middle East." PBS. 2002. Web. 28 Apr. 2015.

[6] Ibid.

[7] United Nations Relief and Works Agency for Palestine Refugees in the Near East. "Palestine Refugees." Web. 28 Apr. 2015.

[8] "Global Connections: The Middle East." PBS. 2002. Web. 28 Apr. 2015.

[9] "Camp David Accords: Fast Facts." CNN. 3 Nov. 2014. Web. 28 Apr. 2015.

[10] Council on Foreign Relations. "Crisis Guide: The Israeli-Palestinian Conflict." Web. 28 Apr. 2015.

[11] Asser, Martin. "Obstacles to Arab-Israeli Peace: Palestinian Refugees." BBC News. 2 Sep. 2010. Web. 28 Apr. 2015.

[12] Hasson, Nir. "Despite It All, Most Israelis Still Support the Two-State Solution." *Haaretz.* 7 Jul. 2014. Web. 28 Apr. 2015.

[13] U.S. Department of State, Bureau of Near Eastern Affairs. "U.S. Relations with Israel." 10 Mar. 2014. Web. 28 Apr. 2015.

[14] Sharp, Jeremy. *U.S. Foreign Aid to Israel.* Congressional Research Service. 11 Apr. 2014. Web. 28 Apr. 2015.

[15] U.S. Department of State, Bureau of Near Eastern Affairs. "U.S. Relations with Israel." 10 Mar. 2014. Web. 28 Apr. 2015.

[16] U.S. Department of State, Office of the Historian. "The 1973 Arab-Israeli War." 31 Oct. 2013. Web. 28 Apr. 2015.

[17] U.S. Department of State, Office of the Historian. "The Reagan Administration and Lebanon: 1981–1984." Web. 28 Apr. 2015.

[18] U.S. Department of State, Bureau of Near Eastern Affairs. "U.S. Relations with Israel." 10 Mar. 2014. Web. 28 Apr. 2015.

[19] Office of the U.S. Trade Representative. "U.S.-Israel Trade Facts." 29 Apr. 2014. Web. 5 May 2015.

[20] U.S. Department of State, Bureau of Near Eastern Affairs. "U.S. Relations with Israel." 10 Mar. 2014. Web. 28 Apr. 2015.

21 "Global Connections: The Middle East." PBS. 2002. Web. 28 Apr. 2015.

22 Council on Foreign Relations. "Crisis Guide: The Israeli-Palestinian Conflict." Web. 28 Apr. 2015.

23 U.S. Department of State, Office of the Historian. "The Oslo Accords and the Arab-Israeli Peace Process." Web. 28 Apr. 2015.

24 "A Look at Israeli Settlers, By the Numbers." Associated Press. 18 Aug. 2013. Web. 28 Apr. 2015.

25 "West Bank Settlement Expansion Surged Under Netanyahu." Associated Press. 15 Dec. 2014. Web. 28 Apr. 2015.

26 Jackson, David. "Obama Team Warns Israel Over Settlements." *USA Today.* 1 Oct. 2014. Web. 28 Apr. 2015.

27 Booth, William. "Israel Announces New Settlement Construction in Occupied West Bank, East Jerusalem." *Washington Post.* 10 Jan. 2014. Web. 28 Apr. 2015.

28 "Creeping Construction: Israel to Build 600 New Settlements in the West Bank." RT. 26 Dec. 2014. Web. 28 Apr. 2015.

29 Lazaroff, Tovah. "Israel Lands Authority Publishes Tenders for 450 West Bank Homes." *Jerusalem Post.* 30 Jan. 2015. Web. 28 Apr. 2015.

30 Moore, Jack. "Israel Settlement Tenders Reach 10-Year High." *Newsweek.* 24 Feb. 2015. Web. 28 Apr. 2015.

31 Heilprin, John. "UN Panel: Israeli Settlements Are Illegal." Huffington Post. 31 Jan. 2013. Web. 28 Apr. 2015.

32 Vick, Karl. "Obama Warns Netanyahu on Peace Talks." *Time.* 3 Mar. 2014. Web. 28 Apr. 2015.

33 Shimoni Stoil, Rebecca. "US Envoy Indyk Insists Peace Process Not Dead." *The Times of Israel.* 9 May 2014. Web. 28 Apr. 2015.

34 Rudoren, Jodi. "Israel: Settlement Plans Renew Palestinian Outrage." *New York Times.* 20 Mar. 2014. Web. 28 Apr. 2015.

35 Goldberg, Jeffrey. "Netanyahu Says Obama Got Syria Right." Bloomberg View. 22 May 2014. Web. 28 Apr. 2015.

36 Ibid.

37 Rudoren, Jodi, and Jeremy Ashkenas. "Netanyahu and the Settlements." *New York Times.* 12 Mar. 2015. Web. 28 Apr. 2015.

38 Hersh, Joshua. "Mitt Romney Says Israel Settlements 'Should Be Discussed in Private.'" Huffington Post. 30 Jul. 2012. Web. 28 Apr. 2015.

39 Moran, Michael. "Terrorist Groups and Political Legitimacy." Council on Foreign Relations. 16 Mar. 2006. Web. 28 Apr. 2015.

40 "The Iran-Contra Affair." PBS. Web. 28 Apr. 2015.

41 Moran, Michael. "Terrorist Groups and Political Legitimacy." Council on Foreign Relations. 16 Mar. 2006. Web. 28 Apr. 2015.

42 Lamothe, Dan. "Bowe Bergdahl, Once-Missing U.S. Soldier, Charged with Desertion." *Washington Post.* 25 Mar. 2015. Web. 28 Apr. 2015.

43 Gomez, Alan. "Is It Ever Right to Negotiate with Terrorists?" *USA Today.* 2 Jun. 2014. Web. 28 Apr. 2015.

44 *Hamas Covenant* 1988. Yale Law School Lillian Goldman Library. Web. 28 Apr. 2015.

45 B'Tselem. "The Siege on Gaza." 1 Jan. 2011. Web. 28 Apr. 2015.

46 Al-Mughrabi, Nidal. "Palestinian Unity Frays, Hurting Gaza's Rebuilding and Statehood Aims." Reuters. 14 Jan. 2015. Web. 28 Apr. 2015.

47 "Palestinian Unity Government Sworn In." Reuters. 2 Jun. 2014. Web. 28 Apr. 2015.

48  Weisman, Steven, and Craig Smith. "U.S. and Europe Halt Aid to Palestinian Government." *New York Times.* 8 Apr. 2006. Web. 28 Apr. 2015.

49  "Crisis in Gaza." Oxfam International. 18 Sep. 2014. Web. 28 Apr. 2015.

50  Byman, Daniel. "How to Handle Hamas." *Foreign Affairs.* Sep./Oct. 2010. Web. 28 Apr. 2015.

51  Eiland, Giora. "A New Approach to Gaza." Ynet News. 3 Jun. 2010. Web. 28 Apr. 2015.

52  Carter, Jimmy. "Support the Palestinian Unity Government." *Washington Post.* 3 May 2011. Web. 28 Apr. 2015.

53  "Kerry Defends U.S. Decision to Work With 'Palestinian Unity Government.'" AFP and Arutz Sheva. 4 Jun. 2014. Web. 28 Apr. 2015.

54  "Khaled Meshaal, Hamas Leader, Vows to Never Recognize Israel." Reuters. 8 Dec. 2012. Web. 28 Apr. 2015.

55  *Hamas Covenant 1988.* Yale Law School Lillian Goldman Library. Web. 28 Apr. 2015.

56  Israel Defense Forces. "Rocket Attacks on Israel from Gaza." Web. 28 Apr. 2015.

57  McCoy, Terrence. "How Hamas Uses Its Tunnels to Kill and Capture Israeli Soldiers." *Washington Post.* 21 Jul. 2014. Web. 28 Apr. 2015.

58  Zanotti, Jim. *U.S. Foreign Aid to the Palestinians.* Congressional Research Service. 3 Jul. 2014. Web. 28 Apr. 2015.

59  Goodenough, Patrick. "Israel 'Deeply Disappointed' U.S. Will Fund Palestinian-Hamas Unity Gov't." *CNS News.* 2 Jun. 2014. Web. 28 Apr. 2015.

60  Levi, Yaakov. "PA Govt. Members Are 'Terrorists in Suits.'" Arutz Sheva. 2 Jun. 2014. Web. 28 Apr. 2015.

# HUMAN RIGHTS AROUND THE WORLD

## CURRENT CONTROVERSIES

- Should the United States do more to compel other nations to address human rights abuses?

- Should the United States take steps to protect homosexuals from persecution abroad?

# INTRODUCTION

> *"To deny people their human rights is to challenge their very humanity."*
> —Nelson Mandela

> *"Every step towards the goal of justice requires sacrifice, suffering, and struggle; the tireless exertions and passionate concern of dedicated individuals."*
> —Martin Luther King, Jr.

In 1776, the United States declared its independence from Great Britain by proclaiming "that all men are created equal, that they are endowed by their Creator with certain unalienable Rights, that among these are Life, Liberty and the pursuit of Happiness."[1] The Declaration of Independence represented a landmark commitment to the protection of human rights and helped inspire democratic movements around the globe for years to come. But over the centuries, Americans have also disagreed over the extent of their responsibilities to protect human rights abroad. In this chapter, we will consider several enduring tensions in human rights policy and examine two current controversial issues:

- Should the United States do more to compel other nations to address human rights abuses?

- Should the United States take steps to protect homosexuals from persecution abroad?

**Why Is the Protection of Human Rights Controversial?** Human rights are rights that are inherent to all people, no matter their gender, race, religion, language, nationality, ethnicity, sexual orientation, place of residence, or any other status. This concept, the origins of which date back thousands of years to ancient Greece and Rome, is famously enshrined in the founding documents of the United States.

But the protection of human rights has also been embraced by the international community, both through the laws adopted by individual nations and through the Universal Declaration of Human Rights (UDHR) of 1948. Proclaimed by the United Nations (UN) General

Assembly in the aftermath of the Holocaust, the UDHR outlined a series of fundamental human rights that required universal protection, including the rights of life, liberty, and security of person; the equal protection of laws; freedom of thought, expression, assembly, and religion; the right to education, work, and representative government; and freedom from slavery, torture, and arbitrary arrest or detention.[2]

Although the UDHR is not a legally binding document, it is the foundation of international human rights law, having inspired more than 80 binding treaties, declarations, laws, and constitutional provisions.[3] Chief among them are the International Covenant on Civil and Political Rights—which had 167 state parties, including the United States, as of 2013[4]—and the International Covenant on Economic, Social, and Cultural Rights—which had 164 state parties, but not the United States, as of 2015.[5]

So why are human rights, a concept embraced by nations around the world, controversial? Some leaders and policymakers disagree with the validity or urgency of certain human rights for practical, philosophical, or political reasons. In China, for example, concerns about rapid population growth led the government to implement a mandatory one-child policy in 1979—a violation of the human right to create a family. The leaders of some theocracies, meanwhile, believe religious laws prohibit equality among the sexes, rights for religious dissenters, or rights for homosexuals. And some authoritarian regimes believe representative government and self-rule threaten political stability, security, and the individual power of leaders.

Meanwhile, the role of the United States in defending human rights around the world also has the potential to ignite controversy. While some policymakers believe the United States—the leader of the free world—has a responsibility to intervene when human rights are violated in foreign nations, others insist Americans have no place interfering in the domestic affairs of sovereign countries.

**Why Is the Protection of Human Rights So Complicated?** Protecting human rights around the world is a vast and complex task. As of 2014, there were a total of 195 sovereign states—and 195 sovereign governments that varied greatly in their structures, intentions, and treatment of their citizens.[6] That same year, Freedom House concluded that only 40 percent of the global population was living in one of the 88 "free" countries; meanwhile, nearly 2.5 billion people, or an astonishing 35 percent of the global population, were living in one of the 48 "not free" countries.[7]

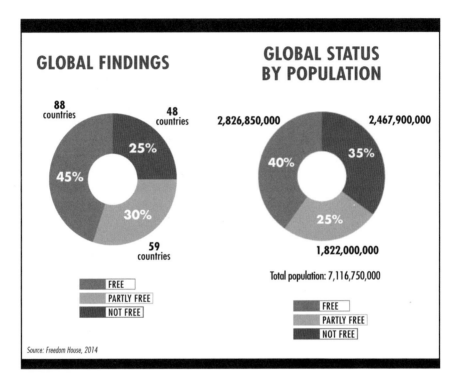

GLOBAL FINDINGS

88 countries
48 countries
25%
45%
30%
59 countries

- FREE
- PARTLY FREE
- NOT FREE

GLOBAL STATUS BY POPULATION

2,826,850,000
2,467,900,000
35%
40%
25%
1,822,000,000

Total population: 7,116,750,000

- FREE
- PARTLY FREE
- NOT FREE

Source: Freedom House, 2014

The preservation of human rights is further complicated by the fact that it is only one of several competing interests that must be balanced by world leaders. The United States, for example, has broad constitutional provisions that protect the liberty and individual rights of its citizens—but at times, the government has encroached upon those rights in the name of national security. The United States and other nations have also used war and military interventions to protect democracy and human rights abroad—but at the same time, those actions have resulted in the deaths of innocent civilians.

With the human rights of so many people at risk in 2015, the international community faces the difficult task of responding to violations. Should the United States take the lead in defending human rights around the world? Or is this a responsibility best left to international bodies and regional allies? Which tools are the most effective in changing the behavior of violating nations? And who has the moral authority to lead this international discussion?

## THE ONGOING DEBATE

### How should the United States respond to foreign human rights abuses?

At the time of its founding, the United States stood alone as the only nation founded on the universal ideas of liberty and equality. And these fundamental principles endured for years to come, encouraging Americans to speak out against injustice and to hold the government accountable when it fell short—sometimes woefully so—of its promises.

But just as the United States has worked to correct human rights violations at home, it has also encountered abuses by its counterparts in the international community. These violations of human rights— committed by both allies and adversaries—have included civil wars, the suppression of speech, the subjugation of women and minorities, arbitrary arrest and detention, and genocide. And as these abuses have been revealed, American officials have weighed whether, and with which tools, to respond.

**Military Action.** At times, the United States has launched military operations, such as combat missions or air strikes, in response to human rights violations abroad. The United States has traditionally employed such action when civil wars or other violent conflicts have urgently threatened the lives of civilians. In recent years, the United States used human rights violations to justify military interventions to combat the Islamic State of Iraq and the Levant (ISIL) in 2014–2015, to help depose long-time dictator Moammar Gaddafi in Libya in 2011, to prevent further ethnic cleansing and violence in the Bosnian War of 1992–1995, and to provide famine relief in war-torn Somalia in 1993.

**Sanctions.** Sanctions are a diplomatic tool used to persuade governments or individuals to change their behavior by restricting trade, financial assistance, or other commercial activity with those governments or individuals. As of April 2015, the United States had 28 sanctions programs in place, many of them in response to human rights violations.[8] For example, Americans sanctioned the authoritarian leader of Syria, Bashar al-Assad, for violently cracking down on pro-democracy protests in 2011 and igniting a civil war. And in early 2015, the United States expanded sanctions against officials in Venezuela for violently suppressing free speech and abusing other human rights.

**Foreign Aid.** Approximately one percent of the United States' annual budget goes toward various foreign aid programs, which include initiatives to improve public health, spur economic development, enhance military readiness, bolster humanitarian assistance, and aid democratic elections.[9] Because many foreign governments depend on this assistance, the United States has used the suspension of foreign aid to punish human rights abusers. Between late 2013 and early 2015, for example, the United States suspended the $1.3 billion in annual military aid it provided to Egypt, in response to the ouster of President Mohamed Morsi and a violent crackdown on members of the Muslim Brotherhood.[10] At other times, the United States has boosted foreign aid to assist the victims of human rights abuses. Between 2011 and early 2015, for example, the United States gave more than $3 billion in humanitarian assistance to Syrians affected by the civil war.[11]

**Diplomatic Negotiations.** The United States has also sought to defend human rights abroad by engaging in diplomatic negotiations, or discussions between high-level government representatives. Since 1990, for example, the United States has held regular talks with the Chinese government, which has violated human rights through the suppression of speech and religious practice, the one-child policy, the overuse of capital punishment, and the confiscation of property. China suspended the dialogue between 2002 and 2008 in response to American criticism of its human rights record at the UN.[12]

**International Action.** The United States does not always lead the response to international human rights abuses, leaving room for international bodies, such as the UN, to play an important role. Over the years, the UN has investigated claims of human rights violations, provided electoral assistance in more than 100 nations, helped forge international human rights agreements, and imposed sanctions on violators.[13]

Each potential course of action, however, presents benefits and drawbacks for the United States and the international community. Proponents of military action, for example, believe it can quickly save countless civilian lives and neutralize dangerous threats, but critics argue that innocent men, women, and children are often caught in the crossfire. Sanctions, meanwhile, can have crippling economic effects on human rights violators, but they can also have unintended effects on oppressed populations. And while diplomatic action preserves important relationships with other governments, it does not always lead to forceful and immediate change.

# THE CURRENT CONTROVERSY

## Should the United States do more to compel other nations to address human rights abuses?

The United States and the international community have witnessed several recent victories on behalf of human rights around the world. The pro-democracy movement took hold of Hong Kong in 2014, drawing hundreds of thousands of demonstrators to protest against the Chinese government. Tunisia, which ousted its dictator and launched the Arab Spring in 2010, held its first ever democratic presidential election in 2014.[14] And in Morocco, lawmakers unanimously amended an article of the penal code that had allowed rapists of underage girls to avoid prosecution by marrying their victims.[15]

But at the same time, human rights were being ignored, revoked, and violently abused in nations around the world. As of early 2015, the Syrian civil war had killed an estimated 210,000 people and displaced more than 3.9 million.[16] In Nigeria, the Islamist insurgent group Boko Haram had killed nearly 10,000 people by the end of 2014.[17] In China, the government continued to suppress free speech, dissent, and religious practice.[18] And in Russia, the government enacted a series of policies aimed at discrediting, monitoring, and silencing political opposition, independent media, and non-governmental organizations.[19]

As people across the globe struggled to protect their human rights in 2015, they helped ignite a national debate over whether the United States should do more to assist them. Some policymakers believe the United States has a moral obligation to ensure that its international partners are protecting the human rights of their citizens—an action that will contribute to greater global stability and prosperity. Supporters also argue that the United States is the only world power with the military, economic, and diplomatic standing necessary to compel violating nations to change their behavior.

But opponents of increased American action disagree, and believe it would be counterproductive for the United States to lecture its international partners about human rights violations. Critics say it would be more effective for the United States to lead by example and to avoid damaging the valuable alliances and relationships it has worked to maintain. Critics also note that the United States already provides enormous support for human rights through military action, sanctions, and foreign aid—and further action must be left to international bodies, regional allies, and the violating nations themselves.

## Should the United States do more to compel other nations to address human rights abuses?

### YES: The United States must use its unmatched resources and influence to stand up for human rights.

"In the early morning hours of August 21, 2013, artillery and mortar shells equipped with sarin gas exploded amidst the agricultural neighborhoods of Ghouta on the outskirts of Damascus. Those exposed to the nerve agent foamed from the nose and mouth, convulsing, desperate for air. Rows of victims, covered in white burial shrouds, soon lay motionless on hospital floors. At least 1,429 Syrian civilians, including 426 children, and many of the brave activists who had raced to the scene with video cameras to show the world what had happened, died on that day."[20]

This abhorrent poison gas attack, carried out by the Syrian army, was only one of the abuses outlined by the State Department in 2013. And in the face of such gross violations of human dignity, the United States has a moral obligation to act decisively, through either military, economic, or diplomatic force.

As the most formidable economic power and the leader of the free world, the United States is the only nation with the resources and influence needed to persuade human rights violators to change their behavior—an action that would have lasting positive effects on global stability. "It is false to suggest that the greater a country's relative power, the less the U.S. can afford to confront its human rights failings," Mark Lagon, a senior fellow at the Council on Foreign Relations, wrote, citing China as an example. "Indeed, if it is too inflexible in absorbing societal demands, China's autocracy could face a rupture threatening global stability."[21]

The United States also has a responsibility to hold its allies accountable for human rights violations—something it has largely failed to do. In 2012, for example, the United States resumed arms sales to Bahrain despite efforts by the regime to silence political opposition; in 2015, the United States also resumed military aid to Egypt, despite the rise of a new authoritarian dictatorship.[22] And Saudi Arabia continues to receive American aid despite the fact that its laws deny equal rights for women, outlaw blasphemy and apostasy, and allow the liberal use of corporal punishment and executions. "The fact is that the United States has never really pushed Saudi Arabia, except in a very sort of broad rhetorical or cosmetic way," said Tom Porteous of Human Rights Watch. "And that's mainly for commercial reasons."[23]

In the end, Americans should remember the words of former UN Secretary General Kofi Annan, who said, "We will not enjoy security without development, we will not enjoy development without security, and we will not enjoy either without respect for human rights."[24]

## NO: The United States does not have the ability, credibility, or right to dictate to sovereign nations.

"China is a developing country with a huge population, and also a developing country in a crucial stage of reform," former Chinese President Hu Jintao said. "In this context, China still faces many challenges in economic and social development. And a lot still needs to be done in China, in terms of human rights."[25]

As rightly concerned as Americans are about human rights violations in China and other nations around the world, they should consider Hu's words. Many countries that currently struggle with the protection of human rights are developing nations in the throes of political upheavals and civil wars. And in many cases, these conflicts can only be solved internally—not through military interference, punitive sanctions, or lectures by the United States. "Americans tend to forget that after Iraq, after Abu Ghraib, after Guantanamo, the U.S. credibility around the world is a lot less than it used to be when the United States says this is the country that's just speaking in the name of human rights," said Princeton University professor Gary Bass. "That's something that's a harder sell these days than it used to be."[26]

Hong Lei, spokesman for the Chinese Foreign Ministry, added, "The United States has no right to pose as arbiters and, at every turn, point their fingers at other countries' human rights as racism and mistreatment of prisoners and other serious problems in the United States are facts now known to all."[27]

By increasing pressure on its international partners to protect human rights, the United States would only expose itself to accusations of hypocrisy and risk its relationships with powerful players in developing regions. "It is essential that the United States and China have a positive, cooperative relationship," former Secretary of State Hillary Clinton said in 2009, as she vowed to continue to press the Chinese on human rights issues. "But our pressing on those issues can't interfere with the global economic crisis, the global climate change crisis, and the security crisis."[28]

As of 2015, Americans were already engaged in military operations against ISIL militants in Iraq and Syria, and had 28 sanctions programs in place against foreign governments and individuals. In 2013, the United States donated an astounding $16.4 billion to alleviate human suffering in other countries, making it the global leader in humanitarian aid.[29] And in the wake of such forceful American action, the onus now falls on international bodies, regional allies, and individual governments to defend human rights around the world.

# THE ONGOING DEBATE

## To what extent should ideological interests influence American foreign policy?

Just as the United States must weigh a variety of tools when combating human rights violations around the world, it also must delicately balance its competing foreign interests. Over the course of American history, policymakers have acted on behalf of the United States' economic, security, and ideological interests, while also debating which should primarily influence foreign policy.

**Economic Interests.** The economic interests of a nation encompass its ability to produce and acquire goods and services; trade policies, such as tariffs, subsidies, quotas, import and export taxes, and product safety regulations; and monetary policies. Nations may act on behalf of their economic interests by signing trade agreements or forging alliances to open new import or export markets.

**Security Interests.** The security interests of a nation are policies aimed at keeping citizens safe. Actions driven by security interests can include domestic military development, the installation of military bases abroad, or foreign interventions intended to boost global security and protect American lives.

**Ideological Interests.** When a nation pursues its ideological interests, it acts on behalf of the values and way of life of its people. But because each and every nation has its own unique worldview, the ideological interests of different countries often conflict with one another, especially when they relate to forms of government, civil rights, and the appropriate role of religion.

At times, the United States' competing interests have overlapped, providing economic, security, and ideological justifications for American actions abroad. During the Iraq War, for example, some Americans cited the economic interest of protecting oil supplies in the Middle East; others cited the security interest of preventing Iraqi dictator Saddam Hussein from using weapons of mass destruction;

Protestors in Berlin rally against human rights violations perpetrated against gays and lesbians, focusing on laws in Russia.

and some cited the ideological interest of deposing Hussein and bringing democracy to Iraq. But at other times, the United States has been forced to choose between its competing interests when acting abroad. The United States maintains a strong economic relationship with China, for example, despite the fact that the Chinese violate Americans' ideological commitment to human rights. And as a genocidal civil war took hold of Rwanda of 1994, the United States—having recently lost troops in its famine-relief mission in Somalia—chose to avoid intervention, therefore prioritizing security interests over ideological interests.[30]

Some policymakers have argued that if the United States is truly committed to freedom, universal equality, and human rights, it has a responsibility to risk its own economic and security interests in pursuit of its ideological goals. But at the same time, others have noted that each sovereign country has its own worldview and is entitled to determine its own actions without American interference.

# THE CURRENT CONTROVERSY

## Should the United States take steps to protect homosexuals from persecution abroad?

The United States has been the site of several significant victories for the gay rights movement in recent years. As of April 2015, 37 states and the District of Columbia had authorized same-sex marriages; in May 2012, President Barack Obama became the first U.S. president to express his support for same-sex marriage; and in 2013, the Supreme Court ruled that gay couples married in states where same-sex marriage is legal must receive the same federal benefits that heterosexual couples receive.[31]

But in much of the rest of the world, the gay community faces a more hostile landscape. As of 2013, only six nations had enacted constitutional prohibitions against discrimination based on sexual orientation. Homosexual acts were illegal in 77 countries, including much of Africa, the Middle East, south Asia, and the Pacific. And in five nations—Iran, Mauritania, Saudi Arabia, Sudan, and Yemen—as well as parts of Nigeria and Somalia, homosexual acts were punishable by death.[32]

Russia, meanwhile, did not make homosexuality illegal, but President Vladimir Putin signed a 2013 law banning the distribution of "propaganda of nontraditional sexual relations" to minors. The law—which carried fines as high as $156 for individuals and $31,000 for media organizations—was also used to ban gay rights parades and to curb the discussion of gay issues on television, in newspapers, and in schools.[33]

These anti-gay laws in foreign countries have sparked a national debate in the United States over whether Americans should take additional steps to protect homosexuals from persecution abroad. Proponents of such action argue that the battle for gay rights is the battle for human rights, and that the United States has a moral obligation to follow its ideological interests and set an example for the rest of the world. But opponents worry that American interference could inspire defiant leaders to dig in, contribute to widespread foreign resentment of the United States, and hinder the global campaign for human rights.

## Should the United States take steps to protect homosexuals from persecution abroad?

### YES: Gay rights are human rights, and the United States must stand up for the persecuted.

In January 2014, the government of Nigeria enacted the Same Sex Marriage Prohibition Act, a law punishing members of gay organizations with as many as ten years in prison and married same-sex couples with as many as 14 years in prison. Within days, police had arrested dozens of gay men—and, according to human rights groups, tortured several into naming others. "Rarely have I seen a piece of legislation that in so few paragraphs directly violates so many basic, universal human rights," said UN High Commissioner for Human Rights Navi Pillay.[34]

The struggle for gay rights is, in fact, the struggle for human rights, and this struggle is hardly limited to Nigeria. In Saudi Arabia, for example, a young gay man was sentenced to 450 lashes and three years in prison in 2014. His crime? Using Twitter to post "immoral" photographs and to meet other gay men.[35] Elsewhere in 2014, eight men in Egypt were accused of participating in a gay marriage ceremony; each was sentenced to one year in prison.[36]

At a time when the mere act of being gay is a crime in 77 countries, the United States has a responsibility to shield innocent people from persecution. In 2014, Senator Edward Markey, D-Mass., introduced the International Human Rights Defense Act, which would direct the State Department to make the protection of gay rights and the prevention of gay discrimination a foreign policy priority. "For the United States to hold true to our commitment to defending the human rights of all people around the world, we must stand with the LGBT community in their struggle for recognition and equality everywhere," Senator Markey said.[37]

If the United States fails to respond forcefully to gay discrimination and persecution, it will only signal to other world powers that such behavior is acceptable. "Mr. Putin's campaign against lesbian, gay, and bisexual people is one of distraction, a strategy of demonizing a minority for political gain taken straight from the Nazi playbook," playwright Harvey Fierstein wrote in the *New York Times*. "Can we allow this war against human rights to go unanswered? Although Mr. Putin may think he can control his creation, history proves he cannot: his condemnations are permission to commit violence against gays and lesbians. In May, a young gay man was murdered in the city of Volgograd. He was beaten, his body violated with beer bottles, his clothing set on fire, his head crushed with a rock. This is most likely just the beginning."[38]

## NO: Foreign interference by the United States can be counterproductive, and even harmful.

Homosexual acts have been illegal—and punishable by life imprisonment—in Uganda since 1950.[39] But in 2014, long-time Ugandan President Yoweri Museveni signed the Anti-Homosexuality Act, which criminalized aid to gays and lesbians, banned the "promotion of homosexuality," and allowed life imprisonment for homosexual acts as minor as touching in public.[40]

The Ugandan law represented a vile affront to the rights of gays and lesbians—but the American response also demonstrated the risks of foreign intervention. In the aftermath of the law's passage, the United States suspended some foreign aid to Uganda, imposed visa restrictions, and canceled a regional military exercise.[41] Museveni, however, was defiant in the face of international criticism. "If the West doesn't want to work with us because of homosexuals, then we have enough space here to live by ourselves and do business with other people," he said. "We are sorry to see that you live the way you live, but we keep quiet about it. Now you say, 'You must also live like us'—that's where we say no."[42]

When the United States seeks to impose its values on other nations, it runs the risk of antagonizing oppressive leaders, angering local citizens and lawmakers, and hindering the vital work of local human rights advocates. In Uganda, for example, the Anti-Homosexuality Act was struck down in 2014 on a narrow technicality—but lawmakers quickly began drafting a new version that focused more intently on outlawing the "promotion" of homosexuality. "People don't realize that the 'promotion' part of it will affect everybody," said gay rights activist Frank Mugisha. "If newspapers report about homosexuality it could be seen as promotion."[43]

In 2013, the Pew Research Center found that 60 percent of Americans believed society should accept homosexuality—but a mere four percent of Ugandans, three percent of Egyptians, and 16 percent of Russians felt the same way.[44] Therefore, the United States must tread carefully when criticizing homosexuality laws in these nations—or risk being attacked for explicitly ignoring the will of the people.

In the end, frustrating as it may be, it is simply not up to the United States to determine the legitimacy of laws passed in other nations. The most the United States can do is ensure justice for its own citizens, keep its doors open for those seeking asylum, and convince the rogue states of the world to follow the American example.

# CONCLUSION

The protection of human rights abroad and the battle against homosexual persecution are only two examples of the human rights policy debates Americans have engaged in for years. And although the fate of these two policies remains far from certain, lawmakers and advocates will undoubtedly continue to debate the goals and priorities of the American human rights strategy— and which government policies best reflect and achieve them.

---

[1] *U.S. Declaration of Independence.*

[2] United Nations. *The Universal Declaration of Human Rights.* Web. 15 Apr. 2015.

[3] United Nations. "The Foundation of International Human Rights Law." Web. 15 Apr. 2015.

[4] Office of the United Nations High Commissioner for Human Rights. "Ratification of the International Covenant on Civil and Political Rights, January 2013." Jan. 2013. Web. 15 Apr. 2015.

[5] United Nations Treaty Collection. "International Covenant on Economic, Social, and Cultural Rights." Database. 15 Apr. 2015. Web. 15 Apr. 2015.

[6] U.S. Department of State, Bureau of Intelligence and Research. "Independent States in the World." 30 Dec. 2014. Web. 15 Apr. 2015.

[7] Freedom House. *Freedom in the World 2014.* 2014. Web. 15 Apr. 2015.

[8] U.S. Department of the Treasury, Resource Center. "Sanctions Programs and Country Information." 14 Apr. 2015. Web. 15 Apr. 2015.

[9] Rutsch, Poncie. "Guess How Much of Uncle Sam's Money Goes to Foreign Aid. Guess Again!" NPR. 10 Feb. 2015. Web. 17 Mar. 2015.

[10] Ryan, Missy. "Obama Administration Ends Long Hold on Military Aid to Egypt." *Washington Post.* 31 Mar. 2015. Web. 15 Apr. 2015.

[11] United States Agency for International Development. "Syria." Web. 17 Mar. 2015.

[12] Voice of America. "U.S., China Begin Human Rights Dialogue." 30 Jul. 2013. Web. 15 Apr. 2015.

[13] United Nations. "60 Ways the United Nations Makes a Difference." Web. 15 Apr. 2015.

[14] Gonzalez, Geysha. "The Best and Worst Human Rights Developments of 2014." Freedom House. 16 Dec. 2014. Web. 15 Apr. 2015.

[15] BBC. "Morocco Amends Controversial Rape Marriage Law." 23 Jan. 2014. Web. 15 Apr. 2015.

[16] United Nations High Commissioner for Refugees. "Syria Regional Refugee Response." 17 Mar. 2015. Web. 17 Mar. 2015.

[17] Connect SAIS Africa. "Social Violence in Nigeria." Johns Hopkins School of Advanced International Studies. Web. 15 Apr. 2015.

[18] Human Rights Watch. "China." *World Report 2014.* Web. 15 Apr. 2015.

[19] Human Rights Watch. "Russia." *World Report 2014.* Web. 15 Apr. 2015.

20  U.S. Department of State, Bureau of Democracy, Human Rights and Labor. *Country Reports on Human Rights Practices for 2013.* Web. 15 Apr. 2015.

21  Lagon, Mark. "Promoting Human Rights: Is U.S. Consistency Desirable or Possible?" Council on Foreign Relations. Oct. 2011. Web. 15 Apr. 2015.

22  Chick, Kristen. "U.S. Resumes Arms Sales to Bahrain. Activists Feel Abandoned." *Christian Science Monitor.* 14 May 2012. Web. 15 Apr. 2015.

23  Porteous, Tom. Interview with Judy Woodruff. "NewsHour." PBS. 27 Jan. 2015. Web. 15 Apr. 2015.

24  United Nations Population Fund. "Quotes on Human Rights." 2004. Web. 15 Apr. 2015.

25  Richburg, Keith. "Hu's Remarks Censored Back Home." *Washington Post.* 21 Jan. 2011. Web. 15 Apr. 2015.

26  Bass, Gary. Interview with Neal Conan. "Talk of the Nation." NPR. 7 May 2013. Web. 15 Apr. 2015.

27  Reuters. "China Says U.S. Can't Slam Others on Rights When It Has Racism Problems at Home." 11 Dec. 2014. Web. 15 Apr. 2015.

28  CNN. "Clinton: Chinese Human Rights Can't Interfere with Other Crises." 22 Feb. 2009. Web. 15 Apr. 2015.

29  Swithern, Sophia. Global Humanitarian Assistance Report 2014. Global Humanitarian Assistance. Web. 15 Apr. 2015.

30  Baldauf, Scott. "Why the U.S. Didn't Intervene in the Rwandan Genocide." *Christian Science Monitor.* 7 Apr. 2009. Web. 15 Apr. 2015.

31  Human Rights Campaign. "Marriage Center." Web. 15 Apr. 2015.

32  Itaborahy, Lucas Paoli, and Jingshu Zhu. *State-Sponsored Homophobia. A World Survey of Laws: Criminalisation, Protection, and Recognition of Same-Sex Love.* International Lesbian Gay Bisexual Trans and Intersex Association. May 2013. Web. 15 Apr. 2015.

33  Associated Press. "Russian Anti-Gay Bill Passes, Protestors Detained." 11 Jun. 2013. Web. 15 Apr. 2015.

34  Legge, James. "Nigeria's Anti-Gay Laws: Homosexuals Rounded Up and Beaten, Rights Groups Claim." *The Independent.* 15 Jan. 2014. Web. 15 Apr. 2015.

35  Piggott, Mark. "Saudi Man Gets 450 Lashes and 3 Years Jail After Posting 'Gay Tweets.'" *International Business Times.* 24 Jul. 2014. Web. 15 Apr. 2015.

36  Reuters. "Egypt Reduces Sentence for Eight Men Over Gay Marriage Video." 27 Dec. 2014. Web. 15 Apr. 2015.

37  Rizzuto, Robert. "Sen. Ed Markey Introduces Legislation Affirming LGBT Rights as Foreign Policy Priority of the United States." MassLive. 13 Jun. 2014. Web. 15 Apr. 2015.

38  Fierstein, Harvey. "Russia's Anti-Gay Crackdown." *New York Times.* 21 Jul. 2013. Web. 15 Apr. 2015.

39  Itaborahy, Lucas Paoli, and Jingshu Zhu. *State-Sponsored Homophobia. A World Survey of Laws: Criminalisation, Protection, and Recognition of Same-Sex Love.* International Lesbian Gay Bisexual Trans and Intersex Association. May 2013. Web. 15 Apr. 2015.

40  Smith, David. "Uganda Anti-Gay Law Declared 'Null and Void' by Constitutional Court." *The Guardian.* 1 Aug. 2014. Web. 15 Apr. 2015.

41  Gettleman, Jeffrey. "Uganda Anti-Gay Law Struck Down by Court." *New York Times.* 1 Aug. 2014. Web. 15 Apr. 2015.

42  Karimi, Faith, and Nick Thompson. "Uganda's President Museveni Signs Controversial Anti-Gay Bill into Law." CNN. 25 Feb. 2014. Web. 15 Apr. 2015.

43  Johnston, Chris. "Uganda Drafts New Ant-Gay Laws." *The Guardian.* 8 Nov. 2014. Web. 15 Apr. 2015.

44  Pew Research Center. "The Global Divide on Homosexuality." 4 Jun. 2013. Web. 15 Apr. 2015.

# ISIL'S QUEST FOR POWER: IRAQ, SYRIA, AND TURKEY

## CURRENT CONTROVERSIES

- Should the United States deploy ground troops to combat ISIL?

- Should the United States demand more of its Middle East allies in seeking regional stability?

# INTRODUCTION

> "God has ordered us to fight. For that reason the soldiers of ISIL are fighting. ... They will never leave fighting, even if only one soldier remains."
> —Abu Bakr al-Baghdadi

> "The only language understood by killers like this is the language of force."
> —Barack Obama

On August 8, 2014, the United States launched its first military action in Iraq since withdrawing troops from the nation in 2011. This time, American air strikes were aimed at destroying a violent fundamentalist group called Islamic State of Iraq and the Levant (ISIL)—also known as Islamic State or ISIS—that had gained control of large strategic sections of Iraq and Syria. In this chapter, we will consider several enduring tensions in American diplomatic and military policy, and examine two current controversial issues:

- Should the United States deploy ground troops to combat ISIL?

- Should the United States demand more of its Middle East allies in seeking regional stability?

**Why Is Combating ISIL Controversial?** For decades, American intervention in the Middle East has been a controversial and complicated issue. This diverse intersection of Africa, Asia, and Europe has long been of vital interest to the United States and the international community, as it is home to several important U.S. allies and nearly half of the proven crude oil reserves in the world, and it is the source of many cultural, ethnic, and religious conflicts and tensions.[1] The population of the Middle East is primarily Arab—a reference to those who speak Arabic as their first language—but it also comprises other, smaller cultural and ethnic groups, such as Persians, Turks, Jews, and Kurds. The region is overwhelmingly Muslim, but religiously diverse as well—the majority of Middle Eastern Muslims belong to the Sunni branch of Islam, while Muslims in Bahrain, Iran, and Iraq largely adhere to the Shia branch of Islam.

In recent years, the United States has employed a wide range of diplomatic and military tools to pursue its goals in the Middle East— methods that have generated controversy at home and abroad, while achieving mixed results. The Iraq War of 2003–2011, for example, toppled the brutal dictatorship of Saddam Hussein but cost the lives of 4,412 American soldiers, wounded 31,949 more, and fiercely divided public opinion.[2] In Syria, meanwhile, the United States resisted intervening militarily in the violent civil war that broke out in 2011—a conflict that had killed an estimated 210,000 people by early 2015[3] and displaced more than 3.9 million refugees.[4]

But in 2013, a radical and violent group of Sunni Muslim militants began seizing territory in Iraq and Syria, seeking to establish a caliphate—an Islamic state ruled by a single religious leader—under strict Islamic law. The group, which calls itself ISIL, has engaged in what the United Nations (UN) called "widespread ethnic and religious cleansing" of Christians, Shia Muslims, Yazidis, and other religious and ethnic groups.[5] ISIL militants have also gained international notoriety for their brutality—by using beheadings and mass killings in their efforts to spread fear and gain territory.

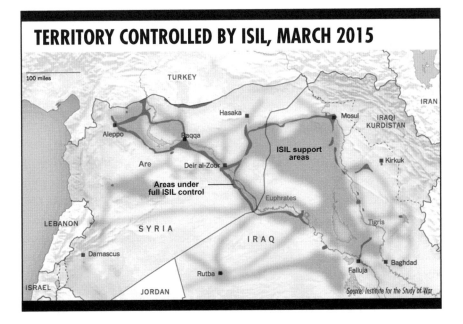

**TERRITORY CONTROLLED BY ISIL, MARCH 2015**

Although U.S. officials have been united in their denunciations of ISIL, they have failed to agree on several key policy points: Just how great a threat does ISIL pose to the United States? And does that threat outweigh the potential consequences of another American intervention in the Middle East?

**Why Is Combating ISIL So Complicated?** Ever since the morning of September 11, 2001—when 19 terrorists from the Islamic extremist group al-Qaeda hijacked four commercial airliners and killed 2,977 people in the deadliest act of terrorism in American history—the United States has dedicated much of its military strength and foreign policy to combating global terrorism.[6] But terrorism is not easy to prevent or to defend against, because terrorists are not officially aligned with national military

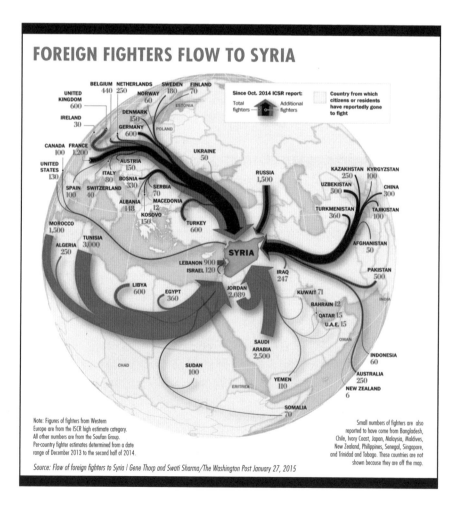

# FOREIGN FIGHTERS FLOW TO SYRIA

Since Oct. 2014 ICSR report:
Total fighters — Additional fighters

Country from which citizens or residents have reportedly gone to fight

BELGIUM 440  NETHERLANDS 250  SWEDEN 180  FINLAND 70
UNITED KINGDOM 600
NORWAY 60
DENMARK 150
IRELAND 30
GERMANY 600
CANADA 100  FRANCE 1,200
AUSTRIA 150
UNITED STATES 130
ITALY 80
BOSNIA 330
SPAIN 100  SWITZERLAND 40
SERBIA 70
ALBANIA 118  MACEDONIA 12
KOSOVO 150
MOROCCO 1,500
TUNISIA 3,000
ALGERIA 250
UKRAINE 50
RUSSIA 1,500
KAZAKHSTAN 250  KYRGYZSTAN 100
UZBEKISTAN 500
CHINA 300
TURKMENISTAN 360  TAJIKISTAN 100
TURKEY 600
SYRIA
LEBANON 900
ISRAEL 120
IRAQ 247
AFGHANISTAN 50
PAKISTAN 500
LIBYA 600
EGYPT 360
JORDAN 2,089
KUWAIT 71
BAHRAIN 12
QATAR 15
U.A.E. 15
SAUDI ARABIA 2,500
SUDAN 100
YEMEN 110
INDONESIA 60
AUSTRALIA 250
NEW ZEALAND 6
SOMALIA 70

Note: Figures of fighters from Western Europe are from the ISCR high estimate category. All other numbers are from the Soufan Group. Per-country fighter estimates determined from a date range of December 2013 to the second half of 2014.

Small numbers of fighters are also reported to have come from Bangladesh, Chile, Ivory Coast, Japan, Malaysia, Maldives, New Zealand, Philippines, Senegal, Singapore, and Trinidad and Tobago. These countries are not shown because they are off the map.

Source: Flow of foreign fighters to Syria | Gene Thorp and Swati Sharma/The Washington Post January 27, 2015

forces and therefore do not wage war on open battlefields. They instead maintain their power to intimidate government officials and civilians by acting unpredictably, through assassinations, bombings, kidnappings, and hijackings. In 2013 alone, the State Department recorded a total of 9,707 terrorist attacks worldwide, resulting in more than 17,800 deaths and nearly 32,500 injuries.[7]

ISIL has presented several new and significant counterterrorism challenges for the international community. By early 2015, ISIL militants controlled thousands of square miles of territory in Iraq and Syria—an area of land larger than some countries that included strategic oil fields, dams, border crossings, and cities. The organization was believed to be collecting millions of dollars each month from oil holdings, organized crime operations, and wealthy sympathizers. According to Central Intelligence Agency (CIA) estimates, ISIL encompassed as many as 31,500 militants by September 2014.[8] This included more than 20,000 foreign fighters by January 2015, nearly one-fifth of whom were from Western Europe.[9] By 2015, the United States and the international community were facing a ruthless, decentralized, and well-funded adversary that was seeking to expand its global reach.

## THE ONGOING DEBATE

### Should the United States use diplomacy or military force to combat international threats?

Over the years, the United States has faced a wide variety of international dangers, including attacks on, and threats against, U.S. citizens and allies; threats against democratic governments around the world; the proliferation of nuclear weapons; terrorism; and genocide and other humanitarian crises. The founding fathers foresaw Americans operating in this global landscape and empowered both the executive and legislative branches of government to conduct foreign policy by splitting war powers between Congress and the president. Congress has the power to declare war and is enabled by the Constitution to control and approve spending, including foreign aid and military budgets. The president has the power to direct war, negotiate international agreements, respond to foreign events, and make statements of foreign policy.

# TOOLS TO COMBAT FOREIGN THREATS

When dangers materialize outside the United States, the executive and legislative branches have used a variety of foreign policy tools to respond, including the following:

**Military Combat.** The United States can fight its enemies by deploying armed forces to carry out large-scale combat missions. For example, the United States invaded Iraq in 2003 after collecting intelligence that suggested the Hussein regime possessed weapons of mass destruction. The dictatorship fell, but a violent insurgency prolonged the American combat mission through 2011.

**Targeted Military Operations.** American armed forces also conduct limited actions, such as air strike campaigns and special forces operations. As civil war tore through Libya in 2011, for example, the United States supported the rebellion against long-time dictator Moammar Gaddafi by joining Operation Odyssey Dawn—a series of air strikes by members of the North Atlantic Treaty Organization (NATO). Gaddafi was captured and killed by Libyan rebel forces following a NATO air strike in October 2011.

**Military Support.** The government can deploy American military advisers to help train and equip local military forces. Following its invasion of Iraq, for example, the United States spent approximately $25 billion over eight years to help build and train a new Iraqi army.[10]

**Sanctions.** Sanctions are a diplomatic tool used to persuade a government to change its policies by restricting trade, financial assistance, or other commercial activity. Since 1979, for example, five American administrations have levied sanctions against Iran for supporting terrorism and developing a secret nuclear program. The United States also imposed sanctions on Syria's authoritarian leader, Bashar al-Assad, for violently cracking down on pro-democracy protests in 2011 and igniting a civil war.

**Diplomatic Negotiations.** The United States can seek to eliminate international threats by engaging in diplomatic negotiations, or discussions between high-level government representatives. Since 2009, for example, the United States has sought to dismantle the Iranian nuclear program by engaging in talks with Iran and the five permanent members of the UN Security Council plus Germany (P5+1).

**Foreign Aid.** Approximately one percent of the United States' annual budget goes toward various foreign aid programs, which include initiatives to improve public health, spur economic development, bolster humanitarian assistance, and aid democratic elections.[11] Between 2011 and early 2015, for example, the United States gave more than $3 billion in humanitarian assistance to those affected by the Syrian civil war.[12]

For centuries, American policymakers have debated the effectiveness of these various diplomatic and military actions. And as ISIL gained strength and territory, the president and Congress pondered how to respond.

## THE CURRENT CONTROVERSY
### Should the United States deploy ground troops to combat ISIL?

On August 8, 2014, President Barack Obama launched the United States' first military action in Iraq in nearly three years—a series of limited air strikes against ISIL targets to protect American personnel. But in the following months, as ISIL militants released videos showing the beheadings of American journalists James Foley and Steven Sotloff, and British aid workers David Haines and Alan Henning, the president:

- Authorized expanded air strikes in Iraq and Syria beginning in September 2014.

- Deployed an additional 1,500 non-combat military personnel to train Iraqi forces in November 2014, bringing the total number of American troops in Iraq to nearly 3,000.[13]

- Asked Congress to authorize military personnel to train and equip moderate Syrian rebels who oppose ISIL. In spring 2015, the Pentagon said it would begin deploying 400 trainers and hundreds of troops to train and equip Syrian rebels in Qatar, Saudi Arabia, and Turkey.[14]

President Obama made it clear, however, that the United States would not engage in a ground war against ISIL. "I want the American people to understand how this effort will be different from the wars in Iraq and Afghanistan," he said in September 2014. "It will not involve American combat troops fighting on foreign soil."[15] Critics of such a ground war believe the United States would only be dragged into another Middle Eastern quagmire—all to fix a problem that must be solved by regional powers such as Saudi Arabia and Turkey.

But others insist the battle against ISIL can be won only with American boots on the ground—and troops that are uniquely skilled in counterinsurgency. They believe that if the United States does not commit fully to fighting this genocidal threat, it will only erase the democratic gains that Americans fought for in Iraq and destabilize the entire Middle East.

## Should the United States deploy ground troops to combat ISIL?

### YES: The U.S. military should intervene to stop this dire global threat.

Since late 2014, ISIL militants have released videos showing the brutal executions of American aid worker Peter Kassig, Japanese hostages Haruna Yukawa and Kenji Goto, Egyptian Christians, and hundreds of Syrian soldiers. ISIL militants killed Muath al-Kaseasbeh, a 26-year-old Jordanian pilot, by confining him to a cage and burning him alive. And in March 2015, ISIL released photographs of men in Syria being thrown from buildings because they were suspected of being gay.

Yet these atrocities are only a fraction of the war crimes committed by ISIL, which killed an estimated 8,493 Iraqi civilians and wounded 15,782 more in the first eight months of 2014 alone. In the face of such a dire threat to human rights and political stability, the United States must enhance its military response by deploying ground troops to Iraq and Syria.

"I think if American and Western values are in jeopardy and U.S. troops working with the coalition force is how you stop ISIS, I think the bulk of the American people are going to say, 'Thank you, Mr. President, for standing up for our values. Thank you for stopping this face of evil,'" said former Governor Rick Perry, R-Texas.[17] And a Quinnipiac University poll released in March 2015 supported his point: Americans favored using ground troops to fight ISIL by an overwhelming two-to-one margin.[18]

President Obama's strategy, however, has largely failed to stop ISIL from gaining territory, murdering innocent people, recruiting foreign fighters, and reversing the democratic progress so many Americans fought and died for in Iraq. "Frankly, I know of no military expert who believes we are going to defeat ISIL with this present strategy," said Senator John McCain, R-Ariz., chairman of the Senate Committee on Armed Services. "We may be able to 'contain,' but to actually defeat ISIL is going to require more boots on the ground, more vigorous strikes, more special forces, further arming the Kurdish *peshmerga* forces, and creating a no-fly zone and buffer zone in Syria."[19]

And Americans cannot settle for merely containing ISIL. As civil war broke out in Syria in 2011, the absence of strong American support for the anti-Assad rebels created chaos—allowing extremists such as ISIL to fill the void. We cannot repeat this mistake. If the United States is truly the leader of the free world, it must use its military—uniquely skilled in counterinsurgency tactics in the wake of the Iraq War—to eliminate this growing global threat.

## NO: Americans cannot afford another lengthy war and must encourage a regional solution.

Between 2003 and 2011, as American ground troops fought to liberate Iraq from the Hussein regime and a violent insurgency, 4,412 U.S. soldiers lost their lives and another 31,949 were wounded.[20] In the 13 years American ground troops fought to eradicate the terrorist threat in Afghanistan, 2,215 U.S. soldiers were killed and another 20,026 were wounded.[21] And if the United States sends ground troops to Iraq and Syria to fight ISIL, the only consequences Americans can truly count on are casualties.

The eight-year Iraq War proved that American ground troops are not a quick fix for violent insurgencies—and that open-ended and unfocused military campaigns only risk the lives of soldiers while solidifying anti-American sentiments. "My fear, even before we begin the invasion ... is that large conventional forces on the ground can win a big, quick, conventional victory, but then you're in the midst of a political and insurgency nightmare, which happened in Iraq," said Senator Jack Reed, D-R.I., the ranking Democrat on the Senate Committee on Armed Services.[22]

Although there is no denying the shocking brutality of ISIL, it cannot fall solely on the shoulders of U.S. troops to combat these violent extremists. "After a decade of massive ground deployments, it is more effective to use our unique capabilities in support of partners on the ground so they can secure their own countries' futures," President Obama said in September 2014. "When we do things alone and ... the people of those countries aren't doing it for themselves, as soon as we leave, we start getting the same problems."[23]

The United States has already implemented a comprehensive strategy to combat ISIL—one that engages international and regional partners while utilizing a variety of diplomatic and military tools. "In addition to the military campaign, it will be equally important for the global coalition to dry up ISIL's illicit funding, to stop the foreign fighters who carry passports from countries around the world, including the United States, [and] to continue to deliver urgently needed humanitarian assistance," said Secretary of State John Kerry.[24]

Furthermore, the United States' strategy has produced positive results. In March 2015, Army General Lloyd Austin announced that the American-led coalition had killed more than 8,500 ISIL fighters since air strikes began in August 2014. "The fact is that he can no longer do what he did at the outset, which is to seize and to hold new territory," Austin said.[25]

# THE ONGOING DEBATE

### Should the United States act alone or in cooperation with international partners to defuse global threats?

Just as the United States has historically employed a variety of diplomatic and military tools against international threats, it has also worked in varying levels of cooperation with other nations. Over the course of American history, the United States has pursued policies of both unilateralism and multilateralism in its foreign affairs.

**Unilateralism.** "It is our one true policy to steer clear of permanent alliances with any portion of the foreign world," President George Washington said in his 1796 farewell address. "It is unnecessary and would be unwise to extend them."[26] The words of the first American president have helped promote the practice of unilateralism—the idea that nations must rely on their own resources and abilities, rather than depend on foreign alliances, to carry out global affairs. Unilateral action, which allows a government to act without the approval or support of other nations, has been employed in the past when leaders have believed international cooperation to be unnecessary or unhelpful, or when nations have been attacked or faced immediate national security threats.

Arab allies and U.S.-coordinated air strikes drove ISIL to retreat from Kobani, Syria.

At times, the United States has opted to act largely on its own when responding to international crises. The Vietnam War, for example, was a unilateral American action aimed at stopping the spread of communism around the globe. And in the aftermath of the 9/11 attacks, the United States responded by leading the invasion of Afghanistan in 2001, while also supplying a majority of the fighting force and military resources. This practice of acting largely alone has attracted both support and criticism from inside and outside the United States. Advocates of American unilateralism have argued that no other nation should have veto power over an action considered by the United States, especially when it relates to national security. Unilateralism has also allowed the United States to swiftly and forcefully act when other nations could not or would not. In 1999, for example, the United States and NATO intervened in Kosovo to stop human rights abuses because China and Russia used their veto powers to prevent the UN Security Council from doing so. Critics, however, believe unilateral action ignores the lasting benefits of global cooperation, and encourages arrogant policies that fail to serve the international community.

**Multilateralism.** The complex and interconnected nature of the modern world has led some nations to embrace the practice of multilateralism—the idea that multiple countries should work together to address specific issues. Multilateral action requires nations to communicate and compromise with one another to create cohesive policies, and to cede sovereignty in order to ensure international alliance and concerted action.

The United States is a member of several international bodies that seek multilateral cooperation, such as the UN, the World Bank, and NATO, and has taken part in numerous multilateral actions. Since 2009, for example, President Obama has sought a multilateral agreement with the P5+1 nations to stop the Iranian nuclear program. Beginning in 2015, the United States also partnered with Qatar, Saudi Arabia, and Turkey on a joint initiative to train and equip Syrian rebel forces.

Similar to unilateralism, American multilateral action has achieved mixed success throughout history. Advocates argue that international cooperation is necessary in order to address certain regional and global issues, such as environmental quality, international trade, nuclear proliferation, drug and human trafficking, the spread of infectious diseases, and international terrorism. Proponents also note that multilateral actions reduce costs for the United States and legitimize American actions. But detractors argue that multilateral action can be a painstakingly slow and ineffective process—one that depends too heavily on unreliable partners and disinterested parties.

And as the threat of ISIL rapidly expanded in the Middle East in 2014, Americans had to choose once more whether to lead the response—or whether to demand more of their regional allies.

# THE CURRENT CONTROVERSY

## Should the United States demand more of its Middle East allies in seeking regional stability?

Although the Middle East has long been complicated terrain for the United States, it is also home to several important allies who have assisted Americans in the fight against ISIL. Saudi Arabia, for example, has contributed warplanes to strike targets in Syria and agreed in 2014 to help host the training of moderate Syrian rebels to fight ISIL. In 2015, the Saudis also began building a 600-mile fence along the kingdom's border with Iraq, aimed at keeping militants out.[27]

Turkey is the sole member of NATO in the Middle East, meaning it—like the United States—has agreed to help safeguard the freedom and security of other NATO members through political and military means. And because Turkey shares a border of more than 700 miles with Iraq and Syria, it has also taken several actions to help defeat ISIL militants. In November 2014, the Turks began training Kurdish *peshmerga* fighters in northern Iraq to help them combat ISIL; in February 2015, they signed an agreement with the United States to host, train, and equip moderate Syrian rebels, and to match the number of military trainers provided by the United States; and by early 2015, Turkish security

ISIL militants destroy ancient artifacts at Iraq's Nineveh Museum.

officials had enhanced their searches for possible jihadists traveling through Turkey and had compiled a no-entry list of roughly 10,000 names.[28]

But as of early 2015, Turkey had largely resisted intervening militarily in the fight against ISIL, leading some American policymakers to demand more of the United States' regional allies. Supporters of an increased allied effort argue that nations such as Turkey have vast— and relatively unused—military resources, and have a greater interest than the United States in promoting regional stability. However, opponents believe that increasing reliance on regional allies—many of whom have priorities other than defeating ISIL—will only slow and complicate the American effort, while placing an important struggle in the hands of those who cannot be trusted to represent American and global interests.

## Should the United States demand more of its Middle East allies in seeking regional stability?

### YES: Middle East allies must accept their regional responsibilities and utilize their vast military resources.

By January 2015, an estimated 20,730 foreign fighters had joined the ranks of ISIL. Although these militant extremists came from all over the globe, a majority of them had one thing in common—they had reached Iraq and Syria by traveling through Turkey.[30]

"It's very easy—you just walk for five minutes and you are in Syria," said Maher, an Iraqi smuggler who charged as little as $20 in early 2015 to transport foreigners across the Turkish border. "There are a thousand roads, it is all open."[31] And it is not only foreign fighters who are freely crossing the border—ISIL has used the porous Turkish frontier to import military supplies and export oil to sell for revenue.

"Completely shutting down the long border may be impossible, but given the country's large military and well-regarded intelligence service, it is inexcusable that Turkey is not doing a better job," the *New York Times* editorial board wrote. "Turkey should also be making military bases and troops available to the American-led coalition."[32]

Since 2014, the United States has led a comprehensive effort against ISIL; yet Turkey, a NATO ally with a large and skilled military, has offered little tangible assistance. "Turkey could destroy ISIS within a couple of hours using its air force and even military force," said Hüseyin Bagci, a professor at Middle East Technical University.[33] But Turkish officials have done little more than train Kurdish and Syrian fighters and make modest improvements to border and travel security. Turkish forces even went so far as to initially block the transport of reinforcements to Kurdish fighters defending Kobani, a besieged Syrian town on the Turkish border, in late 2014.

Like Turkey, Saudi Arabia has much more at stake than the United States in the struggle against ISIL, and therefore, must play a leading role in the international effort. "The holy cities of Mecca and Medina, the heartland of Arabia, is almost irresistible to Salafi jihadists like ISIS. It is their home base," said Gregory Gause, a Saudi expert at Texas A&M University. "And so I think that there is a sense where ISIS is shooting at Saudi Arabia as an ultimate goal."[34]

If the international community is going to defeat ISIL, it cannot do so without the robust participation of regional powers such as Saudi Arabia and Turkey. The Saudi and Turkish people, who share borders with the countries being swallowed by ISIL, have much more to lose in this fight than the United States—and they should act like it.

# NO: Increased allied involvement will only complicate and threaten the U.S. mission.

In February 2015, James Clapper, the director of national intelligence, was asked in his testimony before Congress if he was optimistic that Turkey would do more to fight ISIL. "No, I'm not," he said. "I think Turkey has other priorities and other interests."[35]

Although the United States is largely focused on combating ISIL, its regional allies do not necessarily share its goals. In Turkey, for example, officials have suggested they are much more concerned with their long-time opposition to the Assad regime and Kurdish autonomy in Syria—competing priorities that have already complicated U.S. efforts. As civil war erupted in Syria in 2011, Turkey opened its borders to Syrian refugees and rebels in order to hasten Assad's fall—but many rebels eventually joined forces with ISIL.[36] "[The Turks] were so determined to take down Assad and essentially have a proxy Sunni-Shia war, what did they do?" Vice President Joe Biden asked. "They poured hundreds of millions of dollars and thousands of tons of weapons into anyone who would fight against Assad—except that the people who were being supplied were al-Nusra and al-Qaeda and the extremist elements of jihadis coming from other parts of the world."[37]

With Turkey so focused on Syria, the United States would likely need to commit to deeper involvement in the Syrian civil war to secure additional Turkish support—a dangerous prospect for a nation still recovering from the Iraq War. "For the Turks, they want a strategy that involves fighting and getting rid of the Assad regime," said Andrew Tabler, a fellow at the Washington Institute for Near East Studies.[38]

The further involvement of other allies also presents complications in the fight against ISIL. In Saudi Arabia, for example, there is some sympathy in the large conservative Sunni Muslim population for ISIL's efforts to take down the Assad regime and the Iraqi Shiite government. And wealthy individuals in Qatar—another American ally—have been among ISIL's most important financiers.

Therefore, instead of compromising the mission against ISIL, the United States must lead and accept the support its allies are able to provide. "The United States has capabilities that no other state or group in the world has, and that is why we must lead this effort," wrote Frederick Kagan, a scholar at the American Enterprise Institute, and Kimberly Kagan, president of the Institute for the Study of War. "The partial commitment of threatened states and groups in the region is not a reason for America to hold back. It's proof that America must lead."[39]

# CONCLUSION

The use of ground troops against ISIL and increased cooperation with regional allies are only two examples of the recent debates Americans have engaged in over counterterrorism policy. With renewed stability in the Middle East far from assured, American policymakers will undoubtedly continue to debate how to defeat ISIL—and which policies best achieve that goal.

1   British Petroleum. *BP Statistical Review of World Energy 2014*. Jun. 2014. Web. 24 Feb. 2015.

2   "Operation Iraqi Freedom (OIF) U.S. Casualty Status." U.S. Department of Defense. 16 Mar. 2015. Web. 17 Mar. 2015.

3   Al-Khalidi, Suleiman. "Syrian Death Toll Now Exceeds 210,000: Rights Group." Reuters. 7 Feb. 2015. Web. 17 Mar. 2015.

4   United Nations High Commissioner for Refugees. "Syria Regional Refugee Response." 17 Mar. 2015. Web. 17 Mar. 2015.

5   UN News Centre. "Iraqi Civilians Suffering 'Horrific' Persecution, Ethnic Cleansing — UN Rights Chief." 25 Aug, 2014. Web. 17 Mar. 2015.

6   CNN. "September 11 Fast Facts." 8 Sep. 2014. Web. 17 Mar. 2015.

7   U.S. State Department, Bureau of Counterterrorism. "National Consortium for the Study of Terrorism and Responses to Terrorism: Annex of Statistical Information." Web. 17 Mar. 2015.

8   Miller, Greg, and Craig Whitlock. "U.S. Weakens al-Qaeda Groups Around the World but Hasn't Wiped Any Out." *Washington Post*. 11 Sep. 2014. Web. 17 Mar. 2015.

9   Neumann, Peter. "Foreign Fighter Total in Syria/Iraq Now Exceeds 20,000; Surpasses Afghanistan Conflict in the 1980s." International Centre for the Study of Radicalisation and Political Violence. Jan. 2015. Web. 17 Mar. 2015.

10  Morris, Loveday. "The U.S. Military Is Back Training Troops in Iraq, but It's a Little Different This Time." *Washington Post*. 8 Jan. 2015. Web. 17 Mar. 2015.

11  Rutsch, Poncie. "Guess How Much Of Uncle Sam's Money Goes To Foreign Aid. Guess Again!" NPR. 10 Feb. 2015. Web. 17 Mar. 2015.

12  United States Agency for International Development. "Syria." Web. 17 Mar. 2015.

13  Carney, Jordain. "Obama to Send More Troops to Iraq in Fight Against Islamic State." *National Journal*. 7 Nov. 2014. Web. 17 Mar. 2015.

14  Payne, Ed. "Pentagon: U.S. to Begin to Train and Equip Moderate Syria Rebels." CNN. 16 Jan. 2015. Web. 17 Mar. 2015.

15  Eilperin, Juliet, and Ed O'Keefe. "Obama Announces 'Broad Coalition' to Fight Islamic State Extremist Group." *Washington Post*. 10 Sep. 2014. Web. 17 Mar. 2015.

16  Smith, Samuel. "UN Report on ISIS: 24,000 Killed, Injured by Islamic State; Children Used as Soldiers, Women Sold as Sex Slaves." 9 Oct. 2014. Web. 17 Mar. 2015.

[17] Perry, Rick. "State of the Union." Interview. CNN. 1 Mar. 2015. Web. 17 Mar. 2015.

[18] Knox, Olivier. "New Poll Finds Major American Support for Sending U.S. Ground Troops to Fight Islamic State." Yahoo News. 4 Mar. 2015. Web. 17 Mar. 2015.

[19] Miles, Kathleen. "McCain Will Push For Ground Troops in Iraq, Syria If GOP Wins the Senate." Huffington Post. 20 Oct. 2014. Web. 17 Mar. 2015.

[20] U.S. Department of Defense. "Operation Iraqi Freedom (OIF) U.S. Casualty Status." 16 Mar. 2015. Web. 17 Mar. 2015.

[21] U.S. Department of Defense. "Operation Enduring Freedom (OEF) U.S. Casualty Status." 16 Mar. 2015. Web. 17 Mar. 2015.

[22] Reed, Jack. "Morning Joe." Interview. MSNBC. 11 Sep. 2014. Web. 17 Mar. 2015.

[23] Acosta, Jim, Kevin Liptak, and Josh Levs. "Obama, Kerry: No U.S. Troops Will Be Sent into Combat Against ISIS in Iraq, Syria." CNN. 17 Sep. 2014. Web. 17 Mar. 2015.

[24] Taylor, Guy. "Kerry to Senate: No Ground Troops Against Islamic State." *Washington Times.* 17 Sep. 2014. Web. 17 Mar. 2015.

[25] "U.S. General Says 8,500 Islamic State Fighters Killed in Iraq." Associated Press. 3 Mar. 2015. Web. 17 Mar. 2015.

[26] Washington, George. Farewell address. 1796. Yale Law School Lillian Goldman Law Library. Web. 17 Mar. 2015.

[27] NPR. "Saudi Arabia Builds Iraq Border Wall To Protect Against ISIS." 20 Jan. 2015. Web. 17 Mar. 2015.

[28] Arango, Tim, and Eric Schmitt. "A Path to ISIS, Through a Porous Turkish Border." *New York Times.* 9 Mar. 2015. Web. 17 Mar. 2015.

[29] Neumann, Peter. "Foreign Fighter Total in Syria/Iraq Now Exceeds 20,000; Surpasses Afghanistan Conflict in the 1980s." International Centre for the Study of Radicalisation and Political Violence. Jan. 2015. Web. 17 Mar. 2015.

[30] Arango, Tim, and Eric Schmitt. "A Path to ISIS, Through a Porous Turkish Border." *New York Times.* 9 Mar. 2015. Web. 17 Mar. 2015.

[31] Trofimov, Yaroslav. "Porous Syria-Turkey Border Poses Challenge in Fight Against Islamic State." *Wall Street Journal.* 19 Feb. 2015. Web. 17 Mar. 2015.

[32] New York Times Editorial Board. "Turkey's Drift From NATO." *New York Times.* 13 Mar. 2015. Web. 17 Mar. 2015.

[33] "Turkey can fight ISIS without external assistance." RT. 7 Oct. 2014. Web. 17 Mar. 2015.

[34] "Saudi Arabia Builds Iraq Border Wall To Protect Against ISIS." NPR. 20 Jan. 2015. Web. 17 Mar. 2015.

[35] Arango, Tim, and Eric Schmitt. "A Path to ISIS, Through a Porous Turkish Border." *New York Times.* 9 Mar. 2015. Web. 17 Mar. 2015.

[36] New York Times Editorial Board. "Turkey's Drift From NATO." *New York Times.* 13 Mar. 2015. Web. 17 Mar. 2015.

[37] Logiurato, Brett. "Turkey's President Demands Biden Apologize over Comments about ISIS." Business Insider. 4 Oct. 2014. Web. 17 Mar. 2015.

[38] Rogin, Josh. "Turkey Still Won't Fight Islamic State." BloombergView. 3 Mar. 2015. Web. 17 Mar. 2015.

[39] Kagan, Frederick, and Kimberly Kagan. "In Fight Against ISIS, the U.S. Must Lead, and Not Rely on Allies." *New York Times.* 16 Sep. 2014. Web. 17 Mar. 2015.

# WEAPONS PROLIFERATION

## CURRENT CONTROVERSIES

- Should the United States continue negotiations with Iran about its nuclear ambitions?

- Should the United States continue to include military equipment and technology in its foreign aid packages?

# INTRODUCTION

> "Nuclear disarmament and nonproliferation are not utopian ideals. They are critical to global peace and security."
>
> —Ban Ki-Moon

> "We maintain the peace through our strength; weakness only invites aggression."
>
> —Ronald Reagan

Ever since the end of World War II, the world has witnessed the widespread proliferation of new weapons and military technology. As the world's leading military and economic power, the United States is in a unique position to help create policies that control just how far these weapons can spread. In this chapter, we will consider several enduring tensions in American policy regarding the proliferation of nuclear and non-nuclear arms, and examine two current controversial issues:

- Should the United States continue negotiations with Iran about its nuclear ambitions?

- Should the United States continue to include artillery and military technology in its foreign aid packages?

**Why Is Weapons Proliferation Controversial?** Over the course of the Cold War (1947–1991), the United States and the Soviet Union vastly expanded their stockpiles of both conventional and nuclear weapons. In the late 20th century, each superpower continuously sought to develop superior military technologies, and by the 1980s, both the United States and the Soviet Union possessed between 30,000 and 40,000 nuclear warheads apiece—enough to destroy the world hundreds of times over.[1]

Today, there are nine nations that possess nuclear weapons.[2] Of these, China, France, Russia, the United Kingdom, and the United States have signed the Treaty on the Non-Proliferation of Nuclear Weapons (NPT), while India, Israel, and Pakistan have not. North Korea, meanwhile, withdrew from the NPT in 2003, after it was confronted by the United States for operating a secret nuclear weapons program it had agreed to dismantle in 1994. The rapid spread of nuclear arms to new nations since the end of World War II included some nations in dangerous and unstable parts of the world. For this reason, the United States has made it a priority to prevent the spread of these weapons and materials to hostile actors, especially terrorist organizations.

Conventional weapons—from rifles to fighter jets—have also become more common over the past several decades. During the Cold War, the United States and the Soviet Union vied for "spheres of influence" in the developing world, and covertly provided arms to various pro-Western or pro-Soviet governments and paramilitary groups. When the Soviet Union collapsed in 1991, Russia and many other former Soviet bloc nations began to sell their extensive arsenals to help pay down their debts.

Although the Cold War has come to an end, the United States continues to provide military aid to many of the nations it supports, often in the form of grants to buy weapons from American manufacturers.[3] While much of this aid has been used effectively to ensure regional stability and to protect American interests, some policymakers have criticized these arms packages for contributing to violence around the world.

Moving forward, American officials must weigh various competing interests and worldviews when crafting arms-related policies:

- *Competing National Interest Priorities.* The debate over whether or not to provide arms and military technology to foreign governments requires American leaders to prioritize and balance economic, ideological, and security interests. Is it better to maintain political and economic stability in fragile parts of the world, even if the leaders we support are undemocratic?

- *Competing Worldviews.* The debate over how to manage weapons proliferation is rooted in the ideology and philosophy of international relations. In crafting foreign policy, which is more important: maintaining fidelity to national values or responding to international realities and events in a practical and effective manner? Should nations act as if they are engaged in an international competition for power, or should they act cooperatively as members of a global community? Under what circumstances can and should the United States intervene in the affairs of other nations?

# WHY IS NONPROLIFERATION POLICY SO COMPLICATED?

Weapons proliferation is perhaps the most serious foreign policy issue facing the United States, but the formation of nonproliferation policies is complicated by several factors.

**Classified Information.** Because most government programs related to nuclear weapons and military aid are classified, only a select few government officials understand the full scope of American policies.

**Long-Term Effects of Military Aid Packages.** Corruption is often an issue when the United States provides military technologies and arms to foreign governments. In the past, some recipient governments have attempted to turn profits by re-selling American weapons to the highest bidder; frequently, foreign leaders pocket the money made by selling these weapons.[4]

Furthermore, because many weapons are durable goods that can function for decades, the United States has little control over what happens to donated weapons once a conflict ends or a government no longer needs them. In the 1980s, for example, the United States covertly supplied weapons and ammunition to *mujahideen* militias fighting in Afghanistan against the Soviet Union. Twenty years later, many of these fighters had joined the ranks of the Taliban, and were using the same weapons against American troops.[5]

**Rise of Non-State Actors.** As non-state actors outside the authority of a formal government play a more prominent role in international relations, many governments fear nuclear materials could soon fall into the hands of terrorist organizations. For this reason, American and other Western leaders have a vital interest in controlling the supply of nuclear materials and technologies, as well as which nations have access to them.

**Moral and Ethical Questions.** There is an ongoing debate over the responsibility of the United States when it comes to the development of nuclear weapons and technology. Some people believe the United States lacks the authority to dictate which countries should or should not obtain nuclear weapons, and have criticized Americans for imposing harsh restrictions on Iran while allowing the covert Israeli nuclear program to go forward. Others believe that as the only nation to have used atomic bombs in warfare, the United States has a moral obligation to do all it can to prevent nuclear proliferation and to reduce the global supply of nuclear arms.

**Domestic Politics.** The sale of arms and ammunition is a multibillion-dollar industry,[6] and changes in military aid policies have a profound impact on American manufacturing. Defense contractors who produce weapons and military equipment provide thousands of jobs and are highly influential in Washington, D.C., meaning any official decision regarding weapons and military technology also significantly affects domestic politics.[7]

# THE ONGOING DEBATE

## How should the United States deal with Iran's nuclear ambitions?

Ever since the Islamic Revolution took hold of Iran in 1979, the United States has made it a priority to confront the perceived threat Iran poses to American interests.[8] Throughout the 1980s and 1990s, Iranian support for militant and terrorist groups in the Middle East was seen as the most significant threat to American interests—and by the early 2000s, concerns arose over a clandestine Iranian nuclear program. If Iran becomes a nuclear power, many American and regional officials fear it would exert a far more assertive role in the Middle East, while providing greater support for governments and organizations that threaten the United States. Some Americans argue that Iranian nuclear ambitions could produce a nuclear arms race in one of the most volatile regions of the world, and many Israelis in particular view an Iranian nuclear weapon as a threat to their very existence. Other leaders worry Iran may transfer nuclear technology to extremist groups or rogue nations.[9]

But Iranian leaders deny they are trying to achieve nuclear weapons capability and assert that Iran's nuclear program is purely for medical and energy-related usage. They argue that uranium enrichment is Iran's "right" as a party to the NPT. Some Iranian leaders have also stated that nuclear weapons are inconsistent with their ideology, citing Supreme Leader Ali Khamenei's 2003 *fatwa*—or religious ruling—that nuclear weapons are un-Islamic.[10]

Yet since the late 1990s, the United States has led a broad coalition of Western powers to place economic pressure—largely in the form of sanctions—on Iran to stop its support of terrorist organizations and to prevent it from advancing its nuclear program.

# AMERICAN-IRANIAN RELATIONS: A BRIEF TIMELINE

### 1953: Prime Minister Ousted in Coup

The U.S. Central Intelligence Agency (CIA) backs a plan, coordinated with British intelligence, to overthrow Iranian Prime Minister Mohammed Mossadegh due to concerns over petroleum exports and Mossadegh's relationship with the Soviet Union. Mohammad Reza Shah Pahlavi becomes the U.S.-backed authoritarian monarch.

### January 1979: The Shah Flees Iran

The U.S.-backed shah is forced to flee Iran following demonstrations against his increasingly authoritarian and secular rule by religious opponents. Within months, the exiled cleric Ayatollah Ruhollah Khomeini, who referred to the United States as the "Great Satan," becomes supreme leader of the new Islamic Republic of Iran.

### November 1979: The Iran Hostage Crisis

After President Jimmy Carter allows the shah into the United States for cancer treatment, a group of Iranian revolutionaries occupy the American embassy in Tehran and take 52 Americans hostage for 444 days. In April 1980, a failed rescue attempt results in the deaths of eight American servicemen, and shortly after, the United States severs diplomatic relations with Iran. The hostage crisis ends with the signing of the Algiers Accords in Algeria on January 19, 1981.

### 1983: Hezbollah Bombings in Beirut

Hezbollah—a terrorist organization backed by Iran—is implicated in the bombing of the American embassy in Lebanon, killing 17 Americans, and the bombing of a Marine compound, killing 241 American servicemen.

### 1986: Iran-Contra Affair

It is revealed that the United States covertly provided weapons to Iran to fund anti-communist forces in Nicaragua and to help free American hostages held by Hezbollah. President Ronald Reagan confirms the weapons sale but denies it was part of an exchange for hostages.

### 1988: Iranian Airbus Shot Down

The *USS Vincennes* shoots down an Iranian commercial airliner, killing 290 civilians from six nations. The United States says the Airbus A300 was mistaken for a fighter jet outside the civilian air corridor.

### 1995: Clinton Administration Embargo

President Bill Clinton imposes a total embargo on dealings with Iran by American companies.

### 2002: "Axis of Evil"

President George W. Bush describes Iran, Iraq, and North Korea as an "axis of evil" in his State of the Union address.

### 2002: Nuclear Program Revealed

An Iranian opposition group reveals secret nuclear facilities in the country, including a uranium enrichment plant and a heavy water reactor. The United States accuses Iran of developing a clandestine nuclear weapons program, which Iran denies.[11]

### 2005: Ahmadinejad Calls for Destruction of Israel

Iranian President Mahmoud Ahmadinejad repeats a quote from Ayatollah Khomeini that Israel "must be wiped out from the map of the world." He says, "And God willing, with the force of God behind it, we shall soon experience a world without the United States and Zionism."[12]

### 2006: Uranium Enrichment

Ahmadinejad announces that Iran has enriched uranium for the first time. The United Nations (UN) Security Council unanimously imposes sanctions on Iran and broadens them in 2008.

### 2010: Sanctions Expanded Again

Ahmadinejad announces Iran has produced uranium enriched to 20 percent purity—a short step from bomb-grade material. The United States, the European Union (EU), and the UN expand sanctions.[13]

### 2013: IAEA Reports on Enriched Uranium

After several years of dead-end international negotiations to end the Iranian nuclear program, the International Atomic Energy Agency (IAEA) concludes that Iran has roughly 410 pounds of uranium enriched to 20 percent purity.[14]

# THE CURRENT CONTROVERSY

## Should the United States continue negotiations with Iran about its nuclear ambitions?

For years, nuclear negotiations between Iran and Western powers ended in disagreement and frustration. But in 2013, the more moderate President Hassan Rouhani was elected to replace Ahmadinejad. And although Rouhani asserted that Iran would maintain its nuclear program, the diplomatic tone largely changed. President Barack Obama even telephoned Rouhani on September 27, 2013, marking the highest-level contact between the United States and Iran since 1979.[15]

The Obama administration has imposed sanctions on Iran, but in 2009, the administration announced it would also fully participate in talks between Iran and the five permanent members of the UN Security Council plus Germany (P5+1)—a change from its previous policy requiring Iran to meet UN demands first. On November 24, 2013, Iran and the P5+1 nations reached a temporary nuclear agreement that halted the expansion of the Iranian nuclear program in exchange for modest sanctions relief. And by April 2015, negotiators announced a tentative framework for a permanent agreement to cut and monitor the Iranian nuclear program and gradually lift sanctions.

Iranians celebrate the tentative agreement on nuclear arms reached between the P5+1 and Iran in April 2015.

AP PHOTO/VAHID SALEMI

But policymakers remained deeply divided over the wisdom of seeking a final deal with Iran.[16]

Supporters claim a comprehensive agreement could significantly improve relations between the United States and Iran, while ensuring that Iranians are unable to develop a nuclear weapon. But many opponents in the Persian Gulf, Israel, and elsewhere in the Middle East worry that easing sanctions on Iran will only enhance its capacity to support terrorist groups and regimes that oppose American interests. Furthermore, some critics—most notably Israeli Prime Minister Benjamin Netanyahu—have taken issue with the preliminary terms of the proposed agreement, which would possibly allow Iran to continue developing uranium in the future if certain conditions are met.[17]

### Should the United States continue negotiations with Iran about its nuclear ambitions?

## YES: We are closer than ever to achieving a peaceful resolution to our nuclear disputes.

The United States cannot achieve international peace by isolating and undermining opposing nations with the hope that they will eventually change their policies. Our troubled history with Iran cannot and should not prevent us from sitting down with Iranian leaders to try to reach a compromise over their nuclear program. The global stakes are simply too high.

The current round of P5+1 negotiations is significant not only because of how close the United States is to securing an equitable nuclear agreement, but also because of the broad coalition involved—including Russia and China, two of Iran's strongest allies. "These six nations came together in 2006 to address Iran's nuclear program and to work as a unified front to try to resolve with diplomacy the concerns that Iran's nuclear program is aimed at developing nuclear weapons," said Shlomo Brom, a fellow at the Center for American Progress.[18] This coalition was not assembled overnight, and if the current negotiations fail, it may take years or even decades to bring these nations back together. For this reason, policymakers should think carefully about the long-term consequences of their opposition to P5+1 negotiations.

Ultimately, there are only two ways to stop Iran from obtaining a nuclear weapon: negotiation or military action. "The alternative to not having a deal is losing inspections, and an Iran ever closer to having the fissile material to manufacture a weapon," a senior White House official said.[19] And at a time when the United States is still reeling politically and financially from the wars in Afghanistan and Iraq, any sort of military strike against Iran could be extremely costly. Iran, unlike many of the United States' recent military opponents, has a large, well-trained, and well-equipped military with the capability to retaliate against American regional interests and allies. The rise of Islamic State of Iraq and the Levant (ISIL) has shown us what can happen in the aftermath of war in the Middle East; therefore, can we really afford to fan the flames in a region already wracked by conflict and extremism?

The United States will never be able to transform Iran into an open and free democracy; only the Iranian people can do that. Average Iranian citizens harbor no ill will toward the people of the United States, and in fact, many are eager to interact with Americans and to build better relations between our two nations. This nuclear agreement is not the end of tension between the United States and Iran, but it will be an important first step toward greater cooperation and peace.

## NO: Iran is simply buying time and will never agree to an equitable resolution.

A nuclear-armed Iran is, in the minds of most American foreign policy experts, the greatest potential threat to our national security. Since 1979, Iran has held our diplomats hostage, covertly attacked our assets overseas, and collaborated with terrorists who are bent on our destruction. Under the current circumstances, there is no good reason why the United States should sit down with Iran to negotiate in good faith.

It is no secret that Iran has a history of collaboration with terrorist groups, most notably Hezbollah in Lebanon. "Iran has been the country that has been in many ways a kind of central banker for terrorism in important regions like Lebanon through Hezbollah in the Middle East, in the Palestinian Territories, and we have deep concerns about what Iran is doing in the south of Iraq," said former Secretary of State Condoleezza Rice.[20] Why should the United States negotiate with a known state sponsor of terrorism, especially when any agreement would most likely boost Iran's economy and allow the government to allocate more resources toward the covert funding of terror?

The harsh sanctions put in place against Iran by the United States, the EU, and the UN have been working. Iran's economy is weak, and the resulting domestic political backlash has placed great pressure on its political leaders. "The problem with this deal . . . is that the sanctions are working. They're doing exactly what we wanted them to do," said former Senator Saxby Chambliss, R-Ga. "The problem is we have given the Iranians relief from sanctions and, in doing that, we got nothing basically in return."[21]

Rouhani has been described by some as a reformer and a moderate, but let us be clear: he harbors many of the same sentiments about the United States and our allies as his predecessors. Under Rouhani's "reformist" administration, Iran has continued to harass and imprison dissenters, homosexuals, and religious minorities. Hardliners continue to cry "Death to America" in public forums, and many are still firm in their commitment to the destruction of Israel.[22] In reality, Rouhani is only a puppet of Iran's supreme leader—an unelected religious authoritarian figure.

"I don't believe that Iran's radical regime will change for the better after this deal," Netanyahu told Congress in 2015. "This regime has been in power for 36 years, and its voracious appetite for aggression grows with each passing year. This deal would only whet Iran's appetite for more."[23]

# THE ONGOING DEBATE

## What are the costs and benefits of providing weapons to foreign governments?

Throughout American history, the United States has often sought to advance its national interests abroad by providing military aid, military technology, and weapons to foreign governments. Under the Foreign Assistance Act (FAA) of 1961, the president and Congress have the authority to provide financial aid, usually in the form of grants or loans, to foreign governments to purchase American arms.[25] In general, the United States provides this type of financing only to close, long-standing military allies or to governments fighting the production and trafficking of drugs intended for the American market.[26] The FAA also allows the Department of Defense and the president to sell or give away stocks of surplus arms, while setting restrictions on the transfer of arms to governments that routinely violate international law.

In 1976, Congress passed the Arms Export Control Act (AECA),[27] which stipulates that weapons may be transferred for self-defense, internal security, or UN operations only, and establishes a process by which the executive branch must give Congress advance notice of major sales. The State Department is responsible for setting regulations on which types of munitions are legal to export, as well as which countries are eligible to receive them.

Foreign nations can receive American arms aid through a variety of programs, but the greatest sum of money is transferred through foreign military financing and the education and training of foreign military services.[28] Since 1950, the United States has provided more than $91 billion in financing to the armed forces of countries around the world.[29] The United States also provides assistance in counternarcotics, counterterrorism, and land mine removal programs in numerous countries, as well as substantial backing to UN peacekeeping operations.[30]

Military aid has the potential to advance the national interest of the United States in a variety of ways. These weapons often serve to strengthen the power of allied governments in unstable regions of the world, ensuring that the United States does not have to shoulder the entire responsibility of maintaining international security. In cases where the United States is supporting another government's efforts to fight drug cartels or terrorist groups, Americans are directly supporting their own security interests. These packages have even been used to secure peace agreements; the two largest recipients of American arms—Israel and Egypt—began receiving this support after they signed a peace treaty in 1979.[31]

Yet there is no guarantee foreign governments will use American military aid in the exact manner the United States specifies. American national interests are often vastly different from those of the nations the United States supports. In Pakistan, for example, the goals of the U.S. military and those of the Pakistani military are markedly dissimilar. "We are supporting the Pakistani military because we are interested in al-Qaeda," said Marina Ottaway, director of the Middle East program at the Carnegie Endowment for International Peace. "Yet the Pakistani military wants the Pentagon's training and funds to better defend against or attack India."[32]

# THE CURRENT CONTROVERSY

## Should the United States continue to include military equipment and technology in its foreign aid packages?

The United States is in a unique position when it comes to the development and distribution of arms—it provided global military aid that totaled $14.5 billion in 2010.[33] American defense industries are on the cutting edge of military technology and therefore, the United States has the ability to ensure its allies and partners have the resources they need to maintain modern and skilled military services. Supporters of these programs, such as the Department of Defense, believe military aid programs can provide a substantial return on American investments, both as a bulwark against terrorism and as a tool to convince foreign governments to support American interests. Furthermore, because these aid programs almost exclusively include the sale of American arms and military technologies, they also provide a substantial boost to the U.S. economy.

But there is also a great deal of controversy and criticism surrounding the nations the United States chooses to equip, as well as unintended consequences that come with arms assistance. Critics of American arms transfers have noted that weapons can fail to achieve their aims and often outlast the regimes they are intended to support. In the 1980s, for example, the United States provided weapons support and heavy artillery to Somali President Siad Barre in exchange for access to port facilities in the Gulf of Aden. But when civil war broke out in Somalia in 1991, those weapons were used against American forces during their 1993 humanitarian intervention. During the second half of the 20th century, the United States provided military aid to several Latin American dictatorships and paramilitary groups to prevent the spread of communism.[34] And in the Middle East, the United States even supported dictators such as Saddam Hussein in Iraq and Hosni Mubarak in Egypt because they kept more radical movements and terrorist groups in check.[35] These cases demonstrate some of the key uncertainties that can arise when considering the costs and benefits of military aid.

## Should the United States continue to include artillery and military technology in its foreign aid packages?

### YES: The United States has an obligation to maintain global security.

The United States has a global advantage when it comes to the size, scope, and technological capabilities of its military. And Americans must recognize that the alternative to sharing these resources is for American troops to maintain a global presence at all times. We can either bankrupt our country by acting as the world's police force, or we can provide friendly governments with the means to maintain their own security.

"The U.S. will ultimately be more secure if capable democratic countries take charge of problems in their own regions," said Doug Bandow, a scholar at the Cato Institute.[36] Would we rather our allies be underequipped and underprepared to face the security challenges of the modern world?

The threats facing the United States and its allies around the world are far too real, and American military aid packages have saved countless lives. Israel, for example, has long been one of the chief recipients of U.S. military aid, much of which has gone toward the development of its Iron Dome missile defense system. "Iron Dome has been a genuine life saver for Israelis enduring round-the-clock barrages of Hamas rockets and missiles from Gaza," said David Harris, executive director of the American Jewish Committee.[37]

The reluctance of the United States to provide military aid packages to Ukraine in its fight against Russian-backed separatists has only emboldened Russia and encouraged President Vladimir Putin to view Americans as weak. If the United States and its allies fail to support Ukraine, Russia will only believe it can make similar acts of aggression elsewhere. Americans do not need to provide so much military aid that Ukraine has the ability to defeat a full-scale Russian attack—but they must give enough to force Russia to reconsider such an attack.[38]

Military aid packages have also helped build popular support for the United States and its policies. Choosing to withhold military aid to countries such as Egypt or Pakistan could lead to a rise in anti-American sentiment, or to the belief that close ties with the United States are not necessary. And these unstable governments may choose to get their arms elsewhere—from Russia or China, for instance. "The United States needs an ally in the [the Middle East]," said David Francis of the *Fiscal Times*. "The United States has provided some $85 billion in aid to Egypt over the last three decades for this very reason: Egypt is a rent-an-ally."[39]

Policymakers should not rush to the conclusion that simply providing weapons will solve every security crisis but, when used appropriately, American military aid packages will ensure not only American national security—but global security as well.

## NO: We cannot bring about peace by selling more weapons.

Over the course of the past century, the United States has, time and time again, provided weapons to governments and non-governmental groups across the globe, naively hoping Americans will somehow be safer as a result. Despite the fact that billions of dollars have been spent—and countless lives lost—because of these weapons packages, there is no evidence the United States has achieved its national security goals. And in fact, many would argue we are less safe as a result.

Throughout the Cold War, the United States took it upon itself to arm various governments and paramilitary groups with the hope they would help prevent the spread of communism. But looking back, these weapons packages did little to bring about the collapse of the Soviet Union or to promote democratic ideals in the places Americans were trying to defend. In central Asia, the Middle East, and elsewhere, many of the weapons Americans donated are still in circulation, and through their proliferation have been used to crush democratic dissent, overthrow governments, and fight against American soldiers.[40]

There is simply no way to know what will happen to the weapons Americans provide as "aid" in the long run. The government has limited stipulations on whether foreign governments may sell American arms once they no longer have a need for them or acquire newer models. American officials also have very little control over who foreign governments might sell these weapons to, and once the weapons are out of Americans hands, they are extremely difficult to track.[41]

"It's difficult to produce a single example in modern history of a strategy of arming rebels actually succeeding," said George Washington University professor Marc Lynch. "Meanwhile, there are plenty of examples of the overt or covert provision of arms to a rebel group prolonging and intensifying conflicts, and lots of cases of rebel groups happily taking our money and guns to 'fight communists' and then doing whatever they like with them."[42]

The Syrian civil war, which erupted in 2011, demonstrates many of the potential problems that can arise from weapons transfers. For several years, the Obama administration has been debating whether to arm moderate Syrian rebels to assist in the fight against President Bashar al-Assad's tyrannical regime and the spreading influence of ISIL militants. However, because the Syrian opposition comprises countless factions fighting for supremacy, it is nearly impossible to determine which groups could be considered "moderate." It is also nearly impossible to prevent American arms from getting into the hands of extremist groups, such as al-Qaeda and ISIL, which are also seeking to overthrow Assad.

"The expectation has always been that countries that receive U.S. military aid and training will be bulwarks of stability and will further U.S. interests in a particular country or region," said Ted Galen Carpenter, vice president for foreign policy studies at the Cato Institute. "Those expectations have often proved excessive."[43]

# CONCLUSION

Nuclear negotiations with Iran and American military aid packages are only two examples of the debates Americans have engaged in for decades over the proliferation of nuclear and non-nuclear weapons. Although the fate of these negotiations and policies remain far from certain, American policymakers, military officials, and citizens will undoubtedly continue to debate the goals and priorities of our national security policies—and what our government can do to best ensure peace, security, and global stability.

---

[1]  Norris, Robert S., and Hans M. Kristensen, "Global nuclear stockpiles, 1945–2006." *Bulletin of the Atomic Scientists.* Vol. 62, no. 4. Jul./Aug. 2006.

[2]  Macias, Amanda. "Nine Nations Have Nukes — Here's How Many Each Country Has." *Business Insider.* 17 Jul. 2014. Web. 26 Mar. 2015.

[3]  "Foreign Military Financing Account Summary." U.S. Department of State. Web. 26 Mar. 2015.

[4]  "Governance, Corruption, and Conflict." United States Institute of Peace. 2010. Web. 26 Mar. 2015.

[5]  Marshall, Andrew. "Terror 'blowback' burns CIA." *The Independent.* 1 Nov. 1998. Web. 26 Mar. 2015.

[6]  Shanker, Tom. "U.S. Arms Sales Make Up Most of Global Market." *New York Times,* 26 Aug. 2012. Web. 26 Mar. 2015.

[7]  Hartung, William D. "Tools of Influence: The Arms Lobby and the Super Committee." Center for International Policy. 31 Oct. 2011. Web. 26 Mar. 2015.

[8]  Katzman, Kenneth. "Iran: US Concerns and Policy Responses." Congressional Research Service. 26 Jan. 2015. Web. 26 Mar. 2015.

[9]  Ibid.

[10]  Eisenstadt, Michael and Mehdi Khalaji. "Nuclear Fatwa: Religion and Politics in Iran's Proliferation Strategy." The Washington Institute for Near East Policy. Sep. 2011. Web. 26 Mar. 2015.

[11]  Whale, Sebastian. "Timeline of Tensions Between Iran and the United States." *The Telegraph.* 7 Nov. 2014. Web. 26 Mar. 2015.

[12]  Bozorghmehr, Shirzad. "Iranian leader: Wipe out Israel." CNN. 27 Oct. 2005. Web. 26 Mar. 2015.

[13]  "Timeline of Nuclear Diplomacy with Iran." Arms Control Association. Dec. 2014. Web. 26 Mar. 2015.

[14]  "Iran nuclear talks: What you need to know about uranium enrichment." *The Telegraph.* 11 Aug. 2013. Web. 26 Mar. 2015.

[15]  Mason, Jeff, and Louis Charbonneau. "Obama, Iran's Rouhani hold historic phone call." Reuters. 28 Sep. 2013. Web. 26 Mar. 2015.

[16]  "Timeline of Nuclear Diplomacy with Iran." Arms Control Association. Dec. 2014. Web. 26 Mar. 2015.

[17]  Davis, Julie Hirschfeld, and Michael D. Shear. "Netanyahu Speech Raises Burden for Obama on Iran Nuclear Talks." *New York Times,* 3 Mar. 2015. Web. 26 Mar. 2015.

[18]  Brom, Shlomo. "Nuclear Negotiations with Iran: The Path Forward." Center for American Progress. 17 Nov. 2014. Web. 26 Mar. 2015.

19  Sanger, David E. and Michael R. Gordon. "White House Offers Rebuttal Before Netanyahu's Speech." *New York Times*. 27 Feb. 2015. Web. 26 Mar. 2015.

20  Bruno, Greg. "State Sponsors: Iran." Council on Foreign Relations. 13 Oct. 2011. Web. 26 Mar. 2015.

21  "Sen. Chambliss: Why Reduce Iran Sanctions When They're Working?" NPR. 26 Nov. 2013. Web. 26 Mar. 2015.

22  "Despite Nuclear Talks, U.S. Seen a 'Great Satan' in Iran." Radio Free Europe. 5 Nov. 2014. Web. 26 Mar. 2015.

23  "The complete transcript of Netanyahu's address to Congress." *New York Times*. 3 Mar. 2015. Web. 26 Mar. 2015.

24  "Egypt protests: Police clash with demonstrators demanding the end of Mubarak's rule." *The Telegraph*. Web. 26 Mar. 2015.

25  "U.S. Foreign Military Assistance." Federation of American Scientists. Web. 26 Mar. 2015.

26  "Foreign Military Financing Account Summary." U.S. Department of State. 2015. Web. 26 Mar. 2015.

27  "The Arms Export Control Act." U.S. Department of State. Web. 26 Mar. 2015.

28  "U.S. Foreign Military Assistance." Federation of American Scientists. Web. 26 Mar. 2015.

29  Ibid.

30  Ibid.

31  "Camp David Accords." Israeli Foreign Ministry. 17 Sep. 1978. Web. 26 Mar. 2015.

32  Mulrine, Anna. "US military assistance for foreign forces: a wise investment?" *Christian Science Monitor*. 1 Mar. 2011. Web. 26 Mar. 2015.

33  Shell, Elizabeth, and Matt Stiles. "Where Does U.S. Military Aid Go?" PBS. 30 Aug. 2012. Web. 26 Mar. 2015.

34  Adams, Francis. "Deepening Democracy: Global Governance and Political Reform in Latin America." Greenwood Publishing Group, Inc. 2003. Web. 26 Mar. 2015.

35  Knell, Yolande. "The complicated legacy of Egypt's Hosni Mubarak." BBC News. 25 Jan. 2013. Web. 26 Mar. 2015.

36  Bandow, Doug. "Free Rider: South Korea's Dual Dependence on America." The Cato Institute. 19 May 1998. Web. 26 Mar. 2015.

37  Stoil, Rebecca Shimoni. "Obama approves $225 million in Iron Dome funding." *The Times of Israel*. 5 Aug. 2014. Web. 26 Mar. 2015.

38  Daalder, Ivo et al. "Preserving Ukraine's Independence, Resisting Russian Aggression: What the United States and NATO Must Do." The Atlantic Council. Feb. 2015. Web. 26 Mar. 2015.

39  Francis, David. "Why Cutting Foreign Aid to Egypt Would Backfire." *The Fiscal Times*. 15 Aug. 2013. Web. 26 Mar. 2015.

40  Gabelnick, Tamar and Anna Rich. "In Focus: Globalized Weaponry." Federation of American Scientists. Vol. 5, No. 16. May 2000. Web. 26 Mar. 2015.

41  Ibid.

42  Lynch, Marc. "Shopping Option C for Syria." *Foreign Policy*. 14 Feb. 2013. Web. 26 Mar. 2015.

43  Mulrine, Anna. "US military assistance for foreign forces: a wise investment?" *Christian Science Monitor*. 1 Mar. 2011. Web. 26 Mar. 2015.

# WOMEN'S RIGHTS AROUND THE WORLD

## CURRENT CONTROVERSIES

- Should the United States impose sanctions on countries that deny equal protection for women?

- Should the United States make it a priority to combat human trafficking abroad?

# INTRODUCTION

"Whether women are better than men I cannot say. But I can say they are certainly no worse."

—Golda Meir

"For my brothers it was easy to think about the future, they can be anything they want. But for me it was hard and for that reason, I wanted to become educated and I wanted to empower myself with knowledge."

—Malala Yousafzai

Recent years have seen several significant achievements for the international women's rights movement. As women have secured their rights to vote, to education, and to make the decisions that affect their lives, they have also assumed positions of political and economic leadership all over the world. Yet in many countries, women are still married as children, forced into slavery, denied access to education or political participation, or refused their basic human rights. The United States has made great strides to protect the rights of women over the centuries, but many Americans still disagree over the extent of their responsibilities to protect those rights abroad. In this chapter, we will consider several enduring tensions in women's rights policy and examine two current controversial issues:

- Should the United States impose sanctions on countries that deny equal protection for women?

- Should the United States make it a priority to combat human trafficking abroad?

**Why Is the Protection of Women's Rights Controversial?** The United States has historically been at the forefront of the crusade for equal rights for women. Eleanor Roosevelt, the former first lady and the first American delegate to the United Nations (UN), served as the chairwoman of the UN Human Rights Commission as it drafted the Universal Declaration of Human Rights (UDHR), adopted by the General Assembly in 1948.[1] This landmark document, which became the foundation of international human rights law and had inspired more than 80 binding treaties as of 2015,[2] affirmed that "all human beings are born free and equal in dignity and rights," and that "everyone is entitled to all the rights and freedoms set forth in this Declaration, without distinction of any kind, such as race, colour, sex, language, religion, political or other opinion, national or social origin, property, birth, or other status."[3]

The UN, which counted 193 nations as members in 2015, has also been a leader in the international women's rights effort, as Article I of its charter promises "to achieve international co-operation in solving international problems of an economic, social, cultural, or humanitarian character, and in promoting and encouraging respect for human rights and for fundamental freedoms for all without distinction as to race, sex, language, or religion."[4]

So why is the protection of women's rights controversial? Some policymakers disagree with the validity or urgency of ensuring equal rights for women for practical, philosophical, or political reasons. The leaders of some theocracies, for example, believe religious law prohibits equality among the sexes. Some cultures, meanwhile, believe education for women and girls interferes with their traditional female roles as wives and mothers. And while policymakers in most democratic nations agree that equal rights for women are important, they do not always agree on whether or how to intervene abroad when violations are taking place. Instead, they must reconcile several competing standards, priorities, and means for protecting women's rights.

- *Competing Standards.* What constitutes equal rights for women? Should other nations be punished for upholding what they view as religious or cultural standards? What types of women's rights violations warrant American intervention? How severe must these violations be?

- *Competing Priorities.* Should U.S. foreign policy focus primarily or solely on ideological interests? Or should the United States take security and economic interests into account before defending women's rights abroad?

- *Competing Means.* What means and methods should the United States employ to protect women's rights? Are sanctions effective in changing other nations' behavior? Does the United States have the law enforcement resources necessary to combat human trafficking abroad?

**Why Is the Protection of Women's Rights So Complicated?** In 2014, the Census Bureau estimated that there were 3.56 billion women and girls around the world, representing slightly less than half of the global population of 7.18 billion people.[5] And these women lived in 195 sovereign states, under 195 sovereign governments that varied greatly in their structures, intentions, and treatment of their citizens.[6]

Ensuring the protection of 3.56 billion people is not an easy task for international organizations such as the UN, and it can be even more complicated for an individual country such as the United States. Although Americans have been regarded as global leaders for many decades, citizens of other countries do not necessarily welcome the United States imposing its values on the rest of the world. The protection and preservation of women's rights is further complicated by the fact that this is only one of several competing interests that world leaders must balance. The United States, for example, has hesitated to intervene in international rights violations at times when Americans' economic or security interests would have been placed in jeopardy.

But in 2015, women around the world were experiencing infringements and outright violations of their basic human rights, and the United States and the international community faced the difficult task of responding to these violations. Should the United States take the lead in defending women's rights around the world? Or is this a responsibility best left to international bodies? Which tools are the most effective in changing the behavior of violating nations? And who has the moral authority to lead this international discussion?

# THE ONGOING DEBATE

## Do international violations of women's rights warrant an American response?

The United States has an extensive history of working to promote and protect equal rights for women. The 14th Amendment to the Constitution guarantees, "No state shall make or enforce any law which shall abridge the privileges or immunities of citizens of the United States; nor shall any state deprive any person of life, liberty, or property, without due process of law; nor deny to any person within its jurisdiction the equal protection of the laws."[7] And the 19th Amendment promises, "The right of citizens of the United States to vote shall not be denied or abridged by the United States or by any state on account of sex."[8]

But as the United States has worked to protect women's rights—and correct violations of women's rights—at home, it has also encountered abuses by its counterparts in the international community. These violations, committed by both allies and adversaries, have included limits on the right to vote, unequal access to education, high rates of child marriage, violence against women, and the failure to protect reproductive rights.

**Voting Rights.** In 1893, New Zealand became the first independent nation in which women were guaranteed the right to vote.[9] And although the 20th century saw women's suffrage spread across the globe, in 2015 there remained two sovereign nations—Saudi Arabia and Vatican City—where only men enjoyed voting rights.[10]

In Vatican City, the 450-citizen seat of the Roman Catholic Church, women cannot be ordained as priests or hold leadership positions within the church, thus preventing them from joining the all-male College of Cardinals in electing the pope.[11] Saudi Arabia, as the birthplace of Islam, has largely derived its societal gender roles from *Sharia*—Islamic law—and from tribal traditions and customs. As a result, the 12 million women who live in Saudi Arabia have been forbidden from driving and from sharing many public spaces with men, and must have a male guardian—typically a father or husband—from whom they must obtain permission to marry, attend universities, travel abroad, hold certain jobs, and undergo elective surgery.[12] But in September 2011, the late King Abdullah bin Abdulaziz Al Saud decreed that Saudi women would be permitted to vote and run in municipal elections for the first time in 2015. Nonetheless, some advocates remained wary because of the kingdom's long history of stalled royal decrees.[13]

**Education.** In 2011, UNICEF estimated that 31 million girls of primary school age, as well as 34 million girls of lower secondary school age, were not enrolled in school.[14] Meanwhile, of the 774 million adults who could not read or write in 2014, an astounding two-thirds were women.[15]

Sub-Saharan Africa has become a region of particular concern when it comes to female illiteracy. Between 2005 and 2009, the UN Educational, Scientific, and Cultural Organization (UNESCO) determined that the ten nations with the lowest female youth literacy rates in the world—Niger, Mali, Burkina Faso, Ethiopia, Chad, Benin, Sierra Leone, Guinea, Senegal, and the Central African Republic—were all in sub-Saharan Africa. In the Central African Republic, the best of the group, only 57 percent of girls could read and write, and in Niger, the worst of the group, only 23 percent of girls were literate.[16]

So why are women and girls lagging behind in education? In short, girls around the world face a wide variety of disruptions to schooling, such as armed conflicts, fears of sexual violence, limited family resources, negative classroom environments, discriminatory education policies, and early marriages.

**Child Marriage.** The practice of child marriage—a formal or customary union in which at least one partner is under the age of 18—was alarmingly common in 2015, as one-third of girls in developing countries were married as children. And in 2015 alone, the UN Population Fund (UNFPA) expected 13.5 million child marriages to take place, or nearly 37,000 such unions each day.[17]

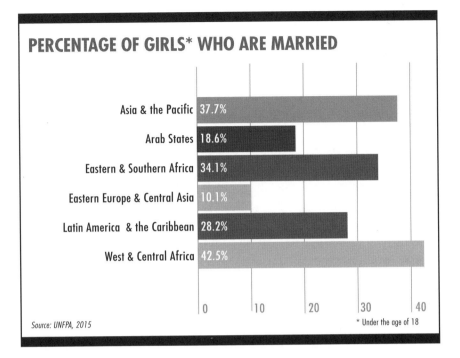

## PERCENTAGE OF GIRLS* WHO ARE MARRIED

Asia & the Pacific — 37.7%
Arab States — 18.6%
Eastern & Southern Africa — 34.1%
Eastern Europe & Central Asia — 10.1%
Latin America & the Caribbean — 28.2%
West & Central Africa — 42.5%

0   10   20   30   40

Source: UNFPA, 2015                                          * Under the age of 18

In 2012, the UNFPA documented 41 countries—most of them in southern Asia and west and central Africa—in which at least 30 percent of young women had been married as children. The highest rates were found in Niger (75 percent), Chad (72 percent), Bangladesh (66 percent), Guinea (63 percent), the Central African Republic (61 percent), Mali (55 percent), Mozambique (52 percent), and Malawi (50 percent).[18] The effects of child marriage are dangerous and far-reaching. Child brides are more likely to become pregnant before their bodies are mature, increasing the risks of childbirth; they are less prone to go to school, as are their children;[19] and they are more likely to experience domestic violence.[20]

**Violence Against Women.** According to the World Health Organization, more than one-third of women around the world have experienced either intimate partner violence or non-partner sexual violence in their lifetime.[21] Yet some nations still fail to protect the victims of rape—and some go so far as to punish women for being alone with an unrelated man or for becoming pregnant.

In 2012, for example, the nation of India was rocked when a 23-year-old woman was raped by a group of men while riding a bus home from the movies in New Delhi. Her injuries were so severe that she died 13 days later while undergoing emergency treatment in Singapore. Within months, India's government had approved an anti-rape law that implemented new punishments for acid attacks, stalking, and voyeurism; introduced death sentences for certain rape crimes; and expanded the definition of rape, so the absence of a physical struggle could no longer be considered consent. [22] But the law failed to criminalize marital rape—an act that remained legal in India in 2015.[23]

**Reproductive Rights.** In 1979, in an attempt to curb population growth, China implemented a mandatory family planning policy, more commonly known as the one-child policy. For decades, the law restricted urban Chinese couples from having more than one child, while allowing additional children to ethnic minorities, rural couples whose first-born was either a girl or disabled, and couples who both

Girls, often blocked from attending school by the Taliban and other religious extremists, study in a school for refugees near Islamabad, Pakistan.

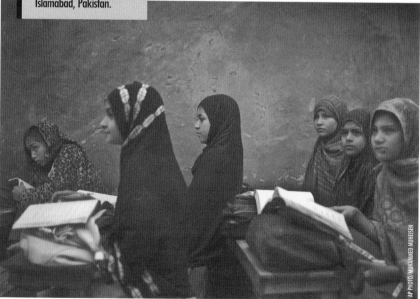

lacked siblings themselves. As of 2015, the policy remained in place, although the Chinese government decided in 2013 to allow a second child to families in which either parent is an only child.[24] Human rights advocates have long argued that the one-child policy violates the basic human right to determine the size of one's own family; many also claim the policy has subjected Chinese women to forced abortions and sterilizations.

In the face of these violations of women's rights, some Americans believe the United States has a responsibility as a global leader to intervene forcefully. But others insist it is not the job of Americans to police the world and that the United States must respect the sovereignty of other nations.

## THE CURRENT CONTROVERSY

### Should the United States impose sanctions on countries that deny equal protection for women?

Sanctions are a diplomatic tool used to persuade governments or individuals to change their behavior by restricting trade, financial assistance, or other commercial activity. As of April 2015, the United States had 28 sanctions programs in place against foreign governments or individuals in response to human rights violations, the proliferation of weapons, the trafficking of narcotics, and the sponsorship of terrorism.[25] Since 1979, for example, five U.S. administrations have levied sanctions against Iran for supporting terrorism and developing a clandestine nuclear program. And beginning in 2011, the United States sanctioned the authoritarian leader of Syria, Bashar al-Assad, for violently cracking down on pro-democracy protests and igniting a civil war.

Yet in 2015, as Saudi Arabia continued to disenfranchise women, China continued to implement its one-child policy, and dozens of other nations allowed girls to be excluded from school, married as children, or disproportionately targeted by violence, policymakers debated whether the United States should extend its sanctions to include countries that deny equal protection for women. Supporters of expanded sanctions argue that women's rights are human rights, and that the United States has a responsibility as the leader of the free world to stand up for equality. But opponents insist that sanctions only harm the vulnerable women and girls who need assistance the most, and destroy vital economic and security relationships with foreign governments.

Human trafficking survivor Shandra Woworuntu shares her story with university students in Texas.

## Should the United States impose sanctions on countries that deny equal protection for women?

### YES: The United States must take a forceful stand and protect women around the world.

In 2006, a teenage girl was raped by seven men near the city of Qatif, Saudi Arabia. The assailants received sentences ranging from ten months to five years in prison, as well as 80 to 1,000 lashes. But in a move that sparked international outrage, the Saudi court sentenced the victim to 90 lashes as well. Why? She had been alone in a car with a man to whom she was not married—a crime in Saudi Arabia.[26]

Although the girl from Qatif was pardoned in 2007, Saudi Arabia remained one of the world's worst violators of women's rights in 2015. Saudi women are still forbidden from driving, from going out in public without wearing a long cloak known as an *abaya*, and from marrying, working, or attending school without the permission of a male guardian.[27]

The United States, however, has largely turned a blind eye to these flagrant abuses of women's rights. "On the one hand, the Obama administration condemns the beheadings, torture, and crackdowns conducted by the armed group Islamic State," said Sunjeev Bery, advocacy director at Amnesty International USA. "On the other hand, the White House is relatively quiet when Saudi Arabian authorities engage in some of the exact same human rights abuses."[28]

If the United States were to impose sanctions on Saudi Arabia and other nations that deny equal protection to women, it would be exercising a powerful tool that has the ability to elicit potent results. American sanctions against Iran, for example, helped compel Iranian leaders to negotiate with the international community over halting its nuclear program.

Sanctions against women's rights violators would also help the United States correct its troubling history of ignoring the wrongdoing of its allies. "Authoritarian regimes on friendly terms with the West are less likely to be punished for democratic wrongdoings," wrote Christian von Soest, a fellow at the German Institute of Global and Area Studies, and Michael Wahman, a fellow at the London School of Economics. "The lack of sanctions or other external pressure against countries such as Saudi Arabia, Egypt, or Qatar represents a broader pattern: Strategic allies are often spared from Western pressure to democratize, and enforcement of democratic norms is much more selective where geostrategic interests prevail."[29]

The United States is in a unique position to change the behavior of a long-time ally and to send a powerful message to the world that women deserve equal protection of the laws.[30]

## NO: Sanctions are unnecessary and only hurt the people who need help the most.

"Before imposing such measures, it is always imperative to foresee the humanitarian consequences of sanctions, without failing to respect the just proportion that such measures should have in relation to the very evil which they are meant to remedy," the late Pope John Paul II said.[31]

Offending governments often respond to sanctions by simply finding alternate trading partners, conducting business on the black market, or rallying public support against the nation imposing the sanctions. And the far-reaching economic consequences are often felt by the poor and the vulnerable instead of by the governing elite, thus doing little to change the behavior of governments. "In Iran the impact of sanctions has been devastating," filmmaker Beheshteh Farshneshani wrote in the *New York Times*. "Over the last year and a half, families living in poverty rose from 22 percent to more than 40 percent, the Rial plummeted at least 40 percent, and the price of food regularly consumed by Iranians—for example, milk, tea, fruits and vegetables—skyrocketed. Moreover, the health of millions of Iranians has been compromised due to the shortage of western medical drugs and supplies."[32]

Sanctions do not only have devastating effects on the countries they target—they can also have devastating effects on the United States. Placing economic sanctions on a regional power such as Saudi Arabia would only increase tensions and risk delicate American alliances in the volatile Middle East.

Much remains to be done to protect innocent women all over the world, but government sanctions are not necessary to enact social change—people all over the world just need to stand up for what they believe. In March 2012, the international community was outraged when Amina Filali, a 16-year-old Moroccan girl who had been raped and then forced to marry her rapist, committed suicide. At the time, the Moroccan penal code allowed those convicted of "kidnapping" a minor to go free if they married the victim—an option Amina's father said was suggested by court officials.[33] The tragedy inspired widespread protests and petitions on Amina's behalf, and by early 2014, Moroccan lawmakers had unanimously amended the law in question.[34]

Despite its position as a world leader, the United States cannot command other countries to follow its cultural and ideological standards. Equal protection of the laws is an important principle. But Americans will have more success defending women's rights by cultivating positive economic relationships and inspiring others to follow its example—not by implementing harsh and punitive measures.

# THE CURRENT CONTROVERSY

## Should the United States make it a priority to combat human trafficking abroad?

Human trafficking is the act of recruiting, harboring, or transporting a person for compelled labor or commercial sex acts by using force, fraud, or coercion. This form of modern-day slavery can include the following crimes:

- *Sex Trafficking.* When a person is coerced, forced, or deceived into prostitution, that person is a victim of trafficking, no matter whether he or she initially consented or not.

- *Forced Labor.* Forced labor traffickers often use physical threats, deception, and coercion to force their victims to work. Migrants are particularly vulnerable to forced labor. Female victims of forced labor—especially those who work as domestic servants—are often sexually exploited as well. Some traffickers prey upon victims by demanding forced labor as a form of payment for a debt, known as debt bondage, incurred by either the victim or his or her family.

- *Involuntary Domestic Servitude.* Environments of informal work in a private residence are conducive to exploitation because workers are isolated and authorities cannot inspect homes as easily as they can formal workplaces.

- *Child Soldiers.* Children are the victims of trafficking when they are recruited by armed forces to serve as soldiers, porters, cooks, guards, servants, or spies.

Although human trafficking affects every nation in the world—whether they are countries of origin, transit, or destination—the exact number of victims remains unknown. In 2014, the State Department estimated that 20 million men, women, and children were enslaved around the world.[35] And in 2012, the UN Office on Drugs and Crime (UNODC) concluded that women and girls accounted for 76 percent of all detected trafficking victims between 2007 and 2010.[36]

The United States has attempted to fight human trafficking by passing the Trafficking Victims Protection Act of 2000 (TVPA) which, along with its reauthorizations, explicitly defines what makes someone the victim of a trafficking crime. The TVPA also established the State Department Office to Monitor and Combat Trafficking in Persons, which coordinates with foreign governments to protect victims and prosecute traffickers, and provided new protections such as the "T-Visa," a visa available to some victims who assist in the prosecution of their traffickers.[37]

On the international level, the major instrument to combat human trafficking is the Protocol to Prevent, Suppress, and Punish Trafficking in Persons, Especially Women and Children—a measure more commonly known as the Palermo Protocol. Adopted by the UN General Assembly in 2000 and entered into force in 2003, the Palermo Protocol defined a global standard for the crime of human trafficking and offered assistance to nations in drafting and implementing anti-trafficking strategies. It also committed its ratifying states to work to prevent human trafficking, protect and assist victims, and promote cooperation among states. As of 2015, 166 countries had become parties to the Palermo Protocol.[38]

But as millions of people remained in bondage in 2015, American policymakers debated whether the United States should do more to combat human trafficking abroad. Supporters argue that only the United States has the resources and international standing necessary to lead the fight against human trafficking. But opponents insist that Americans have already done so much to address this issue—and that now, the international community must step in to address this international problem.

## Should the United States make it a priority to combat human trafficking abroad?

### YES: The United States must use its vast resources to help end modern-day slavery.

In 2014 alone, the State Department identified more than 44,000 survivors of human trafficking crimes, from sexual exploitation and forced labor to debt bondage and involuntary domestic servitude. But at the same time, the State Department estimated that 20 million men, women, and children remained enslaved around the world, proving that there is so much more to be done to combat this terrible crime.[39] As the most prosperous nation and the leader of the free world, the United States is best placed to assume this responsibility.

"It ought to concern every person, because it is a debasement of our common humanity," President Barack Obama said in 2012. "It ought to concern every community, because it tears at our social fabric. It ought to concern every business, because it distorts markets. It ought to concern every nation, because it endangers public health and fuels violence and organized crime. I'm talking about the injustice, the outrage, of human trafficking, which must be called by its true name—modern slavery."[40]

Between 2007 and 2010, the UNODC found trafficking victims of 136 nationalities in 118 countries—the United States included.[41] This is an issue that deserves the full attention of both Americans and the international community. "The unfortunate reality is that women's issues are marginalized, and in any case sex trafficking and mass rape should no more be seen as women's issues than slavery was a black issue or the Holocaust was a Jewish issue. These are all humanitarian concerns, transcending any one race, gender, or creed," Pulitzer Prize–winning journalists Nicholas Kristof and Sheryl WuDunn wrote.[42]

To be sure, the United States has already implemented several policies to assist victims and prosecute their traffickers, but more are desperately needed. In order to be eligible for a T-Visa, for example, a victim must assist in the prosecution of his or her trafficker—but some do not apply out of fear of retaliation. In fiscal year 2013, the Office to Monitor and Combat Trafficking in Persons spent nearly $21 million on foreign assistance resources, but that budget has remained flat, and even decreased at times, since 2009.[43]

Meanwhile, it is especially important for prosperous nations such as the United States to lead the crusade against human trafficking because developing nations—the source of most victims—simply do not have the law enforcement resources necessary to identify and combat these crimes.[44] And if the United States fails to take decisive action, no one will step up in its stead.

## NO: The United States should focus on problems at home; the international community must step up to address trafficking globally.

"Human trafficking happens throughout the world, with millions of victims falling through the cracks of their own societies only to be exploited by traffickers," UNODC executive director Yury Fedotov wrote in 2012. "They can be found in the world's restaurants, fisheries, brothels, farms, and homes."[45]

It is precisely because of the global nature of human trafficking that the international community—not the United States—must take the lead in this important fight. International slavery can come to an end only if every country does its part to eradicate it, and the United States has already done so much. Congress has passed and repeatedly reauthorized the TVPA, which has allowed the State Department to spend tens of millions of dollars each year to assist victims and prosecute traffickers. And as recently as April 2015, the Senate passed the Justice for Victims of Trafficking Act, which expands law enforcement tools against sex trafficking and creates a new fund to assist victims. "We have not fallen deaf to the cries of those who actually need our help," Senator John Cornyn, R-Texas, said.[46]

"Prevention programs have combined public awareness and education campaigns with education and employment opportunities for those at risk of trafficking, particularly women and girls," the Congressional Research Service said of American anti-trafficking efforts in 2013. "Protection programs have involved direct support for shelters, as well as training of local service providers, public officials, and religious groups. Programs to improve the prosecution rates of traffickers have helped countries draft or amend existing anti-[trafficking] laws, as well as provided training for law enforcement and judiciaries to enforce those laws."[47]

Although there is certainly more work to be done to combat human trafficking abroad, it is now time for the United States to turn its focus inward. With a skyrocketing national debt, topping $18 trillion in early 2015, the United States cannot afford to police the crimes that occur in countries all over the world.[48] This is an international problem, and it requires an international response.

Therefore, the United States should focus on combating human trafficking within its borders before sending its resources abroad. As Senator Cornyn pointed out, "Human trafficking is happening right in our own backyard, and more than 80 percent of sex trafficking victims in America are U.S. citizens."[49]

# CONCLUSION

The use of sanctions to protect women's rights and the prioritization of the fight against international human trafficking are only two examples of the policy debates Americans have engaged in for decades. And although the fate of these two specific policies remains far from certain, rights advocates and lawmakers will undoubtedly continue to debate the goals and priorities of the U.S. strategy on women's rights—and which government policies best reflect and achieve them.

[1] "Document for March 15th: Appointment of Eleanor Roosevelt as U.S. Representative to the United Nations." National Archives. Web. 24 Apr. 2015.

[2] United Nations. "The Foundation of International Human Rights Law." Web. 15 Apr. 2015.

[3] United Nations. *The Universal Declaration of Human Rights.* Web. 15 Apr. 2015.

[4] *Charter of the United Nations.* 26 Jun. 1945. Web. 24 Apr. 2015.

[5] U.S. Census Bureau. "International Data Base, World Population by Age and Sex." 2014. Web. 24 Apr. 2015.

[6] U.S. Department of State, Bureau of Intelligence and Research. "Independent States in the World." 30 Dec. 2014. Web. 15 Apr. 2015.

[7] *U.S. Constitution.* Amendment. XIV.

[8] *U.S. Constitution.* Amendment. XIX.

[9] "Women's Suffrage Petition." Archives of New Zealand. Web. 24 Apr. 2015.

[10] Dewey, Caitlin. "7 Ridiculous Restrictions on Women's Rights Around the World." *Washington Post.* 27 Oct. 2013. Web. 24 Apr. 2015.

[11] "Population." Official Website of Vatican City State. Web. 24 Apr. 2015.

[12] United Nations Economic and Social Commission for Western Asia. "The Demographic Profile of Saudi Arabia." Web. 24 Apr. 2015. Murphy, Caryle. "Saudi Women Still Assigned Male 'Guardians.'" *USA Today.* 9 Dec. 2014. Web. 24 Apr. 2015.

[13] MacFarquhar, Neil. "Saudi Monarch Grants Women Right to Vote." *New York Times.* 25 Sep. 2011. Web. 24 Apr. 2015.

[14] UNICEF. "Girls' Education and Gender Equality." 15 Jul. 2014. Web. 24 Apr. 2015.

[15] Kelleher, Fatimah. "The Literacy Injustice: 493 Million Women Still Can't Read." *The Guardian.* 8 Sep. 2014. Web. 24 Apr. 2015.

[16] UNESCO Institute for Statistics. "10 Countries with the Lowest Female Youth Literacy Rates, 2005–2009." EdStats. Aug. 2011. Web. 24 Apr. 2015.

[17] United Nations Population Fund. "Top 10 Myths About Child Marriage." 12 Feb. 2015. Web. 24 Apr. 2015.

[18] United Nations Population Fund. *Marrying Too Young: End Child Marriage.* 2012. Web. 24 Apr. 2015.

[19] United Nations Population Fund. "Top 10 Myths About Child Marriage." 12 Feb. 2015. Web. 24 Apr. 2015.

[20] International Center for Research on Women. "Child Marriage Facts and Figures." Web. 24 Apr. 2015.

[21] World Health Organization. "Violence Against Women." Nov. 2014. Web. 24 Apr. 2015.

[22] BBC News. "Explaining India's New Anti-Rape Laws." 28 Mar. 2013. Web. 24 Apr. 2015.

23 Sarkar, Monica. "Marital Rape: Why is it Legal in India?" CNN. 9 Mar. 2015. Web. 24 Apr. 2015.

24 Levin, Dan. "Many in China Can Now Have a Second Child, But Say No." *New York Times.* 25 Feb. 2014. Web. 24 Apr. 2015.

25 U.S. Department of the Treasury, Resource Center. "Sanctions Programs and Country Information." 14 Apr. 2015. Web. 15 Apr. 2015.

26 Abu-Nasr, Donna. "Rape Case Roils Saudi Legal System." Associated Press. 21 Nov. 2006. Web. 24 Apr. 2015.

27 *The Economist.* "Saudi Arabia's Dress Code for Women." 28 Jan. 2015. Web. 24 Apr. 2015.

28 Taylor, Adam. "The Facts—and a Few Myths—about Saudi Arabia and Human Rights." *Washington Post.* 9 Feb. 2015. Web. 24 Apr. 2015.

29 Von Soest, Christian, and Michael Wahman. "How the West Selectively Promotes Democracy Through Sanctions." *Washington Post.* 10 Jan. 2015. Web. 24 Apr. 2015.

30 U.S. Department of State. "U.S. Relations with Saudi Arabia." 23 Aug. 2013. Web. 24 Apr. 2015.

31 Sirico, Robert. "Free Trade and Human Rights: The Moral Case for Engagement." Cato Institute. 17 Jul. 1998. Web. 24 Apr. 2015.

32 Farshneshani, Beheshteh. "In Iran, Sanctions Hurt the Wrong People." *New York Times.* 22 Jan. 2014. Web. 24 Apr. 2015.

33 Schemm, Paul. "Amina Filali, Morocco Rape Victim, Commits Suicide after Forced Marriage to Rapist." Associated Press. 14 Mar. 2012. Web. 24 Apr. 2015.

34 BBC News. "Morocco Amends Controversial Rape Marriage Law." 23 Jan. 2014. Web. 15 Apr. 2015.

35 U.S. Department of State. *Trafficking in Persons Report.* Jun. 2014. Web. 24 Apr. 2015.

36 United Nations Office on Drugs and Crime. *Global Report on Trafficking in Persons 2012.* 2012. Web. 24 Apr. 2015.

37 Siskin, Alison, and Liana Sun Wyler. *Trafficking in Persons: U.S. Policy and Issues for Congress.* Congressional Research Service. 19 Feb. 2013. Web. 24 Apr. 2015.

38 "Protocol to Prevent, Suppress and Punish Trafficking in Persons, Especially Women and Children, Supplementing the United Nations Convention against Transnational Organized Crime." United Nations Treaty Collection. 24 Apr. 2015. Web. 24 Apr. 2015.

39 U.S. Department of State. *Trafficking in Persons Report.* Jun. 2014. Web. 24 Apr. 2015.

40 Obama, Barack. Remarks to the Clinton Global Initiative. New York City. 25 Sep. 2012. Web. 24 Apr. 2015.

41 United Nations Office on Drugs and Crime. *Global Report on Trafficking in Persons 2012.* 2012. Web. 24 Apr. 2015.

42 Kristof, Nicholas, and WuDunn, Sheryl. 2009. *Half the Sky: Turning Oppression into Opportunity for Women Worldwide.* New York: Knopf, p. 234.

43 U.S. State Department, Office to Monitor and Combat Trafficking in Persons. "International Programs to Combat Trafficking in Persons." 20 Jun. 2014. Web. 24 Apr. 2015.

44 United Nations Office on Drugs and Crime. "Human Trafficking FAQs." Web. 24 Apr. 2015.

45 United Nations Office on Drugs and Crime. *Global Report on Trafficking in Persons 2012.* 2012. Web. 24 Apr. 2015.

46 "Anti-Human Trafficking Bill Passes Senate." Associated Press. 22 Apr. 2015. Web. 24 Apr. 2015.

47 Siskin, Alison, and Liana Sun Wyler. *Trafficking in Persons: U.S. Policy and Issues for Congress.* Congressional Research Service. 19 Feb. 2013. Web. 24 Apr. 2015.

48 U.S. National Debt Clock. Brillig. Web. 6 Mar. 2015.

49 Rhodan, Maya. "Republican House Takes Aim at Human Trafficking Again." *Time.* 27 Jan. 2015. Web. 24 Apr. 2015.